INDEFENSIBLE:

TEN WAYS THE ACLU IS DESTROYING AMERICA

Bob,

Congratulations on

your graduation!

Blessings,

[signature]

Blessings,

[signature]

SAM KASTENSMIDT

FOREWORD BY DR. GARY CASS

INDEFENSIBLE
10 WAYS THE ACLU IS DESTROYING AMERICA

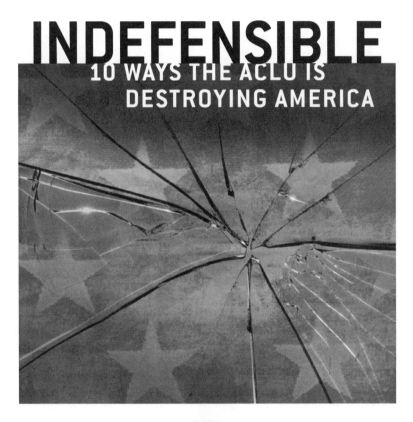

Coral Ridge Ministries
Fort Lauderdale, Florida

Indefensible: Ten Ways the ACLU Is Destroying America

By Sam Kastensmidt

Copyright © 2006 by Coral Ridge Ministries

Published by Coral Ridge Ministries
Printed in the United States of America
ISBN 13 #: 978-1-929626-28-1

Design by Roark Creative: www.roarkcreative.com

Coral Ridge Ministries
Post Office Box 40
Fort Lauderdale, Florida 33302
1-800-988-7884
letters@coralridge.org
www.coralridge.org

Center for Reclaiming America for Christ
P.O. Box 632
Fort Lauderdale, FL 33302
1-877-725-8872
cfra@coralridge.org
www.reclaimamerica.org

Contents

Acknowledgements

For all things I give thanks—first and foremost—to my God and my Redeemer, Jesus Christ. It will never cease to amaze me that the Creator of all things loved me enough to endure the wrath that should have been mine. Knowing that my Savior willingly subjected Himself to the shame and agony of the Cross—to purchase me from sin and death and to redeem me in the sight of God—allows me to rest in the knowledge that He will never leave or forsake me. For that I am truly humbled and immensely grateful!

I would like to thank Dr. D. James Kennedy for allowing God to use him so boldly to speak truth to our culture, and for his many ministries—especially Coral Ridge Ministries, Coral Ridge Presbyterian Church, and Knox Theological Seminary—all of which have deeply impacted my life. I also want to thank the many thousands of people who faithfully partner with these ministries in both prayer and financial assistance. Without you, these ministries would not be possible.

I would also like to thank my mom and dad, who have always been there for me and have helped mold me into who I am today.

To Laura, thank you for your warmth and your patience with me as I worked on this.

I would like to thank Dr. Gary Cass for his leadership at the Center for Reclaiming America for Christ and for his steadfast encouragement throughout the writing process.

To those who helped in editing and fine-tuning the content of this book, especially John Aman, Nancy Britt, Scott Cochran, Laura McClain, Miriam Slagle, and Anthony Urti—thank you for your hard work.

And thanks to the many employees of Coral Ridge Ministries—from the executives to the operations team. This book is the product of a team effort. It would not be possible without your hard work and contributions to the ministry.

Foreword

Long before it was popular to do so, Dr. D. James Kennedy, president and founder of Coral Ridge Ministries, was warning his audience of the American Civil Liberties Union's sinister threat to morality and religion—two arenas George Washington described as the fundamental pillars of American political prosperity.

For his efforts to expose them, the ACLU named Dr. Kennedy one of the most "dangerous" men in America. No higher honor could be bestowed on a true American patriot. In a world where you are known by your friends—and by your enemies—the ACLU is indeed a fine enemy for a Christian patriot to have. Dr. Kennedy considers the indignation of the ACLU a badge of honor.

Due to the sustained efforts of Dr. Kennedy and many others, the tide is turning in the public's perception of this benignly named organization. After all, who could be against civil liberties?

Consider that just 25 years ago, President Jimmy Carter awarded the Presidential Medal of Freedom—the highest award bestowed on American civilians—to Roger Baldwin, the founder of the ACLU—a man who once famously declared, "communism is the goal."

Today, the ACLU's prestige is slipping. After decades of seemingly unstoppable, often unopposed success at bullying communities into submission through threat of lawsuits, the courts are beginning to reject the ACLU's radical agenda. In a recent case involving the public display of the Ten Commandments, a three-judge panel of the 6th U.S. Circuit

Court of Appeals upheld the constitutionality of the display, writing, "Our concern is that of the reasonable person. And the ACLU, an organization whose mission is 'to ensure that the government [is kept] out of the religion business,' does not embody the reasonable person."

While the court grossly understated the ACLU's position (the organization is far more dangerous than being simply "unreasonable"), the ruling is a step in the right direction, due in no small part to the concerted efforts that have been mounted in recent years to challenge the ACLU's preposterous courtroom claims.

In 1994, Dr. D. James Kennedy, along with Dr. James Dobson, Marlin Maddoux, Dr. Bill Bright, and others, co-founded the Alliance Defense Fund to aggressively defend religious liberty. Since then, the organization has trained more than 800 attorneys—men and women who stand ready and willing to defend America from the ACLU's attacks. No longer can ACLU lawyers march into courtrooms, briefcases swinging, to present their arguments unopposed.

As of May 2005, the ADF had funded litigation for more than 1,300 court cases, including many legal disputes that involved communities threatened by the ACLU. In its twelve year history, the ADF has won three out of every four cases litigated to completion, and it has successfully participated in more than 25 U.S. Supreme Court cases.

Dr. Kennedy's leadership in this battle has borne fruit in our United States Congress as well. Rep. John Hostettler of Indiana, whose initial decision to run for Congress was confirmed at a Reclaiming America for Christ conference, is currently sponsoring a bill to defund the ACLU.

It may surprise you to learn that your tax dollars help fund the ACLU's corrosive agenda. Under current law, federal courts can order government entities that lose in court to the ACLU to pay its attorney fees. The state of Alabama, for example, was forced to give $500,000 to the ACLU and other groups that sued Roy Moore because of this law. When Congressman Hostettler's bill is successful, this outrageous taxpayer subsidy of the ACLU will end!

Dr. Kennedy saw through the façade and slick image of the ACLU decades ago and has since been a forerunner in exposing the organization's agenda. In the past fifteen years, *The Coral Ridge Hour* has run at least ten nationally broadcast programs devoted entirely to exposing the evils of the ACLU. Currently, *The Coral Ridge Hour* spotlights the ACLU's activities on a quarterly basis.

This powerful new book by Sam Kastensmidt, a staff researcher and news analyst at the Center for Reclaiming America for Christ, is just the latest installment of Dr. Kennedy's long-standing promise to expose the treacherous work of the ACLU.

This book-length "rap sheet" is a stunning indictment of the ACLU's nefarious activities on a broad set of topics. In each area addressed, Sam reveals how the ACLU is working to weaken and topple those twin pillars of American political prosperity: morality and religion. *Indefensible* will startle and anger you as you discover the many ways this legal organization has used the courts to impose its alien values on a nation.

DR. GARY CASS
Executive Director
Center for Reclaiming America for Christ

Introduction

*For you were once darkness, but now you are light in the Lord.
Walk as children of light (for the fruit of the Spirit is in all goodness,
righteousness, and truth), finding out what is acceptable to the Lord.
And have no fellowship with the unfruitful works of darkness,
but rather expose them. For it is shameful even to speak of
those things which are done by them in secret. But all things
that are exposed are made manifest by the light, for
whatever makes manifest is light.*

– Ephesians 5:8-13 (NKJV)

American Civil Liberties Union. The name alone would lead most Americans to believe that the organization is a noble defender of liberty in the finest tradition of our nation's Founders.

Those familiar with the agenda of the ACLU understand all too well that the organization is not even remotely concerned with advancing or protecting true liberty. Instead, it parades under a false banner of liberty while attacking the very foundations of America. The ACLU is in the business of defending the indefensible—protecting all forms of licentiousness and striving to destroy the boundaries of common decency.

By attempting to mask gross immorality behind stretched definitions of constitutional liberty, the ACLU poses a tremendous threat to America's future stability. Certainly America's Founding Fathers never envisioned a day when groups like the ACLU would be able to distort the clear intentions of the Constitution into justification for travesties like abortion on demand, child pornography, and muzzling religious speech.

UNDERSTANDING OUR ROOTS

Samuel Adams, the Father of the American Revolution, understood the dangers posed by moral anarchy—particularly for a self-governing republic. After witnessing the tumultuous social collapse of European nations, Adams warned:

> Neither the wisest constitution nor the wisest laws will secure the liberty and happiness of a people whose manners are universally corrupt . . . A general dissolution of the principles and manners will more surely overthrow the liberties of America than the whole force of the common enemy.[1]

Adams believed that an America absent of common virtue posed a far greater threat to American liberty than the whole force of its common enemies. Baron de Montesquieu, a famous French political thinker who exerted tremendous influence on our Founding Founders, once advised, "The deterioration of every government begins with the decay of the principle upon which it was founded."[2]

A review of the writings of our Founding Fathers makes it obvious that this philosophy was the rule . . . not the exception. In George Washington's famed 1796 Farewell Address, he offered this parting advice for future generations: "Of all the dispositions and habits which lead to political prosperity, religion and morality are indispensable supports."[3]

The noble philosophy of America's Founders stands in direct opposition to the perverse agenda of the ACLU, which seems largely defined by its efforts to stifle both religion and morality.

JUDICIAL ACTIVISM AND THE ACLU

Thankfully, the majority of Americans could never embrace the debauched agenda of the ACLU. In recognition of this simple fact, the ACLU has opted to undermine the representative will of the American people by saturating the nation with costly lawsuits. Its attorneys have mastered the art of litigious intimidation—threatening American communities with the prospect of expensive court battles, unless they yield to the will of the ACLU and surrender their collective values.

The ACLU's disdain for the countless vestiges of America's Christian heritage helps to explain why the organization handles nearly six thousand court cases each year and claims to "participate in more cases before the Supreme Court than anyone besides the U.S. government itself."[4] Indeed, the ACLU is hard at work challenging the core values of our country and stifling the will of the American people.

Regrettably, the organization has been extremely successful when it comes to bending the meaning the U.S. Constitution. The ACLU lacks the support necessary to mount effective campaigns to actually amend the text of the Constitution, but in the modern era of judicial supremacy this is no longer necessary. Instead, it can rely on a handful of unelected judicial contortionists to stretch the intentions of America's Founders beyond recognition—and impose its own morphing ideologies onto the unchanging text of the Constitution.

U.S. Supreme Court Justice Charles Evans Hughes once arrogantly wrote, "We are under a Constitution, but the Constitution is what the judges say it is."[5] Borrowing from this philosophy, the ACLU is able to circumvent the law by finding judges willing to redefine it to suit its own purposes. Ideologically-driven, unchecked judges are free to offer ridiculous interpretations of standing laws—essentially creating new laws.

Under this prevailing judicial philosophy, which treats the Constitution as an "evolving document," Americans are no longer governed by the Constitution; instead, the nation is ruled by a robed oligarchy! The current system expends no effort toward healthy public debate or discourse. Rather, the discontented few need only appeal to the arrogance of judges who believe they know what is best, rather than the American people and their legislators.

WE THE PEOPLE—OVERRULED!

In this era of judicial activism, popular majorities and common morality have become irrelevant. The American people have expressed tremendous outrage over issues like partial-birth abortion, same-sex marriage, child pornography, parental rights, and the eradication of all public recognition of America's Christian heritage. But with the help of judges, the legal petitions of the ACLU have repeatedly trumped the collective will of America.

The voice of the majority has been utterly ignored:

- 70 percent of Americans support a federal ban on partial-birth abortion.[6]
- 77 percent of Americans support the public display of the Ten Commandments.[7]
- 87 percent of Americans support the right to display nativity scenes on public property.[8]
- 66 percent of Americans oppose same-sex "marriages."[9]
- 59 percent of Americans (ages 27 to 59) support prayer at official public school activities.[10]
- 57 percent of Americans agree with the

statement: "Abortion is murder."[11]

- 75 percent of Americans favor "allowing churches and other houses of worship to apply, along with other organizations, for government funding to provide social services."[12]

- 51 percent of Americans believe that churches "should express their views on day-to-day social and political questions."[13]

- 64 percent of Americans believe that wives should have to inform their husbands before getting an abortion.[14]

- 73 percent of Americans support requiring minors to obtain parental consent before getting an abortion.[15]

- 87 percent of Americans believe that the Pledge of Allegiance should include the words "under God."[16]

- Only 12 percent of Americans support an "evolution only" high school biology curriculum, while 55 percent support the teaching of creationism, intelligent design, and evolution.[17]

- 63 percent of parents support new regulations limiting the amount of sex and violence in TV shows during the early evening hours.[18]

Millions of Americans—all overruled by the legal shenanigans of the ACLU!

Having usurped the role of the legislature, the ACLU and the courts have effectively undermined the text and the original intent of the U.S. Constitution. Each new lawsuit is treated like an opportunity to relaunch the Constitutional Convention, and each subsequent conflicting court decision further erodes and distorts the original intentions of the thirty-nine signers of the U.S. Constitution.

Our Founders never intended for the U.S. Constitution to be treated like an evolving document. Rather, James Madison, the primary architect of the Constitution, once wrote:

> I entirely concur in the propriety of resorting to the sense in which the Constitution was accepted and ratified by the nation. In that sense alone it is the legitimate Constitution. And if that be not the guide in expounding it, there can be no security for a consistent and stable ... exercise of its powers.[19]

America was founded as a constitutional republic with checks and balances, in order to ensure that the steady rule of law would trump the whimsical and often despotic nature of men. As they sought to establish a self-governing nation, the Founders feared the power of an unchecked judiciary. Thomas Jefferson once wrote, "To consider the judges as the ultimate arbiters of all constitutional questions [is] a very dangerous doctrine indeed, and one which would place us under the despotism of an oligarchy."[20]

The *Federalist Papers*, which persuaded Constitutional Convention delegates to ratify the Constitution, specified that "the judiciary is beyond comparison the weakest of the three departments of power. . . . it can never attack with success either of the other two."[21] Nevertheless, our modern unaccountable judiciary has repeatedly struck down laws duly passed by our elected officials. To make matters worse, this repressive branch of government has expressly abandoned the moral compass of mainstream America.

THE AGENDA OF THE ACLU

The ACLU has dismissed the wisdom of our Founding Fathers as archaic and outdated. Into this void of constitutional discipline, the ACLU has launched a number of massive legal campaigns that, if successful, will utterly destroy this country. This is not to say that the ACLU is on the wrong side of every issue. Even a broken clock is right twice a day. For instance, the ACLU opposed overly restrictive campaign finance reforms,[22] it opposed the High Court's reckless eminent domain decision,[23] and the organization—on rare occasions—has even defended the liberties of Christians.[24] Nevertheless, these examples of prudence are the exception—not the rule!

The ACLU's most prominent campaigns focus on ten key areas:

1. Dismissing America's Christian Heritage
2. Attacking Religious Liberties
3. Silencing the Church
4. Advancing Sexual Anarchy
5. Sexualizing America's Children
6. Redefining Marriage and Family
7. Promoting Obscenity
8. Promoting the Culture of Death
9. Impeding America's War on Terror
10. Looting the American Taxpayers

THE DANGERS OF RELATIVISM

John Adams warned of the day when a baseless free society would abandon moral absolutes. He wrote, "Democracy will soon degenerate into . . . [such] anarchy that every man will do what is right in his own eyes and no man's life or property or reputation or liberty will be secure."[25]

This baseless society described by John Adams—where "no man's life or property or reputation or liberty will be secure"— may be coming to fruition in modern-day America. We live in an age when life, private property, reputation, and religious liberty are no longer considered inalienable rights bestowed by our Creator. Rather, these rights are increasingly conditioned upon the capricious discretion of judges.

This is the ACLU's grand design—the creation of a society where every man does what is right in his own eyes. Now that our courts are actively dismissing religion and morality from the law, states are increasingly powerless to oppose the ACLU's quest to legitimize absolute moral chaos—prostitution, polygamy, gay marriage, legalized drugs, euthanasia, abolition of parental rights, the right to sodomy, child pornography, abortion on demand, sexualization of children, censored curriculums, and open endorsement of our country's military opponents.

This is the sort of lunacy that comprises the ACLU's agenda.

CONFUSING LIBERTY WITH LICENSE

Throughout history, the wisest philosophers have all understood that the greatest threat to the prosperity of any self-governing society would be a collapse of common values— when absolute standards of right and wrong are exchanged for the whims of individual opinions. When every man does what is right in his own eyes, the fabric of society is inevitably destroyed.

The Bible, the bedrock of America's common morality, demands respect for absolutes. The prophet Isaiah wrote, "Woe to those who call evil good, and good evil; who put darkness for light, and light for darkness . . . Woe to those who are wise in their own eyes, and prudent in their own sight!"[26]

Apart from Scripture, the Greek philosophers also recognized the dangers of moral relativism, fearing the prospect of a generation with no respect for absolutes. In perhaps the world's most famous treatise on justice, *The Republic*, Plato outlines the traits of a dangerous leader:

> He doesn't admit true speech . . . that there are some pleasures belonging to good desires and some belonging to bad desires, and that ones must be practiced and honored while others checked. . . . Rather, he shakes his head at all this and says that all [desires] are alike and must be honored on an equal basis.[27]

Does this sound familiar? Plato's writings foreshadowed the modern "whatever floats your boat" relativistic mentality.

The great philosophers understood the folly and inevitable collapse looming for societies that harbor no respect for morality, law, or personal accountability. For such societies, Plato concluded, "Too much freedom seems to change into nothing but too much slavery, both for private man and city. . . . Tyranny is probably established out of no other regime than democracy— the greatest and most savage slavery out of the extreme of freedom."

Unquestionably, the ACLU is committed to these most dangerous extremes of freedom—where liberty mutates into licentiousness and serves only as an usher to tyranny. If America cannot recapture its respect for the law and its belief in moral absolutes, this nation will likely be cast onto the ash heap of history, along with all the other empires and civilizations that grew too "enlightened" for absolute standards of right and wrong.

ONE

Dismissing America's Christian Heritage

"Blessed is the nation whose God is the LORD."

— Psalm 33:12

Long before the ACLU began imposing its morally destructive agenda upon the American people, the organization understood that it must first undermine the common bonds of society. If it could strip the nation of its reliance upon a higher law, then the universal truths of right and wrong could be abandoned for the whimsical impulses of men. Hence, it is not surprising that the ACLU has played such an instrumental role in the rise of secularism and blatant hostility toward America's religious heritage.

Francis Schaeffer, a Christian philosopher of the twentieth century, explained, "If there is no absolute beyond man's ideas, then there is no final appeal to judge between individuals and groups whose moral judgments conflict. We are merely left with conflicting opinions."[1]

Dr. D. James Kennedy, president and founder of Coral Ridge Ministries, has likewise warned against the pitfalls of relativism:

> The greatest danger for any government is the temptation to dissociate itself from the

ultimate source and authority of all governing—God Himself—and become a government unto itself. When that happens, there ceases to be a benchmark for morality, and therefore for justice, and a government becomes either tyrannical or anarchical—in any case, immoral.[2]

This was a prevailing fear among America's Founding Fathers. Alexander Hamilton, a signer of the U.S. Constitution and co-author of the *Federalist Papers*, once described man-made moral standards as nothing more than "absurd and impious doctrine." He wrote, "The law of nature . . . dictated by God, Himself, is, of course, superior in obligation to any other. It is binding over all the globe, in all countries, and at all times. No human laws are of any validity if contrary to this."[3]

To understand the gravity of the ACLU's efforts to banish God from government, it is essential to understand the sincere reliance upon faith and religion that characterized the founding era. Indeed, the Church's role in laying the foundations of American liberty was tremendous.

THE CHURCH'S ROLE IN AMERICAN LIBERTY

Consider the life of the Reverend John Witherspoon. Born in 1723 in Scotland and raised during the Great Awakening—the enormous spiritual revival that gripped Europe and the American colonies between 1730 and 1770—he became an ordained Presbyterian minister at the age of 20. Thereafter, he provided such powerful and illuminating sermons that he was awarded an honorary doctorate of divinity from the prestigious St. Andrews University.

At the age of 44, Witherspoon had developed such an impressive reputation that he was invited to America to become the President of Princeton University. Upon arriving in America in 1768, Witherspoon saw a country set ablaze by the powerful sermons of George Whitefield, Jonathan Edwards, and Gilbert Tennent. The fruit of the Great Awakening was so palpable it caused Benjamin Franklin to write in his autobiography:

> It was wonderful to see the change soon made in the manners of our inhabitants. From being thoughtless or indifferent about religion, it seem'd as if all the world were growing religious, so that one could not walk thro' the town in an evening without hearing psalms sung in different families of every street.[4]

As Princeton's new president, the fiery preacher's enthusiasm was well received, and he became an instrumental voice in America's struggle for independence. In fact, Witherspoon often taught about the Christian's duty to fight for the causes of liberty and righteousness. In one famous lesson he told his students, "It is in the man of piety and inward principle that we may expect to find the uncorrupted patriot, the useful citizen, and the invincible soldier. God grant that in America true religion and civil liberty may be inseparable."[5]

Witherspoon's teaching was so widely admired that he was selected to serve as a member of the Continental Congress where he was named to more than one hundred committees. When the time for revolution came, Reverend John Witherspoon did not shrink from signing his name to the Declaration of Independence—a certain death warrant should the Revolution fail.

In fact, Witherspoon was so instrumental in stirring the souls of America's patriots and preachers that upon hearing of "the shot heard around the world," which launched the American

Revolution, British Prime Minister Horace Walpole declared to Parliament: "Cousin America has run off with a Presbyterian parson."[6]

Princeton University still boasts, "The record of Princeton men who studied under Reverend John Witherspoon is outstanding, including President James Madison [primary author of the U.S. Constitution], Vice-President Aaron Burr, nine cabinet officers, 21 United States senators, 39 members of the House of Representatives, three justices of the Supreme Court, 12 governors, and numerous delegates to the Constitutional Convention."[7]

What type of lessons did he teach? On May 17, 1776, weeks before America declared her independence, Reverend Witherspoon proclaimed:

> He is the best friend to American liberty, who is most sincere and active in promoting true and undefiled religion, and who sets himself with the greatest firmness to bear down profanity and immorality of every kind. Whoever is an avowed enemy of God, I scruple not [do not hesitate] to call him an enemy of his country.[8]

Witherspoon was certainly not the exception. Of the 56 signers of the Declaration of Independence, 24 held seminary degrees.[9] Two of the Continental Congress's first actions were to hire military chaplains and to purchase 20,000 Bibles to remedy a national shortage. In fact, America's first Speaker of the House was a minister, the Reverend Frederick Muhlenberg.[10]

The government's religious commitment was so deeply ingrained that America's subsequent treaty with the British (the Treaty of Paris) began with the words, "In the name of the most Holy and undivided Trinity."[11]

DISTORTING THE FIRST AMENDMENT

In an effort to secularize the nation, the ACLU has engaged in a "search and destroy" mission aimed at removing all vestiges of the nation's religious history from the public realm. From displays of the Ten Commandments and nativity scenes to war memorial crosses and religious murals, the ACLU is determined to erase all symbols of America's Christian heritage by perverting the clear intentions of the First Amendment.

Concerning religion, the First Amendment declares, "Congress shall make no law respecting an establishment of religion, or prohibiting the free exercise thereof. . . ."

Despite overwhelming historical evidence to the contrary, the ACLU claims this amendment was intended to create a wall of separation between church and state, thereby prohibiting government officials from honoring America's religious heritage or even allowing Christian values to influence public policy decisions.

THE FRAMERS' VIEW OF THE FIRST AMENDMENT

Both the writings of our Founding Fathers and virtually every U.S. Supreme Court decision on the matter until 1947 prove that the framers of the Constitution never intended to banish faith and religion from government.

James Wilson, a signer of both the Declaration of Independence and the U.S. Constitution, was appointed by President George Washington to serve as one of the original justices of the U.S. Supreme Court. He wrote, "Human law must rest its authority ultimately upon the authority of that law which is Divine . . . Far from being rivals or enemies, religion and law [church and state] are twin sisters, friends, and mutual assistants."[12]

Few people could decipher the purposes of the U.S. Constitution better than President James Madison, whom even most secularists acknowledge to be the document's primary architect. On February 3, 1812, President Madison appointed Joseph Story to serve on the U.S. Supreme Court, deeming him a worthy interpreter of the revered document.[13] He would become the first Supreme Court justice to address the subject of religious freedom in America.[14]

As Justice Story explained:

> We are not to attribute this [First Amendment] prohibition of a national religious establishment to an indifference to religion in general, and especially to Christianity (which none could hold in more reverence than the framers of the Constitution) . . . Probably, at the time of the adoption of the Constitution . . . the general, if not the universal, sentiment in America was that Christianity ought to receive encouragement from the State.[15]

Two centuries later, Americans are confronted by a judiciary that does not permit the slightest mingling of government and religion. This was not always the case. In two centuries of constitutional history, the judicial mandate of devout secularism is a relatively new phenomenon.

158 YEARS WITHOUT A "WALL"

From 1789 (when the language of the First Amendment was approved) to 1947 (when the Supreme Court first elaborated its doctrine of a "high and impregnable" wall between church and state), the government was never expected to be void of religion.

A sampling of court decisions from America's history proves just that:

> **1803**–The Maryland Supreme Court decreed, "By our form of government, the Christian religion is the established religion; and all sects and denominations of Christians are placed on the same equal footing and are equally entitled to protection in their religious liberty."[16]
>
> **1811**–The New York Supreme Court explained, "We are a Christian people and the morality of the country is deeply engrafted upon Christianity."[17]
>
> **1824**–The Pennsylvania Supreme Court ruled, "Christianity, general Christianity, is and always has been a part of the common law."[18]
>
> **1844**–The U.S. Supreme Court declared, "Christianity . . . is not to be maliciously and openly reviled and blasphemed against, to the annoyance of believers or the injury of the public."[19]
>
> **1889**–In its decision upholding laws against polygamy, the U.S. Supreme Court argued, "Bigamy and polygamy are crimes by the laws of all civilized and Christian countries."[20]
>
> **1892**–After reviewing numerous historical records to determine the heritage of the United States, the nation's High Court concluded, "These and many other matters which might be noticed, add a volume of unofficial declarations to the mass of organic utterances that this is a Christian nation. We are a Christian people, and the morality of the country is deeply engrafted

upon Christianity."[21]

1931–The U.S. Supreme Court explained, "We are a Christian people, according to one another the equal right of religious freedom and acknowledging with reverence the duty of obedience to the will of God."[22]

THE FAULTY FOUNDATIONS OF THE WALL

Not long after the High Court acknowledged "the duty of obedience to the will of God," a rising belief in the supreme will of the government and the Court forever altered the national landscape. In 1932, President Franklin D. Roosevelt was inaugurated and zealously championed a wide variety of government programs aimed at pulling the nation from the depths of the Great Depression. As the government grew in size and power, the nation's collective reliance upon God as the source of liberty diminished.

In the mid-1930s, the Supreme Court struck down several of Roosevelt's social programs, starting a vicious feud between the judicial and executive branches. Initially, Roosevelt attempted to squelch the Court through the Court Packing Plan of 1937, a proposal which asked Congress to increase the number of justices on the Court—so the President could appoint enough justices to create a majority in his favor. Congress rejected the request.[23]

Still, Roosevelt remained determined to pack the Court with ideologically-driven judges who would support his proposals for expansive government programs—never imagining that this same Court would eventually issue a decision that sought to replace God with government as the ultimate source of American liberties.

By 1947, the entire Court was composed of Justices appointed by two presidents, Franklin Roosevelt and Harry Truman, who believed strongly in an expanded role for the federal government.[24] In the case of *Everson v. Board of Education* (1947), this skewed Court considered the constitutionality of a New Jersey law allowing financial reimbursements to parents who sent their children to Roman Catholic parochial schools, as opposed to the largely Protestant-oriented public schools. In a 5-4 decision authored by Justice Hugo Black, a former member of the (anti-Catholic) Ku Klux Klan,[25] the Court ruled, "The First Amendment erected a wall between church and state. That wall must be kept high and impregnable. We could not approve the slightest breach."[26]

The *Everson* decision is the epitome of judge-made law. *The "wall between church and state" is never once mentioned in the text of the U.S. Constitution.* In a desperate effort to ignore the clear intentions of the constitutional framers, one ACLU resource offers this convoluted explanation for why it took the Court 158 years to discover the wall: "Although the Bill of Rights was ratified in 1791, it took two centuries for a body of law on the church/state relationship to evolve."[27]

Incredibly, the ACLU expects people to believe that all previous generations, including the generation of men who authored the U.S. Constitution, were incapable of correctly interpreting it because it had not yet "evolved."

In erecting this wall, the Court relied upon an 1802 letter from Thomas Jefferson to a group of persecuted Baptists in Danbury, Connecticut. In this private letter, President Jefferson explained that the First Amendment had erected "a wall of separation between church and state."[28] Placed in its proper context, it is quite obvious that Jefferson was merely using the phrase to state that the Connecticut government should not force its citizens to worship in a particular manner.

If Jefferson had intended for this "wall" to create a secular government with an "impregnable" separation between church and state, it remains quite perplexing to ponder (1) why Jefferson would have allowed church services to be held in the U.S. Capitol building, (2) why, as governor, he drafted resolutions in support of public days of prayer in Virginia, or (3) why he repeatedly approved legislative acts to fund missions "for civilizing the Indians and promoting Christianity."[29]

The *Everson* decision ignored these facts, making a mockery of jurisprudence.

ACLU – THERE FROM THE BEGINNING

Not surprisingly, the ACLU played a pivotal role in the *Everson* case.[30] *The Washington Times* published an opinion article elaborating on the organization's involvement:

> In 1947, the ACLU was responsible for *Everson v. Board of Education* coming before the high court. One of its lawyers, Leo Pfeffer, wrote the draft of the opinion which resulted in the so-called "separation of church and state." This was the first time in history that the Supreme Court did not use precedent in its opinion. It ignored precedent.[31]

In 1971, in the case of *Lemon v. Kurtzman*, the Court compounded the problem by establishing a three-prong test to determine the constitutionality of a government action. The Lemon Test requires that all government actions (1) must have "a secular legislative purpose," (2) must not advance nor inhibit religion, and (3) must not foster "an excessive government entanglement with religion."[32]

The *Everson* and *Lemon* decisions remain the two most lethal arrows in the quiver of the ACLU, providing all the ammunition necessary for the organization to continue its extensive and vigorous legal campaign to rid America of any public reminders of its religious heritage.

In the nearly sixty years since 1947, the ACLU has enjoyed great success in the U.S. Supreme Court, particularly in the arena of recasting America's religious heritage.

- In 1962, the ACLU represented Steven Engel in the case of *Engel v. Vitale*, persuading the High Court to banish prayer from public schools.[33]
- In 1963, the organization represented Edward Schempp in the case of *Abington v. Schempp*, which declared it unconstitutional for schools to require Bible reading.[34]
- In 1968, the ACLU filed an *amicus* (friend of the court) brief in the case of *Epperson v. Arkansas*, which struck down a law prohibiting schools from teaching evolutionary theories.[35]
- In 1985, the ACLU filed an *amicus* brief in the case of *Wallace v. Jaffree*, which struck down an Alabama law requiring a moment of silence in public schools.[36]
- In 1987, in the case of *Edwards v. Aguillard*, the organization convinced the Supreme Court to strike down a Louisiana state law requiring creationism to be taught alongside evolution.[37]
- In 1989, in the case of *Allegheny v. ACLU*, the organization successfully argued that nativity scenes should be banished from a

Pittsburgh courthouse lawn.[38]

- In 1992, in the case of *Lee v. Weisman*, the ACLU filed an *amicus* brief with the Court, convincing five justices to forbid public prayer during graduation ceremonies.[39]

- In 2003, the ACLU filed an *amicus* brief in the case of *Locke v. Davey*, opposing a college student's right to use state scholarship funds to pursue a degree in theology.[40]

Frustrated by the disastrous consequences unleashed by the *Everson* and *Lemon* rulings, U.S. Supreme Court Chief Justice William Rehnquist wrote in 1985:

> The greatest injury of the "wall" notion is its mischievous diversion of judges from the actual intentions of the drafters of the Bill of Rights. . . . No amount of repetition of historical errors in judicial opinions can make the errors true. The "wall of separation between church and state" is a metaphor based on bad history, a metaphor which has proved useless as a guide to judging. It should be frankly and explicitly abandoned.[41]

DISMISSING THE DECALOGUE

In 1980, the ACLU used the *Lemon* precedent to urge the U.S. Supreme Court to strike down a Kentucky statute which required public schools to display privately-funded copies of the Ten Commandments in all classrooms. In the case of *Stone v. Graham*, the High Court issued a 5-4 decision declaring that "the posting of the Ten Commandments in public school rooms has no secular legislative purpose, and is, therefore, unconstitutional."

The Court noted:

> If the posted copies of the Ten Commandments
> are to have any effect at all, it will be to induce
> the school children to read, meditate upon, per-
> haps to venerate and obey, the Commandments.
> . . . [This] is not a permissible state objective.[42]

In 1995, fifteen years after the *Stone* decision, the ACLU threatened Etowah County (Ala.) Circuit Judge Roy Moore with a lawsuit, unless he agreed to remove a small wooden plaque of the Ten Commandments from his courtroom wall. In response to the ACLU's intimidation tactics, Judge Moore emphatically vowed, "I'm not taking down the Ten Commandments plaque."[43]

Consequently, the ACLU proceeded with a lawsuit, igniting an emotional firestorm. When asked about the controversy, then-Alabama Governor Fob James told reporters, "The only way those Ten Commandments and prayer would be stripped from that courtroom is with the force of arms. I will use all legal means at my disposal, including the National Guard and State Troopers, to prevent the removal of the Ten Commandments from Judge Moore's courtroom."[44]

In 1998, the Alabama Supreme Court dismissed the ACLU's case on a technicality, but Judge Moore, affectionately nicknamed "the Ten Commandments Judge," had gained the respect and admiration of Alabama residents. Moore launched a campaign to run for the Supreme Court of Alabama. In November 2000, after promising to bring the Ten Commandments into the Alabama Supreme Court building and to "restore the moral foundation of law," Moore was elected to serve as the chief justice of the

Alabama Supreme Court, receiving over seventy percent of the vote.[45]

In August 2001, Chief Justice Moore kept his promise, unveiling a privately-funded Ten Commandments monument in the rotunda of the Alabama Supreme Court building. Three months later, the ACLU filed a federal lawsuit, demanding that the monument be removed.[46]

On November 18, 2002, U.S. District Judge Myron Thompson sided with the ACLU, ordering the monument's removal. In complete disregard for America's religious heritage, Judge Thompson arrogantly declared, "The state may not acknowledge the sovereignty of the Judeo-Christian God and attribute to that God our religious freedom."[47]

Judge Thompson's decision abandoned the spirit of the nation's Founders, who hinged the entire prospect of American liberty on the philosophy that all men "are endowed *by their Creator* with certain unalienable rights."[48] Indeed, the very first sentence of the Declaration of Independence makes it abundantly clear that the Founders based their claim to freedom upon "laws of nature and of nature's God."[49]

Justice Moore appealed this ruling, but a unanimous three-judge panel of the Eleventh U.S. Circuit Court of Appeals affirmed Judge Thompson's decision. The appellate court elaborated that some acknowledgments of God (e.g. the national motto or legislative prayer) are permissible, but only "because they have lost through rote repetition any significant religious content."[50]

In other words, the government may acknowledge God so long as it does so in a manner that is repetitious and insincere. In response, Chief Justice Moore declared, "For federal courts to adopt the agenda of the ACLU and remove the knowledge of God and morality from our lives and our law is wrong."[51] Ironically, following his heroic efforts to "restore the moral foundation of law," Chief Justice Moore was removed from office by a judicial "ethics" panel for refusing to obey a court order.[52]

FLOOD OF TEN COMMANDMENTS LITIGATION

Rather than recognizing the role of a higher law in protecting American liberties, ACLU lawyers consider the law of God to be "offensive and intimidating."[53] One ACLU official stated, "Under our Constitution, the government has no business erecting, accepting, or maintaining religious monuments on public property. Such symbols of faith belong in churches, synagogues and homes, not courthouses and other seats of power of our secular government."[54]

With this philosophy, the ACLU has inundated hundreds of communities throughout America with lawsuits aimed at removing displays of the Ten Commandments from public settings.[55] One city mayor likened the ACLU to a "snake that's crawling around, looking for religious markers to devour."[56]

In Kentucky alone, the ACLU has filed lawsuits to remove displays of the Commandments from Clark County, Garrard County, Grayson County, Harlan County, Jackson County, Mc-Creary County, Mercer County, Pulaski County, Rowan County, and the Kentucky state capitol building.[57]

SUPREME COURT CONFUSES COMMANDMENTS ISSUE

In 2005, the ACLU's lawsuit against McCreary County, Kentucky, went all the way to the U.S. Supreme Court. In the case of *McCreary v. ACLU*, the organization demanded that two Ten Commandments displays be removed from public property. In its legal brief, the ACLU cited a multitude of existing precedents and even went so far as to insinuate that the displays could convey a chauvinistic message "by using the masculine God over the feminine Goddess."[58]

In June 2005, the High Court issued a 5-4 decision, ordering government officials to remove the displays. In an attempt to explain the Court's departure from the original intent of the Constitution, Justice David Souter explained, "Applications unanticipated by the Framers are inevitable."[59]

Thankfully, the *McCreary* decision was not the final word. On the very same day, the very same Court issued a decision unmistakably contradicting the *McCreary* ruling and revealing the unpredictable nature of the modern judiciary. In the case of *Van Orden v. Perry*, the Court upheld the constitutionality of a Ten Commandments display at the Texas State Capitol building.

Responding to the two decisions' embarrassing lack of clarity, Justice Antonin Scalia noted:

> What distinguishes the rule of law from the dictatorship of a shifting Supreme Court majority is the absolutely indispensable requirement that judicial opinions be grounded in consistently applied principle. That is what prevents judges from ruling . . . as their personal preferences dictate. Today's opinion forthrightly . . . admits that it does not rest upon consistently applied principle.[60]

In a press release, Dr. D. James Kennedy echoed Justice Scalia's concerns: "This is not law. This is the consequence of the Court's abandonment of the plain text of the Constitution. . . . It has left a trail of confused and confusing jurisprudence that has left lower courts puzzled and perplexed."[61]

OPPOSING THE PLEDGE

The ACLU has also challenged the constitutionality of the 1954 law that added the words "under God" to the Pledge of Allegiance. This phrase was added during the early days of the Cold War—as Congress and President Dwight D. Eisenhower sought a way to instill in children the concept that American liberty comes from God—not from government.

Explaining that a belief in God was the "unbridgeable gap between America and Communist Russia," one Congressman explained at the time, "Unless we are willing to affirm our belief in the existence of God and His creator-creature relation to man, we drop man himself to the significance of a grain of sand and open the floodgates to tyranny and oppression."[62]

Fifty years later, the ACLU actively seeks to erase this distinction. Thus, the organization has filed numerous lawsuits challenging the constitutionality of the Pledge—and state laws requiring its recitation.[63]

Most notably, the ACLU supported the efforts of atheist Michael Newdow in his legal campaign against the Pledge. On June 26, 2002, a three-judge panel of the Ninth U.S. Circuit Court of Appeals issued a 2-1 decision, striking down the 1954 law that added "God" to the Pledge.[64] Interestingly enough, one of the judges who declared the Pledge unconstitutional (Stephen Reinhardt) is married to the president of the Los Angeles chapter of the ACLU.[65]

Eventually, the case was appealed all the way to the U.S. Supreme Court, where the ACLU filed an *amicus* brief in support of the plaintiff. The ACLU argued that the Pledge's "ritual recitation is not a device for achieving . . . secular purposes."[66] According to such logic, the practice must be declared unconstitutional.

In June 2004, the Supreme Court refused to consider the

merits of the case, dismissing it on a technicality and explaining that Newdow did not possess sufficient custodial rights over his daughter to challenge the law.

Undeterred, Newdow refiled his lawsuit with eight additional plaintiffs, and in September 2005, U.S. District Judge Lawrence Karlton struck down the constitutionality of the Pledge, citing the previously overturn decisions of the Ninth Circuit. As of this book's printing, an appeal is pending.[67]

ATTACKING A WWI MEMORIAL CROSS

Given the anti-religious fervor of the ACLU and the unpredictable nature of American courts, it seems that no public acknowledgement of God is safe from assault. This has become evident through the organization's campaigns to remove crosses from war memorials.

In 1934, the Veterans of Foreign Wars (VFW) erected a five-foot-tall Latin cross in a remote section of the Mojave National Preserve as a memorial to the more than 116,000 American soldiers who fought and died in World War I.[68] For 65 years not one single complaint was leveled against the memorial. In fact, many area residents used the cross as a venue for Easter services.

In 1999, the ACLU of Southern California sent a letter to the National Parks Service (NPS) threatening to take legal action against the agency unless it agreed to tear down the cross. Upon learning of this threat, Congress passed a law specifying that no federal resources "may be used . . . to remove the five-foot-tall white cross located within the boundary of the Mojave National Preserve."[69]

So, the ACLU filed a federal lawsuit on behalf of Frank Buono, a former Mojave park employee who had since moved to Oregon. In July 2002, U.S. District Judge Robert J. Timlin issued a decision which threatens the security of all federally owned memorials and gravestones that bear the image of a cross. Judge Timlin declared that "the presence of the cross on federal land conveys a message of endorsement of religion."[70] As such, the judge ordered a wooden box to be placed over the cross for the duration of the government's appeals process.

In an effort to save the cross, the government appealed to the Ninth U.S. Circuit Court of Appeals, to no avail. The appellate court acknowledged that the cross had been erected "in memory of veterans who died during World War I," and ordered the government to tear it down anyway, explaining that "the primary effect of the presence of the cross was to advance religion."[71]

As a result, Congress passed further legislation to transfer ownership of the land from the federal government to a private entity, on the assumption that if the memorial were owned by members of the private sector, the issue of government endorsement would not be a problem. The ACLU filed another lawsuit challenging Congress' actions. A determined Judge Timlin declared the land-transfer unconstitutional, and—as of this printing—an appeal is still pending in the Ninth Circuit.[72]

Peter Eliasberg, a staff attorney for the ACLU of Southern California, contends that the government is only wasting its time in its efforts to save the memorial:

> The government has an obligation to take down the cross as soon as possible. . . .[73] The courts have consistently held that a permanent religious fixture on federal land is a violation of the U.S. Constitution. An Act of Congress doesn't change that. The cross must come down, and no amount of political maneuvering or grandstanding will prevent that.[74]

To understand the hypocritical condition of modern American jurisprudence, one needs only to reflect on the treatment given to two different California war memorials. In 2002, the Mojave cross was banished to the darkness of a coffin-like box, in fear that it might offend visitors in the middle of the Mojave Desert. One year later, the state of California was busy dedicating a new memorial paver on the property of the California State Capitol designed to honor gay and lesbian veterans.[75]

REMOVING THE MOUNT SOLEDAD MEMORIAL CROSS

The ACLU's disdain for war memorial crosses is not limited to the Mojave cross. In 1989, a similar situation developed in San Diego, when the ACLU sued to remove a 29-foot-tall cross from the Mount Soledad War Memorial. Though the cross had stood atop Mount Soledad since 1954, the organization argued that it was unconstitutional. On December 3, 1991, U.S. District Judge Gordon Thompson, Jr., ordered the city to tear it down.

The city appealed the decision. In 1998, after nine years of legal wrangling, the city attempted to sell the half-acre of land beneath the cross to a private entity (the Mount Soledad Memorial Association) for $106,000. As expected, the ACLU filed a lawsuit challenging the deal. The sale was struck down by a 7-4 decision of the Ninth U.S. Circuit Court of Appeals, which concluded that the primary motive for selling the land was to aid religion.

Subsequently, San Diego residents presented more than 100,000 petitions to their elected officials, who agreed to allow the voters to determine the fate of the memorial cross. On July 26, 2005, in an effort to both keep the cross and avoid financial liability for the ACLU's lawsuit, seventy-six percent of San Diego voters agreed to transfer ownership of the Mount Soledad War

Memorial to the federal government.

Revealing a clear disdain for the democratic process, James McElroy, an attorney for the ACLU, lashed out: "It still doesn't mean a d*** thing. Voters should have never voted on it. It's a waste of taxpayers' money."[76] Immediately, the ACLU went shopping for an activist judge to overrule the will of San Diego voters. Four months later, California Superior Court Judge Patricia Cowett struck down the ballot measure, calling the election an "unconstitutional aid to religion."[77]

Fifteen years after the original decision in the Mount Soledad case, Judge Thompson announced plans to enforce his original decision, ordering the city on May 3, 2006, to remove the cross within 90 days or face daily fines of $5,000. "It is now time, and perhaps long overdue, for this Court to enforce its initial permanent injunction forbidding the presence of the Mount Soledad cross on City property," he wrote.[78]

On July 7, 2006, Supreme Court Justice Anthony Kennedy intervened, issuing a four-page opinion, allowing the city of San Diego to keep the cross while it pursues an appeal. "The equities here support preserving the status quo while the city's appeal proceeds," Justice Kennedy explained. "Compared to the irreparable harm of altering the memorial and removing the cross, the harm in a brief delay pending the Court of Appeals' expedited consideration of the case seems slight."[79]

In a letter to President Bush, Congressman Duncan Hunter, who represents the San Diego area, warned, "It would be a national travesty to have this veterans' memorial dismantled against the overwhelming majority of San Diego residents and federal legislative intent."[80] Shortly thereafter, both houses of Congress approved legislation to transfer ownership of the land to the U.S. Department of Defense,[81] and President Bush endorsed the bill. "The people of San Diego have clearly expressed their desire to keep the Mt. Soledad Veterans Memorial in its present form," he said. "Judicial activism should not stand in the way of the people."[82]

Immediately, the ACLU pledged to challenge the new law. "The courts will invalidate the transfer," promised McElroy. "This is going to inflame people's emotions, but it won't succeed."[83]

SUING TO BAN BIBLES FROM PUBLIC VIEW

Apparently no public memorial is safe from the ACLU's reach if it acknowledges the faith of the deceased.

For almost five decades, a privately-funded Bible display rested outside Harris County Courthouse in Houston, Texas. The display was erected in 1956 to memorialize the late philanthropist William Mosher for his dedication to the area's hungry and homeless—a dedication which had stemmed from the teachings of Scripture. However, the ACLU filed a lawsuit contending that the memorial violated the First Amendment.

In 1988, the memorial withstood an aggressive barrage of litigation filed on behalf of the American Gay Atheists. After the county successfully defended it, the display was repeatedly vandalized. On one occasion, vandals broke the memorial's glass case, stole the Bible, and replaced it with a gay pornographic magazine.[84]

Later that year, county officials removed the Bible to avoid future conflict. Seven years later, County Judge John Devine campaigned on a "platform of putting Christianity back into government." When Judge Devine was elected, he restored the Bible to its rightful place in the display, and the ACLU filed a federal lawsuit demanding its removal.

On August 10, 2004, U.S. District Judge Sim Lake sided with the ACLU, declaring, "The Bible atop the Mosher monument does not have a secular purpose, and the primary or principal effect of the Bible display is to advance religion. . . . [Therefore], the Bible display violates the Establishment Clause."[85] In August 2006, a three-judge panel of the Fifth U.S. Circuit Court of Appeals upheld Judge Lake's ruling.[86] As of the book's printing, the case was under appeal.[87]

FIGHTING TO BANISH BABY JESUS

The ACLU has also zealously fought to prevent communities from displaying nativity scenes on public property during the Christmas season. Indeed, every year the nation is invariably littered with scores of ACLU lawsuits aimed at forcing communities to forfeit their right to acknowledge the Christmas season.

These lawsuits have been going on for decades. On December 10, 1986, the ACLU of Greater Pittsburgh filed a federal lawsuit aimed at preventing Allegheny County officials from displaying a nativity scene in the county's courthouse. The case made it all the way to the U.S. Supreme Court.

On July 3, 1989, in the case of *Allegheny v. ACLU*, the U.S. Supreme Court issued a 5-4 decision prohibiting the county from displaying a nativity scene in celebration of the federally-sanctioned religious holiday. Incredibly, in the same ruling, the Court actually approved the public display of a Jewish menorah.

In a decision that defies reason, the Court declared:

> [The] government may celebrate Christmas in some manner and form, but not in a way that endorses Christian doctrine. Here, Allegheny County has transgressed this line. It has chosen to celebrate Christmas in a way that has the effect of endorsing a patently Christian message.[88]

Therefore, the Court explained that, in order to be constitutional, a nativity scene must also be accompanied by secular symbols (i.e., reindeer, Santa Claus, or Frosty the Snowman). Armed with the *Allegheny* precedent, the ACLU has harassed hundreds of communities. Though ninety-six percent of all Americans celebrate Christmas, the fear of lawsuits has caused government officials to go to ridiculous lengths to ensure that residents are not exposed to the holiday's actual significance.[89]

As a result of this hysteria, cities across America now celebrate a "winter holiday" rather than "Christmas," and many school districts encourage teachers to avoid the word "Christmas" altogether. One New Jersey school district banned the playing of *instrumental* Christmas music,[90] while a school in Colorado barred students from sharing candy canes with classmates.[91] The city manager in Eugene, Oregon, actually went so far as to issue a directive prohibiting the display of Christmas trees on government property.[92]

By cherry-picking from a hodgepodge of inconsistent court rulings, the ACLU and other advocates of secularism have been able to pressure many counties and school districts to forsake the true reason for the season.

USING LEGAL INTIMIDATION TO ADVANCE SECULARISM

The ACLU has used the momentum generated by these types of court decisions to banish religion from all areas of America's public life. To chronicle each instance would require an entire series of books. The following is just a brief sampling:

The ACLU and Berkley Gardens Elementary School principal Kathleen Madigan filed a lawsuit against Kenneth Roberts, a fifth-grade teacher, for keeping a Bible on his desk and reading it to himself during the students' silent reading time. A judge ordered Roberts to conceal the Bible during the school day.[93]

In October 2001, as the nation mourned the September 11 tragedy, the ACLU sent a letter to administrators at Breen Elementary School in Rocklin, California, threatening to sue the district for displaying a "God Bless America" sign. The ACLU claimed that such signs convey "a hurtful, divisive message."[94]

In February 2003, the ACLU sent a letter to U.S. Park Officials, demanding that they remove three bronze plaques from various locations in the Grand Canyon because the plaques were inscribed with Bible verses.[95]

In April 2004, in response to a threat from the ACLU, the city of Redlands, California, agreed to remove a cross from its official city logo. The image was obscured or removed from all city vehicles, buildings, doors, stationery, and even police badges.[96]

On June 1, 2004, in response to the ACLU's threats of a federal lawsuit, the Los Angeles County Board of Supervisors voted 3-2 to remove a small cross from the county's official seal.[97]

In January 2005, the ACLU threatened to file a lawsuit against the city of Greer, South Carolina, unless the city agreed to stop its annual tradition of publishing a calendar featuring Bible verses. The city agreed to stop.[98]

In September 2005, the ACLU threatened to sue Oglethorpe County, Georgia, unless the county agreed to remove a display of the 23rd Psalm from the county clerk's office. Frustrated by the threat of expensive litigation, one county official ordered the display to be taken down. "I think it is the wrong thing to do, but I have to do it," he told reporters.[99]

In August 2006, Joe Cook, executive director of the ACLU of Louisiana, threatened to file a lawsuit against St. Bernard Parish, after learning that parish officials planned to unveil a cross-shaped memorial to the victims of Hurricane Katrina.[100]

ACLU HYPOCRISY ABOUNDS

In recent decades, the ACLU has used its so-called "wall" to fight tooth and nail to prevent government sponsorship of the Pledge of Allegiance, memorial crosses, Ten Commandments displays, nativity scenes, Bible displays, and virtually every other acknowledgement of America's religious heritage.

At the same time, it is worthwhile to note that there have been some instances in which the ACLU has endorsed public displays of religion. For example, when New York City Mayor Rudy Giuliani threatened to cut taxpayer funding from the Brooklyn Museum of Art for displaying a painting of the Virgin Mary with cow dung and pictures of female sexual organs pasted all over her body, the ACLU was first in line to defend the display.[101] U.S. District Court Judge Nina Gershon ruled that New York City's elected officials were not allowed to place conditions on the museum's funding.[102]

In another instance, the ACLU offered its support to the taxpayer-funded National Endowment for the Arts, after the agency sponsored an art show featuring "Piss Christ"—an exhibit consisting of a crucifix submerged in a jar of urine.[103]

In the ACLU's myopic world, it appears that the only permissible publicly-funded displays of religion are those which blatantly mock or disparage the Christian faith.

A DEPARTURE FROM CONSTITUTIONAL CHAOS?

However, there may be a light at the end of this dark tunnel. With the resignation of Justice Sandra Day O'Connor and the appointments of Chief Justice John Roberts and Justice Samuel Alito, most legal scholars expect a pronounced shift in how the High Court handles cases involving the so-called "wall of separation between church and state."

Already, federal appellate courts appear to be growing increasingly bold in their willingness to reject frivolous ACLU lawsuits. In December 2005, less than one year after the Supreme Court issued its conflicting opinions on the constitutionality of Ten Commandments displays on government property, a unanimous three-judge panel of the Sixth U.S. Circuit Court of Appeals upheld a display at the Mercer County, Kentucky, courthouse and rebuked the ACLU for its "hyper-sensitive" lawsuit.

In an unabashed and refreshing departure from the High Court's flawed post-*Everson* jurisprudence, the federal appellate court declared, "The ACLU makes repeated reference to 'the separation of church and state.' This extra-constitutional construct has grown tiresome. The First Amendment does not demand a wall of separation between church and state."[104]

The court explained:

> Our concern is that of the reasonable person, and the ACLU . . . does not embody the reasonable person. . . . If the reasonable observer perceived all government references to the Deity as endorsements, then many of our Nation's cherished traditions would be unconstitutional, including the Declaration of Independence and the national motto. Fortunately, the reasonable person is not a hyper-sensitive plaintiff.[105]

The panel's decision was upheld in the ACLU's appeal to the full Sixth Circuit.[106]

Mat Staver, president and general counsel of Liberty Counsel, reflected on the recent shift in momentum in the ACLU's quest to rid God from government. "They clearly realize that the landscape has changed," said Staver. "They no longer can count on the U.S. Supreme Court to be their friend in their anti-God campaign. The tide is turning. . . . The ACLU's agenda has been rocked backward. Now more than ever we must increase our efforts to regain lost ground."[107]

"From the 1920s to the 1980s, the ACLU was the only game in town," Staver noted. "They stuffed their briefcases with legal memos promoting their lies and went from one court to the next selling their corrosive agenda. But when Christians show up for battle, by God's grace, we can win. And win we have!"[108]

TWO

Attacking Religious Liberties

Proclaim liberty throughout all the land to all its inhabitants.

– Leviticus 25:10

For decades, the American people have watched in frustration as the ACLU conspires with America's judiciary to eliminate religious expression from every conceivable state-sponsored venue—classrooms, graduations, football games, universities, local government meetings, state legislatures, Congress, courtrooms, military academies, Christmas pageants, state-supported children's homes, and various faith-based initiatives.

Alan Sears, president of Alliance Defense Fund, explains:

> The ACLU desires a secular, faithless America where all memory of faith traditions and religion are absent from the public square, morals are relative, and where parental rights, religious freedom, and the sanctity of human life . . . are nearly non-existent. This is the America we will get unless we stand up to the ACLU.[1]

A review of the ACLU's actions points clearly to a deep-seated hostility toward religion—a hostility that has fueled the organization's drive to trample the religious liberties of Americans.

PROHIBITING PRAYER IN THE PUBLIC SCHOOLS

The campaign to secularize America is a relatively new phenomenon. In a resource still used to teach immigrants about American history, the U.S. Department of State explains:

> For many years, a particular ritual marked the beginning of each school day all across America. Teachers led their students through the Pledge of Allegiance, a short prayer, the singing of "America" or "The Star-Spangled Banner," and possibly some readings from the Bible. The choice of ritual varied according to state law, local custom, and the preferences of individual teachers or principals.[2]

This was the case in Union Free School District No. 9 in New Hyde Park, New York. Prior to 1962, the district's students rose each morning and recited the nondenominational Regents' prayer: "Almighty God, we acknowledge our dependence upon Thee, and we beg Thy blessings upon us, our parents, our teachers and our Country."[3]

However, just fifteen years after the *Everson* decision introduced the "wall" notion, William Butler, an attorney with the New York Civil Liberties Union (an ACLU affiliate), filed a federal lawsuit on behalf of five parents to end school prayer in America.[4] On June 25, 1962, in the case of *Engel v. Vitale*, the High Court did just that—siding with the ACLU and prohibiting school-sanctioned prayer in classrooms across America.[5]

Justice Hugo Black, author of the unfounded *Everson*

decision, also wrote this majority opinion, hinging the entire decision on his recently erected "wall." Justice Black wrote:

> The State's use of the Regents' prayer in its public school system breaches the constitutional wall of separation between Church and State. We agree with that contention, since we think that the constitutional prohibition against laws respecting an establishment of religion must at least mean that, in this country, it is no part of the business of government to compose official prayers for any group of the American people to recite as a part of a religious program carried on by government.[6]

On the very next day, *Newsday* reported:

> The most enthusiastic endorsement of the high court decision came from the New York Civil Liberties Union, which hailed it as "a milestone in the development of guarantees of separation of church and state." George E. Rundquist, executive director of the organization, said that the court's decision is in no way an attack on religion. It simply makes crystal clear that a state-written and imposed prayer has no place in the public schools.[7]

Americans disagreed. In fact, on the twentieth anniversary of the *Engel* decision, a Gallup poll discovered that 81 percent of Americans not only supported school prayer, but favored a constitutional amendment to protect it from the courts.[8] Unfortunately, in the decades following the decision, numerous examples of religious expression—once commonplace in American culture—have been banished from the public realm against the wishes of the American people.

Though the ACLU had vowed that the *Engel* decision was not an "attack on religion," time has proven otherwise. In November 2005, the Anti-Defamation League, an organization staunchly committed to secularism, conducted a nationwide survey and found that 64 percent of American adults believe that "religion *is* under attack."[9]

Unquestionably, the actions of the ACLU have contributed to these sentiments.

SCHOOL PRAYER ALMOST RESURRECTED

In the early 1990s, the High Court agreed to review a case challenging the constitutionality of a Rhode Island middle school's graduation prayers. Steven R. Shapiro, national legal director of the ACLU, co-authored a brief to the U.S. Supreme Court, urging the Court to prohibit the prayers. In the case, *Lee v. Weisman* (1992), most legal scholars expected the High Court to finally overturn the 1962 *Engel* decision. With the Court almost evenly divided on the issue of school prayer, Associate Justice Anthony Kennedy would serve as the deciding vote.

Christian legal scholars were optimistic—and with good reason. Just a few years before the *Weisman* case, Justice Kennedy authored a powerful and persuasive dissenting opinion in the case of *Allegheny v. ACLU* (1989), supporting the public display of nativity scenes:

> Government policies of accommodation, acknowledgment, and support for religion are an accepted part of our political and cultural heritage. . . . Any approach less sensitive to our

heritage would border on latent hostility toward religion, as it would require government, in all its multifaceted roles, to acknowledge only the secular, to the exclusion and so to the detriment of the religious.[10]

After the Court deliberated the facts of the *Weisman* case, Justice Kennedy did, indeed, author a court decision that would have resurrected school prayer, but he discarded it, changing his mind at the last minute and writing Justice Harry Blackmun, "My draft looked quite wrong."[11]

Instead, Justice Kennedy sided with the ACLU, striking down public school graduation prayers. Writing for the 5-4 majority, Justice Kennedy abandoned his previous philosophy, claiming that students should never feel coerced to participate in a religious activity: "Research in psychology supports the common assumption that adolescents are often susceptible to pressure from their peers towards conformity."[12]

In a justifiably fiery dissent, Justice Antonin Scalia noted the danger of whimsical Justices:

> That fortress which is our Constitution cannot possibly rest upon the changeable philosophical predilections of the Justices of this Court, but must have deep foundations in the historic practices of our people. . . . A few citations of "research in psychology" that have no particular bearing upon the precise issue here cannot disguise the fact that the Court has gone beyond the realm where judges know what they are doing.[13]

With regard for neither the text of the Constitution nor the intent of its framers, the Court handed the ACLU another weapon with which it has bullied countless school administrators. Consequently, school districts across America have gone to extremes—trampling the religious liberties of Christian students—to prevent the possibility of an ACLU lawsuit.

ATTEMPTING TO MUZZLE STUDENTS AT GRADUATION

On June 15, 2006, Brittany McComb, valedictorian of her graduating class in Henderson, Nevada, was scheduled to deliver her graduation speech. Midway through, as Brittany began explaining how Jesus Christ had filled the emptiness that had plagued her life, school officials actually pulled the plug on her microphone.

Weeks earlier, when Brittany submitted her speech to school administrators, they requested that she recite a carefully edited version of the speech—with all references to God and Jesus Christ removed. Brittany refused, opting to deliver her speech in its entirety. However, as soon as she deviated from the school's censored version—speaking of God's role in her life—her microphone was turned off.[14]

Halfway through her speech, Brittany told the crowd:

> His love fits. His love is "that something more" we all desire. It's unprejudiced, it's merciful, it's free, it's real, it's huge, and it's everlasting. God's love is so great that he gave His only Son up [*microphone plug pulled here*] to an excruciating death on a cross so His blood would cover all our shortcomings and provide for us a way to heaven in accepting this grace. This is why Christ died.[15]

The U.S. Supreme Court has claimed repeatedly that

students do not "shed their constitutional rights to freedom of speech or expression at the schoolhouse gate."[16] But the ACLU of Nevada applauded the actions of the Clark County School District, arguing that the district was right to silence such speech.[17]

Gary Peck, executive director of the ACLU of Nevada, explained, "We are not talking about a public forum where people have unfettered rights to say whatever they choose. This was a school-sponsored event. The podium should not be turned into a pulpit for the purpose of preaching."[18]

Just three years before, the ACLU demanded that the school district abolish its policy allowing student-led graduation prayers. When the school board refused,[19] the ACLU filed suit. Eventually, the board caved and agreed to rescind its prayer policy to appease the organization. Now, rather than taking a principled legal stand against the ACLU, the district is faced with a federal lawsuit filed on behalf of Brittany McComb.

"This is a clear case of censorship and discrimination and an egregious violation of free speech as protected by our First Amendment," explains John Whitehead, president of the Rutherford Institute. "What happened to Brittany McComb should not happen in a country that prides itself on promoting freedom." As of this book's printing, McComb's case is pending.

MORE YOUTH REJECTING ACLU OPPRESSION

Increasingly, young Americans are growing sick and tired of the ACLU's repressive censorship. In a similar incident, the ACLU filed a petition, asking a federal judge to prevent student-led prayer at Russell County (Ky.) High School's graduation ceremony. On graduation day, U.S. District Judge Joseph H. McKinley granted an injunction, forbidding Megan Chapman, the student-elected senior chaplain, from offering a prayer to open the ceremony.[20]

Russell County High School graduates refused to surrender their liberties. On the morning after graduation, the *Louisville Courier-Journal* reported:

> A federal judge ordered school officials and a student not to include a scheduled prayer at last night's Russell County High School graduation ceremony. About 200 seniors responded at the event by standing during the principal's opening remarks and reciting the Lord's Prayer. That prompted a standing ovation from the standing-room-only crowd.[21]

Most Americans long for the days of unfettered religious freedom, when a student's simple prayer or a valedictorian's speech about the love of God was not considered an act of state defiance! Unfortunately, the ACLU's efforts to muzzle public expressions of religion show no signs of slowing. To the contrary, in recent years the ACLU has ramped up its efforts.

REQUESTING IMPRISONMENT FOR PRAYER

Consider the ACLU's relentless crusade against the Tangipahoa Parish (La.) School Board. In October 2003, the ACLU filed its third unique lawsuit against the school district in nine years.[22] The first two lawsuits successfully (1) prohibited prayers during football games and (2) prevented biology teachers from presenting evidence for creationism. The third lawsuit sought to prohibit the parish school board members from opening their meetings with prayer.[23]

Again, the ACLU found a federal judge sympathetic to its

cause. On February 23, 2005, U.S. District Judge Helen G. Berrigan ordered the school board to discontinue its 32-year-old tradition, because "opening each meeting with a prayer lacks a secular purpose."[24]

The following month, after learning of several instances of prayer at school functions, Joe Cook, executive director of the ACLU of Louisiana, labeled the board's allowance of prayer "un-American and immoral."[25]

On May 18, 2005, the ACLU filed a motion to hold various employees of the district in contempt of court for praying illegally at school functions. In its motion, the ACLU argued that these prayers "must result in [the district employees'] removal from society."[26]

Using language more appropriate for an oppressive regime in Iran or China, the ACLU urged the court to impose severe sanctions upon any board member or teacher who participated in or allowed prayer at a school function. In its motion, the ACLU explained, "Anything short of actual imprisonment would be ineffective to sending that message to these individuals."[27]

In an effort to end any confusion, the board invited Alliance Defense Fund (ADF) attorneys to host a seminar explaining the constitutionally-defined religious liberties of public school faculty and staff. During the conference, Cook again revealed his hostility toward people of faith.

Cook furiously derided the board. "They believe that they answer to a higher power," he told WAFB-TV reporters, "which is the kind of thinking that you had with the people who flew the airplanes into the buildings in this country."[28]

Consider the sentiments of the ACLU expressed in this single case: (1) allowing school prayer is "un-American and im-moral," (2) elected officials must be imprisoned for allowing prayer at school functions, and (3) people who believe in a higher power are like terrorists.

One would hope that the American people see this jargon as the fanatical rhetoric that it is and summarily dismiss it from any sphere of legitimate public discourse. Yet, frighteningly, these sentiments come from an organization that has enjoyed greater access to our nation's Supreme Court than any other entity besides the U.S. government itself.[29]

PRAYER IS A "DEMEANING ACT"

In August 2005, the ACLU filed a federal lawsuit against Cobb County, Georgia, for allowing sectarian prayers during the opening of county commission meetings. In this case, the ACLU requested that the county be prohibited "from knowingly and intentionally allowing sectarian prayers at County government meetings."

Oddly enough, the ACLU's lawsuit did not request an outright prohibition of legislative prayers. Instead, the lawsuit sought only to prohibit sectarian prayers—preventing Christian clergy from praying in the name of Jesus. While cloaking its argument under its "separation of church and state" mantra, the ACLU essentially argued that officials of the "state" must impose a code of censorship on how the ministers of the "church" are allowed to pray.

Arguing on behalf of its clients, the ACLU's brief explained that "the prayer practice is a demeaning act" that had inflicted "irreparable harm" upon the plaintiffs.[30]

On January 13, 2006, U.S. District Judge Richard Story denied the ACLU's request for a preliminary injunction, which would have forced county officials to abandon sectarian prayer for the length of the trial. In a 65-page ruling, Judge Story explained that the ACLU did not have a "substantial likelihood" of prevailing in its case. He concluded:

To be sure, many of these speakers, in offering their invocations, identify the deity to whom they direct their prayer. In that respect, they surely convey their alignment with one religious creed to the exclusion of others. But viewed cumulatively, given the diversity in the denominations and faiths represented, it is difficult to extrapolate from any one speaker's affiliation the preference on the part of the Cobb County government.[31]

In response to the ruling, Maggie Garrett, an ACLU attorney, admitted, "The problem with the prayers is that the overwhelming majority of prayers mention Jesus."[32]

SUING TO STOP SUPPER PRAYERS

Nonsectarian prayers are not safe either, as evidenced in the ACLU's attacks against American military academies.

Founded in 1839, the Virginia Military Institute (VMI) is the nation's oldest military college. For more than 160 years, the state-supported college enjoyed a tradition of saying grace before dinner meals. However, on January 23, 2001, two VMI cadets threatened to take legal action unless the school put a stop to the nondenominational prayers.

In a written response to the cadets, VMI Superintendent General Josiah Bunting, III, refused to abandon tradition, declaring, "The Constitution does not prohibit our saying grace before supper. And we shall continue to do so. . . . [It] is a precious link to our heritage."[33]

In May 2001, upon General Bunting's refusal, the ACLU filed a federal lawsuit on behalf of the two cadets. Eight months later, on January 24, 2002, U.S. District Judge Norman Moon sided with the ACLU, ordering VMI to stop offering corporate prayer before meals. Former Virginia State Attorney General Jerry Kilgore responded, "It's a shame today that while American soldiers are fighting for our liberty in places like Afghanistan, cadets training to be soldiers cannot pray [corporately] for their safety."[34]

The case was appealed to the Fourth U.S. Circuit Court of Appeals. Though the appellate court acknowledged that cadets were "not obliged to recite the prayer, close their eyes, or bow their heads," it concluded, "VMI's supper prayer conflicts with First Amendment principles."[35]

In declaring the prayer unconstitutional, the court conveniently ignored the historical events surrounding the drafting of the Constitution. More specifically, on the very same day that Congress approved the wording of the First Amendment (November 25, 1789), it also voted to recommend a national "day of public thanksgiving and prayer."[36] Certainly our Founders would never have endorsed a government-led call to prayer on the very same day that they intended to prohibit it!

Unfortunately, many of today's judges no longer consider the Founders' intentions a relevant tool in interpreting the Constitution, but Thomas Jefferson once instructed:

> On every question of construction, carry ourselves back to the time when the Constitution was adopted, recollect the spirit manifested in the debates, and instead of trying what meaning may be squeezed out of the text, or invented against it, conform to the probable one in which it was passed.[37]

No reasonable historian or constitutional scholar could legitimately assert that the Founders intended to prohibit corporate prayer at the nation's military academies. Yet, rather than reflecting upon the spirit manifested in the constitutional debates, the Fourth Circuit opted to "squeeze" new meaning from the text.

ATTACKING PRAYER AT THE U.S. NAVAL ACADEMY

The ACLU next tried to use that appellate court decision to force another military academy to abandon its tradition of prayer. Maryland ACLU's Director Susan Goering sent a letter to the Naval Academy in Annapolis warning, "We believe that when you have had a chance to review the Fourth Circuit's opinion, you will agree that the Naval Academy's lunchtime prayer cannot pass constitutional muster and will, therefore, cease the practice."

Thankfully, the Naval Academy refused to cower to the ACLU's threats, announcing that it would vigorously defend its long-standing tradition of prayer before meals. Immediately, a frustrated ACLU announced plans to search for a disgruntled cadet willing to sue the Naval Academy. ACLU lawyer David Rocah whined to reporters, "We tried things the nice way, and they have told us to pound sand. If someone is interested in challenging [prayer at the Naval Academy], we'd be perfectly happy to talk to them about that."[38]

This is the *modus operandi* of the ACLU—legal intimidation and contorting the Constitution!

As a result, U.S. Rep. Walter Jones (NC) sponsored legislation designed to protect voluntary, non-denominational prayer in the nation's military academies.[39] In a press release announcing the new legislation, Rep. Jones declared:

> I find it incredibly ironic that . . . organizations like the ACLU are attempting to take away the very freedoms that these students are willing to

go to war to protect. . . . The principles of faith that guided our founders animate the lives of the men and women training to defend our nation. That tradition and heritage is in trouble. I have seen the federal courts take one right after another away from people of faith in this country, and I think it's time to fight.[40]

Unfortunately, the legislation never made it past the House Committee on Armed Services.[41]

ACLU SUES TO CENSOR INDIANA LEGISLATIVE PRAYER

The ACLU has even fought to impose standards on the religious content of legislative prayers.

In June 2005, the Indiana Civil Liberties Union (ICLU) filed a federal lawsuit against Indiana's Speaker of the House, Brian Bosma, seeking to stop a 189-year-old tradition of offering sectarian prayer at the opening of each session.[42]Though the Indiana House had permitted prayers from Muslims, Jews, and Christians, the ICLU's legal complaint focused solely on prayers that included phrases like "in the strong name of Jesus our Savior," "We pray this in Christ's name," and "I appeal to our Lord and Savior, Jesus Christ."

Speaker Bosma stood on firm legal ground. Already, the Supreme Court had ruled that legislative prayers were constitutional. In the case of *Marsh v. Chambers* (1983), the Court declared:

It can hardly be thought that in the same week Members of the First Congress voted to appoint and to pay a chaplain for each House and also voted to approve the draft of the First Amendment for submission to the states, they intended the Establishment Clause of the Amendment to forbid what they had just declared acceptable.... The opening of sessions of legislative and other deliberative public bodies with prayer is deeply embedded in the history and tradition of this country.[43]

The Court also rejected the ACLU's misguided notion that courts should serve as censors for these prayers, declaring, "It is not for us to embark on a sensitive evaluation or to parse the content of a particular prayer."

With precedent on his side, Speaker Bosma refused to back down, telling reporters, "The day the Indiana Civil Liberties Union dictates free speech on the floor of the Indiana House is the day that democracy begins to decline. . . . This is an important right that we need to preserve."[44]

Tragically, on November 30, 2005, U.S. District Judge David F. Hamilton shunned High Court precedent, ordering the Indiana House to cease its tradition of offering unfettered prayer. Hamilton wrote, "If the Speaker chooses to continue any form of legislative prayer, he shall advise persons offering such a prayer . . . that they should refrain from using Christ's name or title or any other denominational appeal."[45]

In a remarkable display of unity, the Indiana House of Representatives voted 83-0 to pass a resolution denouncing the court's decision.[46] Speaker Bosma declared:

> This resolution not only marks a moment in history for the Indiana House of Representatives to preserve this tradition, but it will continue to remind all of us, for generations to come, that this decision of the federal court to restrict prayer

in the Indiana House of Representatives was intolerable.[47]

Unfortunately, given the rise of judicial activism, even unanimous declarations from America's elected officials cannot match the disproportionate power of one federal judge. In May 2006, Speaker Bosma appealed the case to the Seventh U.S. Circuit Court of Appeals.[48] As of this book's printing, no decision had been reached.

OPPOSING A MINUTE OF SILENCE

In its quest to ensure that prayer is banished from the public realm, the ACLU has even sued to strike down a Virginia statute that required public schools to give students one minute of silence each day to "meditate, pray, or engage in other silent activity."[49]

On June 22, 2000, the ACLU of Virginia filed a federal lawsuit to strike down that statute. Kent Willis, executive director of the ACLU of Virginia, stated, "Every Virginia legislator knows the purpose of this law. It is an attempt to put state-sanctioned prayer back in our public schools, and that is both shameful and unconstitutional."[50]

Rev. Jerry Falwell, a Virginia pastor and resident, responded:

> The ACLU believes students are not emotionally balanced enough to have a moment of their own in which to meditate, daydream, or pray. . . . A moment of silence is dangerous in their minds. The ACLU, in its desperate attempt to regulate silence in Virginia schools, has shown just how vindictive and anti-prayer it really is.[51]

U.S. District Judge Claude M. Hilton rejected the ACLU's lawsuit. The organization appealed the judge's decision to the Fourth U.S. Circuit Court of Appeals, to no avail. A split three-judge panel of the Fourth Circuit rejected its request, concluding, "Just as this short period of quiet serves the religious interests of those students who wish to pray silently, it serves the secular interests of those who do not wish to do so."[52] ACLU attorney Stuart Newberger—perhaps fearing that students might actually pray in silence—called the appellate court's decision "intolerable."[53] The ACLU filed an appeal to the U.S. Supreme Court, but the Justices refused to consider the merits of the case.[54]

SUING TO STOP CHILDREN'S FUNDRAISER

Regardless of national history or public opinion, the ACLU arrogantly ignores the indisputable fact that activities involving both government and religion can be mutually beneficial.

For example, in August 2004, the Franklin County (Ohio) Department of Children's Services planned to sponsor a gospel music concert designed to raise money and awareness for the county's adoption services and foster homes. Upon learning of the event, the ACLU sent a letter to the government agency demanding they cancel the concert.

Doris Calloway-Moore, spokeswoman for the department, was stunned by the unexpected letter. She told reporters, "The only goal is to find homes for kids who need them. When we look at demographics and of the people who adopt, we find most people are of faith."[55]

Despite this, the ACLU of Ohio charged that the gospel concert "constitutes an impermissible and possibly unconstitutional entanglement of government and religion." In a subsequent press release, the organization warned, "Failure to cancel the event may result in litigation to prevent the concert from going forward."[56] As indicated, when the agency refused to cancel the event, the ACLU filed a federal lawsuit seeking to shut it down.

On August 20, 2004, U.S. District Judge Algenon L. Marbley explained that the case was a "close call" but ruled against the ACLU, concluding that the county's one-time gospel concert did not constitute an "excessive entanglement" between government and religion.[57]

John Saros, executive director for the Department of Children's Services, praised the judge's decision noting, "The religious community is part of our community, and we need to work with them and be partners with them as well as civic and other volunteer groups in the community."

On the opposing side, Jeffrey Gamso, legal director for the ACLU of Ohio, responded by calling the judge's decision to allow cooperation between the faith-based community and the children's services agency "wrong, wrong, and wrong."[58]

STAMPING OUT SECULAR BIBLE COURSES

In its unyielding pursuit of a wholly secularized America, the ACLU has also opposed using the Bible as a resource to teach about nonreligious history and ancient culture. When the Lee County (Florida) School Board approved an elective course that would "use the Bible as a historical document," the ACLU quickly filed a federal lawsuit.

Most legitimate historians agree that Scripture offers invaluable historical insights. In his book, *The New Evidence That Demands a Verdict*, Josh McDowell explains:

> The Bible is the only book that was written over about a fifteen hundred year span . . . by more than forty authors from every walk of

life, including kings, military leaders, peasants, philosophers, fishermen, tax collectors, poets, musicians, statesmen, scholars, and shepherds . . . written on three continents [Asia, Africa, and Europe] . . . in three languages [Hebrew, Aramaic, and Greek].[59]

Given its uniqueness in world history, it would be utterly foolish and narrow-minded to dismiss the Bible in a study of world history, simply because a handful of ACLU attorneys are intolerant of anything remotely resembling religion.

Howard Simon, executive director of the ACLU of Florida, argued:

Whether Bible stories are the "gospel truth" is a matter of faith, not literal history. Over a decade ago, the federal courts prevented religious zealots from evangelizing public school children with the teaching of the biblical story of creation as science. We expect the courts to similarly invoke constitutional principles to prevent the Bible from being used as a history text in Lee County.[60]

On January 20, 1998, U.S. District Judge Elizabeth Kovachevich issued a convoluted two-part ruling that allowed Lee County high schools to teach history lessons from the Old Testament while barring them from using the New Testament. Judge Kovachevich explained, "This Court, too, finds it difficult to conceive how the account of the resurrection or of miracles could be taught as secular history."[61]

This case is not unique. The ACLU has opposed countless curricula involving Christian themes in districts throughout America—even when the courses are designed for adults. For example, the Dearborn, Michigan, school district cancelled a 10-week *adult*-education *elective* on the core tenets of Christianity after receiving legal threats from the ACLU.[62]

BARRING AFTER-SCHOOL CHRISTIAN PROGRAMS

To the average observer, it is obvious that the ACLU is interested in squelching the right of religious expression for those engaged in state-sponsored activities. The ACLU has even insisted on "a prohibition of religious speech" in cases where there *might* be a misguided *perception* of government endorsement of religion.

In September 1996, Stephen and Darleen Fournier requested permission from the Milford (New York) School District to use school facilities for meetings of the local Good News Club, a private Christian organization for children ages 6-12. When the district refused to allow access, the Good News Club filed a federal lawsuit claiming that the school district, which allowed other private organizations to meet on campus, violated its rights to free speech and equal protection.

Lower courts sided with the district, upholding its decision to discriminate against the after-school ministry. Incredibly, the Second U.S. Circuit Court of Appeals went so far as to claim that the activities of the children's ministry were "quintessentially religious" and therefore "fall outside the bounds of pure 'moral and character development.'"[63]

The Good News Club appealed the decision to the U.S. Supreme Court. The ACLU was on hand to defend the district's decision to discriminate. Steven R. Shapiro explained, "An elementary school student is unlikely to perceive any separation at all between church and state when religious instruction takes place in the school building immediately after the final school bell."[64]

In its *amicus* brief to the High Court, the ACLU contended that permitting Christian programs to utilize public facilities during after-school hours created "a seamless web between classroom instruction and religious indoctrination." Incredibly, the ACLU argued that if a program with Christian content conveys even the slight resemblance of government endorsement, then the Court should conclude that "a *prohibition on religious speech* reflects a respect for neutrality, rather than a disrespect for religion."[65]

On June 11, 2001, in a 6-3 decision, the U.S. Supreme Court overturned the lower court decisions, siding with the Good News Club. Writing for the Court, Associate Justice Clarence Thomas declared:

> We conclude that Milford's restriction violates the Club's free speech rights and that *no* Establishment Clause concern justifies that violation. . . . When Milford denied the Good News Club access to the school's limited public forum on the ground that the Club was religious in nature, it discriminated against the Club because of its religious viewpoint, in violation of the Free Speech Clause of the First Amendment.[66]

Justice Thomas also addressed the appellate court's appalling decision, noting, "According to the Court of Appeals, reliance on Christian principles taints moral and character instruction in a way that other foundations for thought or viewpoints do not. We, however, have never reached such a conclusion."[67]

SEEING PAST THE RHETORIC

The ACLU often claims to be a proponent of religious liberties, free speech, and the strict separation of church and state. However, countless examples prove just the opposite. Time and again, the organization has taken stances demonstrating that it seems more interested in muzzling religious speech by endorsing the *regulation* of church *by* state.

How else could one explain ACLU attempts to impose court-sanctioned content standards for prayer, its applause for the censorship of graduation speeches, its demands for the "imprisonment" of praying teachers, its efforts to prohibit voluntary corporate prayer in the nation's military academies, its opposition to moments of silence in public schools, or its outright attempt to justify "a prohibition on religious speech"?

Certainly, such actions do not demonstrate a desire for government neutrality in matters of religion. If anything, the ACLU's antics reveal a deep-seated hostility toward religious expression in the public realm.

In 1962, an ACLU attorney involved in the case that prohibited school prayer promised Americans that the decision was "in no way an attack on religion." Four decades of history have only proven him wrong. The rulings hinging upon that 1962 precedent have been used and reused by the ACLU to trample the religious liberties of countless Americans.

THREE

Silencing the Church

*Having brought the apostles, they made them appear before
the Sanhedrin to be questioned by the high priest. "We gave
you strict orders not to teach in this name [Jesus]," he said.
"Yet you have filled Jerusalem with your teaching...."
Peter and the other apostles replied: "We must obey
God rather than men!"*

— Acts 5:27-29 (NIV)

In recent decades, the ACLU has unleashed a massive campaign to undermine America's religious heritage and subvert the influences of faith upon those who serve in public capacities, essentially confining the Church to remain within the stone walls of its sanctuaries. Though the ACLU often claims that its efforts are aimed at "keeping the government out of the religion business,"[1] a closer look at its actions suggest that it is more interested in keeping the religious out of the government business.

As the ACLU fights to purge America's religious roots from the national conscience, it is imperative for Christians to defend the Church's liberties. Ronald Reagan once warned, "Freedom is a fragile thing and is never more than one generation away from extinction. It is not ours by inheritance; it must be fought for and defended constantly by each generation, for it comes only once to a people."[2]

A Dreadful Lesson From the Nazis

Perhaps no other event in recent history has proven the need for vigilance more than the meteoric rise of Adolf Hitler and the subsequent suppression of church liberty in Germany. In the early 1930s, Adolf Hitler and his Nazi regime sought to muzzle the Church's influence in German politics. Hitler was so determined to control the nation's pulpits that he banned publication of Bibles, ordered that crosses be removed from churches, and even established his own national bishop. By monitoring the nation's pulpits, Hitler was able to silence the voices of Christian conscience before their messages could undermine his credibility. Still, some pastors chose to speak out. One of the great voices of dissent was Rev. Friedrich Martin Niemöller.

On January 25, 1934, after Rev. Niemöller and others had begun to question the legitimacy of Hitler's policies, the dictator summoned them to the Reich chancellery in Berlin. Niemöller admitted to the Führer that he had growing concerns about the policies of the Nazi regime, emphasizing his concerns for the Church and the people of Germany. Hitler ominously responded, "You confine yourself to the Church. I'll take care of the German people."[3]

Two years later, this bold pastor endorsed an open letter to Hitler, boldly denouncing the policies of his regime. "Even an exalted cause must, in the end, lead the nation to ruin if it sets itself against the revealed will of God," the letter explained. "Our people threaten to transgress the limits set by God. [Nazism] seeks to make itself the measure of all things. That is human arrogance, setting itself up against God."[4]

In June 1937, the Nazi regime accused Niemöller of a criminal offense for preaching with "malicious and provocative criticism . . . to undermine the confidence of the people in their political leaders." For doing so, this courageous Lutheran pastor was convicted of "abuse of pulpit" and was confined in the Dachau concentration camp until the liberation in 1945.[5]

During the Nuremberg Trials, as the international community investigated the horrific war crimes perpetrated by the Nazi regime, numerous reports were compiled to document its actions. One such report, *The Persecution of the Christian Churches*, explained:

> Throughout the period of National Socialist rule, religious liberties in Germany . . . were seriously impaired. The various Christian Churches were systematically cut off from effective communication with the people. . . . Under the pretext that the churches themselves were interfering in political and state matters, they would deprive the churches, step by step, of all opportunity to affect German public life.[6]

With no competing voice, Hitler's regime was able to brainwash and mislead the German people, invade Poland, launch World War II, and institute a program for the systematic elimination of entire classifications of people. When all was said and done, six million Jews were either piled into mass graves, or their incinerated remains dusted the European countryside. In the absence of a legitimate church voice, World War II led to the death of more than sixty-two million people from fifty different countries.[7]

CENSORING AMERICA'S PULPITS

Tragically, less than a decade after defeating Adolf Hitler and his fascist Nazi regime, the U.S. government began taking steps to silence its own churches.

In the summer of 1954, Senator Lyndon B. Johnson (TX) was concerned about the actions of several anti-Communist organizations which were threatening his bid for reelection. Consequently, on July 2, 1954, as the Senate was considering a major tax code revision, Senator Johnson proposed a floor amendment to prohibit non-profit 501(c)(3) organizations (including churches) from engaging in political activity.[8]

Johnson's proposed revision was approved by a simple voice vote—with no public debate on the matter. Without serious reflection on the potential consequences, churches were stripped of the liberty to engage in the vital issues of American political life.

In an effort to restore the religious liberties of America's clergy, Rep. Walter Jones (NC) introduced the Houses of Worship Free Speech Restoration Act, which sought to amend the existing IRS Code to ensure that churches, synagogues, and mosques would not be taxed or punished simply "because of the content, preparation, or presentation of any homily, sermon, teaching, dialectic, or other presentation made during religious services or gatherings."[9]

Though it claims to be a proponent of free speech, the ACLU vehemently opposed the measure. In a letter distributed throughout the U.S. House of Representatives, the organization stated, "The American Civil Liberties Union strongly urges you to vote 'NO' on H.R. 235, the Houses of Worship Free Speech Restoration Act. The ACLU opposes any proposal, including H.R. 235, which would allow only religious tax-exempt organizations to engage in political activities."[10]

Opposition to this "free speech restoration act" reveals the blatant double standard in the ACLU's support for a strict separation between church and state. The ACLU contends that either: (1) the state should be permitted to regulate the activities and sermons of the Church, or (2) the state should impose taxation upon the Church. In either scenario, the state plows through the so-called "wall" that the ACLU claims should be "impregnable."

Through its opposition to Jones' bill, the ACLU makes clear its support for government monitoring and regulation of speech and activities in America's churches.

Such a stance absolutely ignores the legitimate purpose of the First Amendment. Among the freedoms guaranteed by this Amendment are the rights to freely exercise one's religion, to speak freely, and to petition the government for grievances. Yet when a pastor attempts to *speak* about his church's *grievances* against government policies in light of *religious* convictions, the ACLU somehow fails to see how the First Amendment applies.

Testifying before the Subcommittee on Oversight of the House Committee on Ways and Means, Dr. D. James Kennedy offered his support for lifting restrictions on America's pulpits:

> With so much uncertainty and so much at risk, silence is, regrettably, the only option for the minister who wants to ensure that the IRS does not open a file on his church. But when Caesar's demand for silence confronts the message of God's Word, ministers are forced into hard choices. That is what happened in Nazi Germany a generation ago. Many pastors submitted, and were silent. Others were not, and paid the price.
>
> If, as has been asserted, we owe our liberties to the "moral force" of the pulpit, the censorship of that voice—for reasons that have everything to do with partisan politics and nothing to do with the separation of church and state—is a monumental mistake that should be quickly corrected. In a culture like ours, which

sometimes seems [to be] on moral life support,
the voice of the Church and her message of
reconciliation, virtue, and hope must not be
silenced.[11]

Unfortunately, it seems that many ministers are failing to
heed the call to confront and engage this culture. Bill O'Reilly,
host of Fox News' *The O'Reilly Factor*, quipped, "We are rapidly
losing freedom in America. Judges are overruling the will of the
people, and fascist organizations like the ACLU are imposing
their secular will. And when was the last time you heard your
priest, minister, or rabbi talk about this? For me, the answer is
simple: Never."[12]

On May 28, 2004, at a conference of American bishops,
Pope John Paul II echoed these concerns, expressing an urgent
need for the Church to confront the decline of faith and values
in Western civilization. In particular, he called upon American
Christians to rise up, declaring:

> The Church in the United States is . . . called to
> respond to the profound religious needs and
> aspirations of a society increasingly in danger of
> forgetting its spiritual roots and yielding to a
> purely materialistic and soulless vision of the
> world. . . . [The] widespread spirit of agnosticism
> and relativism has cast doubt on reason's ability
> to know the Truth.[13]

OPPOSING FAITH-BASED INITIATIVES

In its efforts to silence the Church, the ACLU often
contends that government contracts with faith-based ministries
fail to satisfy an adequate secular purpose. In making this claim,

the ACLU ignores the fact that it was largely Christians who gave rise to the abolitionist and women's suffrage movements. It was also the early American Church that established countless hospitals and ministries to help the poor.

In their book, *What If Jesus Had Never Been Born?*, Dr. D. James Kennedy and Jerry Newcombe point out: "Almost every one of the first 123 colleges and universities in the United States has Christian origins. . . . Harvard, Yale, William and Mary, Brown, Princeton, New York University, Northwestern University, and other schools have thoroughly Christian roots."[14]

Given the many historic contributions of the Church to American culture, it would be grossly unfair to claim that its actions unilaterally do not serve secular purposes.

In recognition of this reality, on January 29, 2001, just nine days after his inauguration, President George W. Bush signed an executive order creating the nation's first White House Office of Faith-Based and Community Initiatives.[15] The administration rightly explained, "Federal funds should be awarded to the most effective organizations—whether public or private, large or small, faith-based or secular—and all must be allowed to compete on a level playing field."[16]

Speaking at the 2006 White House National Conference on Faith-Based and Community Initiatives, President Bush addressed the importance of community outreach, pointing to several positive trends in America's cultural landscape:

> There is a quiet transformation taking place. Violent crime rates have fallen to their lowest level since the 1970s. Welfare cases have dropped by more than half. Drug use amongst youth is down 19 percent since 2001. There are fewer abortions in America than at any point in the last three decades. The number of children born to

teenage mothers has fallen for a dozen years in a row. I attribute the success of these statistics to the fact that there are millions of our fellow citizens all working to help people who hurt, working toward a better tomorrow.[17]

Though faith-based initiatives have a proven record of effectiveness, the ACLU's unyielding dedication to undermine the Church's role in society is once again made evident in its vehement opposition to these programs. The ACLU has argued that these taxpayer funded faith-based initiatives are discriminatory and unconstitutional, even though the U.S. Supreme Court would beg to differ: "This Court has never held that religious institutions are disabled by the First Amendment from participating in publicly sponsored social welfare programs."[18]

So, when the Senate introduced the CARE (Charity Aid, Recovery and Empowerment) Act to fund various faith-based programs, the ACLU mobilized opposition to the bill, labeling the faith-based programs as a "formula for discrimination in employment." In particular, the ACLU argued that the proposed faith-based initiatives were unconstitutional because they failed to require employment of homosexuals or people of opposing religious beliefs.[19]

"This new faith-based bill would both further legitimize the President's misguided initiative and promote taxpayer-funded religious discrimination," said Christopher Anders, ACLU Legislative Counsel. "The legislation is a far cry from a compassionate approach. In reality, it will work to institutionalize religious bias in employment."[20]

The ACLU's opposition to such programs is not restricted to the federal level.

In September 2004, the New York Civil Liberties Union, an affiliate of the ACLU, filed a federal lawsuit seeking to revoke city funding from the Salvation Army. During that year, with financial assistance from New York City, the Army served approximately 2,300 residents daily, offering meals, foster care, adoption services, rehabilitation programs, group homes, boarding houses, services for children with developmental disabilities, HIV services, group day care, and a detention facility for juvenile delinquents.[21]

However, because the Salvation Army has ethical standards for its employees, the ACLU filed a complaint, asking a federal judge to declare that "provision of government funds to finance the Salvation Army's discriminatory religious practices is unconstitutional."[22] Donna Lieberman, executive director of the NYCLU, argued, "[W]hen a church takes on the responsibilities of government [social programs] . . . it can't impose a religious litmus test on its employees. It can't require them to sign a loyalty oath."[23]

Thankfully, U.S. District Judge Sidney H. Stein sided with the Salvation Army, declaring:

> The notion that the Constitution would compel a religious organization contracting with the state to secularize its ranks is untenable in light of the Supreme Court's recognition that the government may contract with religious organizations for the provision of social services.[24]

FIGHTING TO HANDICAP RELIGIOUS SCHOOLS

The ACLU has also stood against school voucher proposals, which offer citizens having children in failing school districts the choice of sending their children to private or religious schools, using financial vouchers from the government.

School voucher proponents contend that competition

between the public and private sectors will ultimately benefit education in general. Other proponents deem school vouchers necessary to ensure educational equality. Ted Sizer, professor of education at Harvard and Brandeis universities, explains, "The issue [is whether] all families have the same choice that upper and middle class Americans have, or should the system remain as it is, giving mobility to those who could buy it and leaving the rest as they are."[25]

When the city of Cleveland, Ohio, instituted a school voucher policy, the ACLU filed a federal lawsuit.[26] Steven R. Shapiro, legal director for the ACLU, argued, "The Cleveland voucher program is nothing but a thinly veiled attempt to provide public funding to religious schools."[27]

Thomas Krannawitter, a senior fellow at the Claremont Institute, responded, "For . . . the American Civil Liberties Union, educating American children is not nearly as important as severing any and all ties between the public and religion. . . . The ACLU clings to its twisted, almost laughable interpretation of the First Amendment."[28]

The ACLU's lawsuit, which challenges the constitutionality of a relationship between public education and religion, runs counter to American history. In fact, the very same Congress that adopted the language of the First Amendment also endorsed the Northwest Ordinance, which declared, "Religion, morality, and knowledge—being necessary to good government and the happiness of mankind, schools, and the means of education— shall forever be encouraged."[29]

It is also worth noting the ACLU's double standard in opposing school vouchers. All parents who send their children to religious schools are required by law to pay taxes in order to fund a public education system with curricula that is often hostile to their deeply held religious beliefs, and the ACLU finds no problem with this. Yet when duly elected officials pass laws allotting public funds to help with the tuition of religious school students, the ACLU files lawsuits.

On June 27, 2002, in a display of judicial restraint, the U.S. Supreme Court issued a 5-4 decision upholding the constitutionality of school voucher programs. Supreme Court Chief Justice William Rehnquist authored the opinion:

> We have repeatedly recognized that no reasonable observer would think a neutral program of private choice, where state aid reaches religious schools solely as a result of the numerous independent decisions of private individuals, carries with it the *imprimatur* of government endorsement. . . . The Ohio program is neutral in all respects toward religion. It is part of a general and multifaceted undertaking by the State of Ohio to provide educational opportunities to the children of a failed school district.[30]

In response to the decision, the ACLU unleashed its tired set of talking points, lamenting the decision as a threat to the "wall" and labeling private choice and open competition between public and religious schools as "bad for education and bad for religious freedom."[31]

So much for being pro-choice!

BARRING THE BOY SCOUTS FROM PUBLIC CONTRACTS

The ACLU is even committed to harassing those organizations whose affiliation with Judeo-Christian beliefs is marginal.

For decades, the Boy Scouts of America (BSA) has built a reputation consistent with the best traditions of America. Its name has even become an adjective synonymous with upright behavior. However, because the BSA requires members to pledge an oath to live "morally straight" lives and acknowledge a "duty to God,"[32] it has become a prime target of the ACLU. The ACLU has equated the Boy Scouts' standards for membership to "bigotry."[33]

In December 2002, the ACLU filed a federal lawsuit against the city of San Diego, arguing that the city's relationship with the Boy Scouts violated the Establishment Clause. Specifically, the ACLU asked a federal judge to nullify the Boy Scouts' decades-old lease of Balboa Park in San Diego. Though the BSA had spent millions to improve the land since 1915, the ACLU argued that leasing to the BSA violated the "separation of church and state," because BSA policy excludes homosexuals from leadership and requires its members to pledge a "duty to God."

The ACLU does not believe that organizations with any form of Judeo-Christian beliefs should be able to enter into contracts with the government unless they first agree to surrender those values—namely by enrolling homosexuals and atheists into both membership and leadership positions.

Incredibly, on July 31, 2003, U.S. District Judge Napoleon Jones sided with the ACLU, declaring the lease unconstitutional. In his decision, Judge Jones explained, "Belief in God is and always has been central to the Boy Scouts of America's principles and purposes ... [and] strongly held private, discriminatory beliefs are at odds with values requiring tolerance and inclusion in the public realm."[34]

The San Diego City Council refused to appeal the judge's decision. In fact, two councilwomen (Toni Atkins and Donna Frey) condemned the children's organization for adhering to "discriminatory" values.[35] Jordan Budd, an attorney for the ACLU, issued an "action alert" to area residents, arguing that those defending the Boy Scouts were "defending bigotry." The alert encouraged the city council "to end its affiliation with this discriminatory organization."[36]

To add insult to injury, the inept council also agreed to pay the ACLU $790,000 in legal fees and $160,000 in court costs for its attack on the Boy Scouts.[37] This is but one example; the ACLU has harassed the Boy Scouts in communities across America. Just one year after the San Diego debacle, the ACLU successfully pressured the Pentagon to instruct its military officials to end all official sponsorship of Boy Scout troops and events. The Scouts are still permitted to meet on military bases, but without the official imprimatur of military support.[38] Adam Schwartz, an attorney with the ACLU, gloated, "This agreement removes the Pentagon from direct sponsorship of Scout troops that engage in religious discrimination."[39]

However, when the ACLU demanded that the Pentagon end its annual sponsorship of the National Scout Jamboree, the Pentagon refused. U.S. Secretary of Defense Donald Rumsfeld told Fox News' Bill O'Reilly:

> I was a Cub Scout, a Boy Scout, an Eagle Scout, a distinguished Eagle Scout, and I am for the Scouts. . . . The Department of Defense has had a longstanding excellent relationship with the Boy Scouts. It has been mutually beneficial. It has helped the Department of Defense and the soldiers and sailors, and it helps the Boy Scouts, and that's a good thing. . . . It ought to continue, and as long as I am here, I will do everything to see that it does.[40]

Hans Zeiger, an Eagle Scout and author of *Get Off My Honor: the Assault on the Boy Scouts of America*, responded:

> The ACLU cares nothing about saving taxpayers money, nor that the Scouts perform millions of dollars and thousands of hours worth of public service. . . . The ACLU simply wants to destroy the Boy Scouts of America.[41]

CENSORING SCIENTIFIC TRUTHS

The ACLU often portrays itself as the champion of free speech. The organization has no problem defending distributors of virtual child pornography, but when the Cobb County, Georgia, School Board allowed factual warning labels to be placed inside the district's biology textbooks, the ACLU mounted a vicious legal campaign.

The stickers advised students that "evolution is a theory, not a fact,"[42] but the ACLU argued that this factual statement conveyed an unconstitutional message of religious endorsement. In January 2005, U.S. District Judge Clarence Cooper agreed and ordered the school district to remove the stickers. The judge warned that the stickers might send "a message that the school board agrees with the beliefs of Christian fundamentalists and creationists."

In his decision, Judge Cooper wrote, "The sticker also has the effect of undermining evolution education to the benefit of those Cobb County citizens who would prefer that students maintain their religious beliefs regarding the origin of life."[43]

Under the ACLU's standards, many of the world's most brilliant scientific scholars would be barred from teaching in public school classrooms. Consider for instance, Albert Einstein, who once declared, "Science without religion is lame."[44] Dr. Francis Collins, director of the Human Genome Research Institute (which mapped the human genome) and author of *The Language of God*, once explained, "I think of God as the greatest scientist . . . . I find it completely comfortable to be both a rigorous scientist . . . and also a believer whose life is profoundly influenced by the relationship I have with God."[45]

If the ACLU had its way, such brilliant scientists would never be permitted to teach a rudimentary biology course in public schools without first submitting to a strict gag order to muzzle their core beliefs.

In May 2006, the Eleventh U.S. Circuit Court of Appeals ordered Judge Cooper to conduct evidentiary hearings and reconsider his decision.[46] As of this book's printing, the case is still pending.

DENYING SCHOLARSHIPS TO THEOLOGY MAJORS

The ACLU seems to cringe at the thought of establishing a level playing field for Christians and religious organizations.

In 1999, Joshua Davey, a student at Northwest College in Kirkland, Washington, qualified for the state's Promise Scholarship for scholastic achievement and was awarded over $1,100. However, when he announced his plan to major in theological studies, the state revoked his scholarship. With the assistance of the American Center for Law and Justice, Davey filed a federal lawsuit, contending that the state had discriminated against him on the basis of religion.

On July 18, 2002, the Ninth U.S. Circuit Court of Appeals, well known for its egregious anti-faith rulings [e.g., the Pledge ruling], made a surprising decision, ruling that the state had "impermissibly deprived Davey of his scholarship" and declaring that the state's standard for awarding scholarships "facially discriminates on the basis of religion." Accordingly, the appellate court ordered state officials to amend the scholarship policy so that it would be equitable for all participants.[47]

When Washington appealed the decision to the U.S.

Supreme Court, the ACLU was on hand to file an *amicus* brief supporting the denial of scholarships to theology majors. The brief argued, "The accusation of viewpoint bias is a powerful rhetorical weapon. But the viewpoint label cannot fairly be attached to the Promise Scholarship, which as discussed above is structured to be scrupulously even-handed among religious viewpoints."

In other words, the ACLU contended that the policy should not be considered discriminatory because the state "scrupulously" showed *equal* discrimination against all people of faith.

Unfortunately, the U.S. Supreme Court sided with the ACLU and reversed the lower court decision. In its ruling, the Court all but admitted that the state's scholarship policy demonstrated some hostility toward religion. Explaining why it rejected the defendant's reliance upon another High Court precedent, the Court declared, "In the present case, the State's *disfavor* of religion (if it can be called that) is of a far milder kind."[48]

In his dissenting opinion, Justice Antonin Scalia slammed the Court for ultimately endorsing the state's "disfavor of religion," warning against the nation's rising hostility toward people of faith:

> One need not delve too far into modern popular culture to perceive a trendy disdain for deep religious conviction. In an era when the Court is so quick to come to the aid of disfavored groups, its indifference in this case, which involves a form of discrimination to which the Constitution actually speaks, is exceptional. . . . Davey is not asking for a special benefit to which others are not entitled. He seeks only *equal* treatment. . . . When the public's

freedom of conscience is invoked to justify denial of equal treatment, benevolent motives shade into indifference, and ultimately into repression.[49]

PUSHING CHRISTIANS INTO THE CLOSET

The ACLU is not only an adamant proponent of strict secularism; many of its members are vitriolic toward people of faith. In November 2004, after an election in which "values voters" played a decisive role, Mike Cubelo, president of the Piedmont County chapter of the ACLU of South Carolina,[50] penned an open letter to religious Americans. Cubelo derided President Bush, claiming that he served as a role model to all those who "believe in the baby Jesus" and are "inarticulate, incompetent, drunk, and bigoted." The letter also turned its attention toward other Christians:

> To Bob Jones, Pat Robertson, and James Dobson: Kneel down, shut up, and pray in a church closet somewhere. We'll come and get you when we need a [J]esus jihad. . . .
> To the Moral Value Morons: Why couldn't you just stay home and pray for a "W" victory instead of actually voting? Don't you have faith in God's will?[51]

Such blind hostility toward people of faith is unfortunate, but it is not unique to America.

THE DANGERS OF HATE CRIME LAWS

In recent years, the secularization of the West, coupled with increased relativism and the advancement of the homosexual agenda, has led many nations to impose gag orders on Christians. Of course these governments cloak this religious censorship under the disguise of protecting citizens from "hate," but they are really imposing criminal sanctions on citizens who speak out against homosexuality, cults, or other religions.

Consequently, the freedoms of believers in the Western world have been severely impaired:

- **Canada**—A Saskatchewan court fined a newspaper publisher for running an advertisement that listed various Bible verses dealing with homosexuality.[52]
- **Sweden**—A pastor was arrested at his church for reading Bible verses concerning homosexuality.[53]
- **Italy**—Journalist Oriana Fallaci was indicted for a hate crime after insulting the Muslim faith in her latest book, *The Rage and the Pride*.[54]
- **Britain**—An Anglican bishop was placed under criminal investigation for merely suggesting that homosexuals can change their sexual orientation.[55]
- **Spain**—The Spanish government threatened a Roman Catholic bishop for speaking out against the country's legalization of same-sex marriage.[56]
- **France**—An 82-year-old priest was convicted of "provoking discrimination," after telling his congregation that Muslims promote an "ideology that threatens the whole world."[57]

- **Australia**—Pastor Daniel Scot was arrested, convicted, and imprisoned for teaching an audience about the faults of the Quran. According to police, this violated an Australian law which reads, "A person must not, on the ground of the religious belief or activity of another person or class of persons, engage in conduct that incites 'severe ridicule' of that other person or class of persons."[58]

- **Brazil**—Two Christians were arrested and charged with a hate crime for distributing Bible tracts during a Spiritist festival honoring Iemanja, an African goddess of the sea.[59]

Such egregious violations of liberty should make our nation reticent to embrace hate crime laws, but the ACLU—while claiming to be a proponent of free speech—has repeatedly urged Congress to pass federal hate crime legislation in America.

In recent years, thirty-one states have enacted hate crime laws, offering special protections to homosexuals,[60] and these state laws have already begun to trample the rights of Christians.

In Philadelphia, Pennsylvania, eleven Christians were arrested and jailed for "ethnic intimidation," after preaching on public streets during a gay pride festival.[61] In Tennessee, two men were arrested and charged with "interfering with a special event" when they attempted to carry large wooden crosses during a "Gay Day" parade.[62] In Idaho, a Hewlett-Packard employee was fired after refusing to remove Bible verses on homosexuality from his cubicle. He filed a federal lawsuit, but the Ninth U.S. Circuit Court of Appeals dismissed it declaring, "An employer need not accommodate an employee's religious beliefs if doing so would result in discrimination."[63]

In simpler terms, the court ruled that discrimination against Christians is permissible, if it prevents discrimination against homosexuals. Under such repressive governance, Christians are quickly becoming the pariahs of society.

Despite these despicable examples, several U.S. Congressmen continue to propose bills aimed at providing special protections for homosexuals at the federal level. If passed, this legislation would allow the U.S. Justice Department to allocate additional funding and personnel to prosecute hate crimes against gays, lesbians, transvestites, and transsexuals.[64]

LOBBYING FOR HATE CRIMES LEGISLATION

The ACLU distributed a letter to members of the U.S. House in May 2005, offering its support for hate crimes legislation. The letter explained, "The ACLU supports providing remedies against invidious discrimination and urges that discrimination by private persons be made illegal when it excludes persons from access to fundamental rights. . . ."[65]

Though it is already illegal to deny another person his fundamental rights, the ACLU seeks to offer *special* rights to homosexual victims of crime. This clearly runs counter to the intent of the Fourteenth Amendment, which guarantees "equal protection of the laws" to *all* citizens. Indeed, such a law would actually promote inequality by treating violent crimes against homosexuals as more insidious and worthy of prosecution than violent crimes against heterosexuals.

Robert Knight, director of the Culture and Family Institute, explained:

> Equal protection means your grandma and your
> friend who lives as a homosexual have the same

rights when they walk down the street. Under a hate crimes law, someone who mugs your grandmother will not be prosecuted as vigorously as someone who commits the same crime against a homosexual. . . . Both deserve protection, but certainly the gay guy doesn't deserve more than your grandmother.[66]

The proposed legislation claims to impact only crimes of violence, but it is legitimate to question how a judge might construe the definition of "violence." For instance, when a Catholic Church refused to share Holy Communion with three gay activists, D.C. Superior Court Judge Mildred M. Edwards told them: "*Tremendous violence* was done . . . when the Body of Christ was denied to you."[67]

In the modern age of judicial activism, what is to prevent another judge from qualifying this example of "tremendous violence" as a federal hate crime?

Dr. Gary Cass, executive director of the Center for Reclaiming America for Christ, warned:

The thought police are coming! Hate crimes legislation is the beginning of the government's intrusion into our God-given freedoms of faith and conscience. If passed, the foundation would be laid for the silencing of America's churches and the imprisonment of her faithful pastors. We have already witnessed gross violations of personal liberty in other nations which have embraced such laws. The logical progression of such laws leads to the callous dismissal of our First Amendment rights of free speech and religious exercise.[68]

Thomas Jefferson would have agreed. In his famed letter to the Danbury Baptists he wrote, "The legitimate powers of government reach actions only and not opinions."[69]

The ACLU would beg to differ.

ATTEMPTING TO SHUT DOWN CHAPLAIN PROGRAMS

Some of the ACLU's efforts to stifle the Church's role in society are more blatant. In 1991, the ACLU of Washington filed a lawsuit seeking to prohibit the Pierce County Sheriff's Department from allowing volunteer chaplains to counsel state and county emergency services personnel and victims of crime. Because the county spent an average of $3,000 each year on supplies like liability insurance, photo IDs, and two-way radios to operate this volunteer chaplaincy program, the ACLU contended that "the use of public funds to support the religious counseling of persons . . . violates the First Amendment."[70]

Thankfully, the Washington Supreme Court issued a 5-3 decision, siding with the chaplains. "We conclude that the use of volunteer chaplains by Pierce County Sheriff's Department complies with the First Amendment of the United States Constitution," the court declared. "The chaplaincy does not violate the establishment clause of the First Amendment."[71]

In their opinion, the justices cited Laurence H. Tribe, a Harvard Law professor known for having argued 34 cases in front of the U.S. Supreme Court. Tribe explained:

> The First Amendment does not require—indeed, it does not permit—government to be totally oblivious to religion. Government may sometimes accommodate religion; in some circumstances, it must do so. Thus, the question is not whether government and religion will

interact, but how.[72]

CENSORING CHRISTIAN VIEWPOINTS IN THE PUBLIC SQUARE

Though the ACLU often bills itself as a champion of free speech, a simple review of the facts causes one to legitimately question its sincerity. The facts seem to indicate that the ACLU is motivated by a desire to silence those who are critical of its objectives.

As recently as June 2006, the organization was actually considering a proposal to muzzle its own board members. The proposed internal censorship policy stated, "A director may publicly disagree with an ACLU policy position, but may not criticize the ACLU board and staff."[73] Not until the *New York Times* published an article about the hypocritical measure did the ACLU finally back away from it.[74]

So much for free speech!

Likewise, when the Church speaks out on critical matters of major public policy with a message that differs from the ACLU's viewpoint, the organization seems interested only in squelching the Church's contributions. As for those legislatures that give heed to Christian principles, they too will often find themselves on the receiving end of ACLU threats and lawsuits.

- In April 2003, the ACLU of Florida forced state health department officials to recall over 13,000 AIDS education brochures, simply because the brochures called upon Christians to "answer Jesus' call" by reaching out to people with HIV and AIDS.[75]
- In May 2004, the Connecticut Civil Liberties Union (an affiliate of the ACLU)

forced the Windsor Locks School District to renege on a promise made to area clergy that would have allowed them "equal access and equal time" to rebut claims made by a homosexual advocacy group at a school-sponsored student assembly.[76]

- The ACLU has sued several state-sponsored abstinence education programs, simply because the programs occasionally referred to God. One ACLU official claimed that it was wrong to use taxpayer dollars for "delivering sermons."[77]

- In March 2006, the ACLU of Rhode Island convinced state officials to drop a ministry's religion-free abstinence program because it advised girls not to wear clothing that invites "lustful thoughts." The ACLU argued that by portraying women as "caring" and men as "strong" the state had promoted "sexist viewpoints . . . out of the nineteenth century."[78]

- The ACLU has filed numerous lawsuits seeking to prevent states from producing "Choose Life" specialty license plates.[79]

- The ACLU filed a lawsuit to overturn an Alaska law that offered tax exemptions for property in which churches house parochial/religious school educators.[80]

Having defended numerous communities against the threats of the ACLU, Alan Sears, president of the Alliance Defense Fund, explained, "The ACLU is the foremost religious censor in America. . . . [The] dramatic erosion of religious liberty is the result of the ACLU's deliberate, incremental strategy."[81]

Indeed, the ACLU seems to scour the nation, desperately searching for the slightest whisper of *Christian* ideals in the public arena over which it can file lawsuits. However, when a federal lawsuit was filed against the Byron Union (Calif.) School District for requiring seventh grade students to pretend they were Muslims, wear Islamic garb, memorize verses of the Quran, recite prayers to Allah, and play "jihad games," the ACLU remained noticeably silent, and a federal judge upheld the constitutionality of this *Islamic* curriculum.[82]

To understand the gross double standard on display, try to imagine the furor that would be generated if a school district required students to wear Christian T-shirts, pray to Jesus Christ, memorize the Ten Commandments, and perform a play reenacting the sufferings of Christ.

WILL THE CHURCH REGAIN ITS VOICE?

If the Church is to regain its voice in American culture, citizens must reject the ACLU's arbitrary guidance on who may and may not engage in political speech or contract with government agencies. The twentieth century revealed the disastrous consequences that occur when government hostility toward the principles of faith cause the Church and its message to retreat behind stone walls.

Unfortunately, the ACLU has repeatedly encouraged government officials to muzzle Christian voices—be they explicitly Christian or merely moral—in the public square. This is evident in a vast array of ACLU endeavors, from its support for "thought crimes," to its banishment of the Boy Scouts and its censorship in the classroom.

The actions of the ACLU speak volumes about its motivations. The ACLU seems determined to silence the Church!

FOUR

Advancing Sexual Anarchy

*For this is the will of God, your sanctification: that you
should abstain from sexual immorality.*

– 1 Thessalonians 4:3

The agenda of the ACLU extends far beyond banishing all aspects of religion from the public square. A brief survey of its activities reveals that the organization is vigorously seeking to eliminate any moral influence from American law—particularly in relation to sexual behavior.

In the modern void of moral absolutes, our schools, courtrooms, government halls, and even some of our churches have embraced the misguided notion that all sexual behaviors and lifestyles deserve equal respect. Unfortunately, the contemporary Church has, perhaps unknowingly, made the problem worse. Many pastors have shied away from discussing sensitive issues like cohabitation, premarital sex, adultery, homosexuality, and the sanctity of marriage.

As churches opt to remain silent, outspoken groups like the ACLU have filled the void, unleashing wrecking balls on the foundations of morality. The silence and apathy of an elder generation has thrust America's youth into a devastating era of boundless sexual anarchy, heartbreak, abortion, out-of-wedlock births, and sexually transmitted diseases.

THE EXPLOSION OF SEXUALLY TRANSMITTED DISEASES

To understand the folly of promoting sexual anarchy, one needs only to look at the rotten fruits of the sexual revolution. Just 30 years ago, doctors and scientists recognized only two sexually transmitted diseases—syphilis and gonorrhea. Both diseases were curable. Today there are more than 25 known STDs, generating more than 13 million new cases annually, and half of them are considered incurable.[1]

According to figures released from the Centers for Disease Control (CDC) and the U.S. Department of Health and Human Services:

- One out of every five Americans over the age of 12 has genital herpes. This equates to 45 million Americans, and this number grows by roughly one million people each year.
- An estimated 20 million Americans are infected with the incurable human papilloma virus (HPV). Over half of all unmarried, sexually active people will acquire HPV in their lifetime.[2]
- Each year, roughly three million Americans contract chlamydia.
- Each year, an estimated 650,000 Americans contract gonorrhea. Seventy-five percent are between the ages of 15 and 29.
- There are 1.25 million Americans living with Hepatitis B, and approximately 77,000 additional people contract this disease annually.[3]
- More than one million Americans are

currently infected with the human immunodeficiency virus (HIV), and up to one-third of those infected are unaware of their condition.[4]

- Half of all young Americans will contract a sexually transmitted disease by age 25.[5]
- The annual comprehensive cost of sexually transmitted diseases in the United States is estimated to be roughly $17 billion.[6]
- In 2003, nearly 35 percent of all births were to out-of-wedlock mothers.[7]
- In 1970, there were roughly 400,000 out-of-wedlock births. In 2003, over 1.4 million babies were born to unwed mothers. This represents a marked increase of 350 percent.[8]

OPPOSING ABSTINENCE EDUCATION PROGRAMS

To combat this growing epidemic, President George W. Bush submitted a 2006 proposed budget which earmarked nearly $193 million for "abstinence-only until marriage" education programs. This action was predicated on the administration's oft-heralded endorsement of the fact that "abstinence is more than sound science—it's a sound practice . . . [and] has a proven track record of working."[9]

Yet, despite the disastrous consequences of the sexual revolution, the ACLU is absolutely opposed to any effort promoting abstinence-only education. In fact, in July 2005 the ACLU sent a letter to various members of the Senate Appropriations Committee. "Dear Senator," the letter began, "As you consider appropriations for Fiscal Year 2006, the American Civil Liberties Union urges you . . . to oppose appropriation of any new money for abstinence-only until marriage education programs."[10]

Though offering few reasons for its opposition, the ACLU concluded its letter by warning that "many federally funded abstinence-only programs contain religious teachings about proper sexual behavior and values."

If there are two things to which the ACLU is highly allergic, they would be religion and values!

In September 2005, the group organized a nationwide letter-writing campaign that urged constituents to write their elected officials, voicing opposition to abstinence-only education. Jennifer McAllister-Nevins, coordinator of the letter-writing project, told reporters, "For too long the federal government has funded abstinence-only-until-marriage curricula that are based on ideology and religion."

An ACLU press release warned that "many of these programs promote gender stereotypes, discriminate against gay and lesbian youth, and all too often proselytize on the public's dime."[11] In essence, the ACLU was pushing the censorship of Christian ideals—so that the nation's schools could promote homosexual ideals "on the public's dime."

Specifically, the ACLU argued that "abstinence-only until marriage" programs would discriminate against homosexuals, because most states prohibit the marriage of same-sex couples. Therefore, the ACLU demanded that state boards of education begin to formulate new curricula, void of any reference to marriage, so that homosexual students could participate comfortably.

TRAGIC CONSEQUENCES OF HOMOSEXUALITY

This is no surprise. The ACLU is firmly committed to advancing all aspects of the homosexual agenda. In 1986 the

ACLU launched its Lesbian and Gay Rights Project—an outreach specifically designed to "bring impact lawsuits in state and federal courts throughout the country . . . to have a significant effect on the lives of lesbians, gays, bisexuals, transsexuals, and those with HIV/AIDS."[12]

The ACLU has remained a champion of efforts to normalize homosexuality—endorsing a lifestyle that has wreaked havoc on millions of lives.

As devastating as the sexual revolution has been on America's general population, its impact on those engaged in a homosexual lifestyle has been even more destructive:

- According to an article in the *Canadian Medical Association Journal,* homosexuals are 3.7 times more likely to be infected with gonorrhea than are heterosexuals.[13]
- *The Archives of Internal Medicine* reported that homosexuals acquire syphilis at a rate ten times greater than heterosexuals.[14]
- In 2003, gay men comprised roughly 60 percent of new syphilis cases.[15]
- Though homosexual men comprise less than two percent of the population, the CDC has reported, "Among young men aged 13-24 years, 49% of all AIDS cases reported in 2000 were among men who have sex with men."[16]
- The CDC has also reported that men who have sex with men are at a dramatically increased risk to contract Hepatitis B.[17]
- According to research conducted by the Department of Laboratory Medicine at the University of California-San Francisco, HPV

infects 93 percent of HIV-positive and 61 percent of HIV-negative gay and bisexual men.[18]

- According to a study published in the December 2003 issue of the *British Journal of Psychiatry*, homosexual men are significantly more likely to suffer from mental disorders, drug abuse, domestic violence, self-inflicted harm, and they are far less likely to remain monogamous in relationships.[19]

Undeniably, the risks associated with the homosexual lifestyle constitute an enormous threat to the homosexual community and to public health in general. Despite clear evidence proving the tragic consequences of this lifestyle, the ACLU continues to promote this agenda in the courtrooms and classrooms of America.

KNOCKING AT THE DOOR OF SEXUAL ANARCHY

In the 1986 case of *Bowers v. Hardwick*, homosexual activists petitioned the U.S. Supreme Court to strike down a Georgia statute criminalizing homosexual sodomy. The plaintiffs argued that homosexual sodomy should be protected under the umbrella of rights guaranteed by the U.S. Constitution. Thankfully, the High Court rejected their request.

Writing for the Court's majority, Justice Byron White explained:

> The issue presented is whether the Federal Constitution confers a fundamental right upon homosexuals to engage in sodomy and hence

invalidates the laws of the many states that still
make such conduct illegal and have done so for
a very long time.[20]

Indeed, for the vast majority of our nation's history,
virtually every state prohibited sodomy. When the Bill of Rights
was ratified in 1791, each of the original thirteen states had
criminal laws against sodomy. In fact, eight of the thirteen
original states (Connecticut, Massachusetts, New Jersey, New
York, North Carolina, South Carolina, Rhode Island, and
Virginia) imposed death sentences on those found guilty of
engaging in homosexual sodomy.

No honest scholar, regardless of legal philosophy, could
legitimately claim that the original intent of our Founders was to
create a right to sodomy.

In 1986, the Court agreed. In a rare act of judicial restraint,
the High Court refused to advance an ideological agenda not
rooted in law. Justice White wisely warned, "The Court is most
vulnerable and comes nearest to illegitimacy when it deals with
judge-made constitutional law having little or no cognizable roots
in the language or design of the U.S. Constitution."[21]

OPENING THE FLOODGATES

After losing the *Bowers* case, an ACLU-led coalition of
pro-homosexual organizations began pressuring states to repeal
their anti-sodomy statutes. Under this pressure, state courts in
Georgia, Kentucky, Minnesota, Montana, and Tennessee struck
down such laws.

The ACLU and Lambda Legal (a legal advocacy group
dedicated to furthering the homosexual agenda) then launched
a "concerted effort" to challenge the constitutionality of
anti-sodomy laws in federal court, with hopes of once again

reaching the U.S. Supreme Court. The ACLU filed lawsuits challenging statutes in Kansas, Maryland, Oklahoma, and Puerto Rico. Lambda Legal challenged laws in Arkansas and Texas.[22]

The Supreme Court eventually agreed to consider the constitutionality of a Texas anti-sodomy statute in the case of *Lawrence v. Texas.* The ACLU's legal team filed a 30-page *amicus* brief supporting the plaintiffs.[23]

Keep in mind that in order for the Court to side with the plaintiffs and the ACLU, it would have to take several fairly drastic measures: (1) ignore the *Bowers'* precedent, (2) dismiss the clear intentions of the Constitution's drafters, (3) extract new interpretations from an unchanging text, (4) banish the role of common morality from the law, and (5) reject the Tenth Amendment right of Texans to govern themselves.

The Court did exactly that!

On June 26, 2003, in a 6-3 decision, it sided with homosexual activists and the ACLU—and created a constitutional right to engage in homosexual sodomy.[24]

ABANDONING RESPECT FOR *STARE DECISIS*

The High Court's decision to overturn such a young precedent shocked many legal scholars. Their astonishment was magnified by the fact that only eleven years earlier, in the 1992 case of *Planned Parenthood v. Casey*, the Court upheld the central tenets of *Roe v. Wade*, emphasizing the importance of *stare decisis* (Latin: "let the decision stand") in politically charged cases. Justice Sandra Day O'Connor authored the majority opinion for the 5-4 *Casey* decision.[25]

Unfortunately, honoring precedent in politically charged cases seemed far less important to the Court when it overturned the *Bowers* decision and struck down Texas' anti-sodomy law. In particular, legal scholars were perplexed by Justice O'Connor's decision to overturn the *Bowers* precedent—not only because of her previously stated respect for *stare decisis*, but because she was actually one of the original Justices who signed the *Bowers* decision.

Essentially, Justice O'Connor overruled herself and thumbed her nose at her own precedent!

SUPPORTING THE INCLUSION OF INTERNATIONAL LAW

Incapable of justifying the *Lawrence* decision with the actual text of the Constitution, the Court opted to import international law into its decision to justify this travesty of jurisprudence. Incredibly, in the majority opinion, the Court referenced the European Court of Human Rights, the European Convention of Human Rights, and a 1957 recommendation of the British Parliament.

This reliance on international law ignited a firestorm of complaint among concerned citizens. If American courts consider international laws when interpreting the U.S. Constitution, they could then justify a broad spectrum of sexual abominations. Looking to Mexico, they could justify reducing the age of sexual consent to twelve.[26] If they looked to Sweden, they could justify repealing criminal statutes prohibiting bestiality.[27] They could justify the legalization of prostitution via the laws of the Netherlands.[28] A judge could cite laws from a handful of nations that have embraced same-sex marriage.[29]

Considering the rapid advancement of secularism and moral anarchy in Europe, it is not surprising that the ACLU has emerged as one of the most ardent supporters of this practice of referencing international law when rendering domestic court decisions.

In response to public outcry in the aftermath of the *Lawrence* decision, Congress introduced legislation designed to prevent judicial activists from looking outside the United States for justification to advance perverted ideologies. The legislation stated that "judicial determinations regarding the meaning of the Constitution of the United States should not be based on judgments, laws, or pronouncements of foreign institutions."

The ACLU fought this measure vigorously, sending letters of opposition to every member of Congress: "We urge you to oppose H. Res. 97, which condemns courts' use of international law when interpreting the United States Constitution."[30]

The ACLU's eager defense of international law revealed what little respect the organization harbors for the U.S. Constitution. It is irrational to think that international law could possibly assist in interpreting the meaning of the U.S. Constitution. As different countries with different laws in different governing systems, the proposition is clearly ludicrous. Using foreign law to interpret the U.S. Constitution is like using a cookbook to interpret a car manual. Still, the ACLU's letter to Congress concluded that it would be foolish "to have Congress dictate to judges what sources of law they can consider when they make constitutional judgments."[31]

Apparently, the ACLU's legal contortionists cannot understand why Congress would want American courts to focus on the Constitution "when they make *constitutional* judgments."

If our courts are permitted to import fashionable international law, what prevents the judiciary from importing the rigid laws of Saudi Arabia, Cuba, or China? To allow judges to devise constitutional interpretations by cherry-picking from a broad range of foreign laws undoubtedly opens the door to disastrous consequences. Unfortunately, Congress failed to pass the bill.

Morality Banished From the Law

Still, the inclusion of international law was not the most

disturbing aspect of the *Lawrence* decision. Rather, that "honor" is reserved for the Court's utter contempt for common morality. In the ACLU's *Lawrence amicus* brief, it urged the Court to declare that a "state's asserted interest in morality" cannot serve as an acceptable reason to justify the existence of criminal statutes prohibiting immoral behaviors.

In the decision written by Justice Anthony Kennedy, the Court concurred with the ACLU's arguments, declaring that the moral fabric of a state's electorate should no longer have a seat at the legislative table. In an astonishing act of judicial arrogance, the Court declared, "The fact that the governing majority in a State has traditionally viewed a particular practice as immoral is not a sufficient reason for upholding a law prohibiting the practice."[32]

Immediately, concerned legal scholars warned that the Court's reckless language would open the floodgates for a myriad of cases challenging state and federal statutes criminalizing various immoral behaviors. Supreme Court Associate Justice Antonin Scalia warned:

> State laws against bigamy, same-sex marriage, adult incest, prostitution, masturbation, adultery, fornication, bestiality, and obscenity are likewise sustainable only in light of *Bowers'* validation of laws based on moral choices. Every single one of these laws is called into question by today's decision.[33]

Blasting the Court for its faulty reasoning and dangerous language, Scalia concluded, "It is clear from this that the Court has taken sides in the culture war, departing from its role of assuring, as neutral observer, that the democratic rules of engagement are observed."[34]

In following years, Scalia would be proven right. The ACLU has since filed lawsuits to legalize polygamy, same-sex marriage, and obscenity, while fighting against laws prohibiting prostitution and fornication. Indeed, with the assistance of Supreme Court precedents like *Lawrence v. Texas*, the ACLU has been able to unleash a massive campaign of lawsuits and lobbying efforts aimed at normalizing a multitude of sexually deviant behaviors.

SUPPORTING LEGALIZED PROSTITUTION

Having argued more cases in front of the U.S. Supreme Court than any other non-government entity and filing roughly 6,000 lawsuits each year, the ACLU's roots are deeply entangled in America's legal realm—contributing to the legal philosophies of many who wield the gavel, including one U.S. Supreme Court Justice.

Justice Ruth Bader Ginsburg once worked for the ACLU, serving as the organization's general counsel from 1973 to 1980. In April 1977, Ginsburg co-authored a scandalous report for the U.S. Commission on Civil Rights. It was entitled *Sex Bias in the U.S. Code*. Amidst her arguments advocating legalized bigamy, co-ed prisons, and a reduction of the age of sexual consent, Ginsburg argued that "prostitution, as a consensual act between adults, is arguably within the zone of privacy protected by recent constitutional decisions."[35]

Sadly, this woman was deemed worthy of a spot on the nation's highest court. As misguided as her legal philosophies can be, Ginsburg is not alone in her support for legalized prostitution. The ACLU has been making this case for at least thirty years.

PROTECTING PROSTITUTES IN PROVIDENCE

Look to the ACLU's efforts in Rhode Island. In 2005, police officers in Providence complained to state legislators about a loophole in the law that allowed prostitution rings to operate behind closed doors—inside spas and massage parlors. While Rhode Island law prohibited loitering for the purpose of prostitution, as well as transporting prostitutes, a broader felony law criminalizing all prostitution was repealed nearly 30 years ago. This provided prostitutes a loophole, allowing them to work inside ordinary massage parlors. Consequently, in one instance, Providence police officers were left with no alternative but to fine prostitutes for giving "massages" without a proper license.[36]

"We do not have a law criminalizing prostitution indoors," complained Providence Police Lieutenant Thomas Verdi.[37] In response to these complaints, Rhode Island Senator Rhoda Perry introduced legislation to prohibit all forms of prostitution.

Immediately, the ACLU flew into action. In May 2005, ACLU of Rhode Island executive director Steven Brown sent letters to Senator Perry and other state legislators, urging them to oppose any new laws criminalizing prostitution.[38] "This legislation should *not* pass," wrote Brown. "The proposed legislation would be an unfortunate step backwards. . . . We therefore urge you to reject the city's overtures to promote legislation criminalizing prostitution."

Much like Justice Ginsburg's argument from decades earlier, Brown attempted to downplay the offensive nature of prostitution by describing it as "consensual sex" and warning that its prohibition could entail a "serious invasion of privacy."[39]

Unfortunately, the Rhode Island legislature chose to listen to the babble of the ACLU and ignore the needs of the state's police officers. Senator Perry even withdrew her legislation.

ENABLING INDECENCY IN PUBLIC PLACES

The organization has also repeatedly opposed police efforts to crack down on "cruising" (a term commonly used by homosexual men to denote the search for anonymous sexual encounters in public places).

Don't think cruising is a major problem in homosexual communities? Think again. *The Advocate*, a leading gay-oriented magazine, recently published the results of a poll of 1,829 gays, lesbians, bisexuals, and transvestites. Sixty-six percent of its participants admitted they had engaged in sexual acts in public places.[40]

Though the results were not scientific, they indicate that cruising is indeed a common activity in the homosexual community. In fact, this dangerous practice is so common that Lambda Legal (the ACLU's primary ally in the fight to legalize sodomy) actually produced a pamphlet, *Little Black Book,* offering tips to homosexual men who "cruise in parks, bathrooms, or other spaces open to public view."

The pamphlet informs readers that "having sex where others might see you and take offense can subject you to arrest, publicity, and other serious consequences," but promises that "Lambda Legal and other groups are fighting against the ways police target [homosexual] men."[41]

The ACLU is one of these "other groups" fighting the police. In 2002, when the Detroit Police conducted a number of undercover sting operations to reduce the incidence of "cruising" in a public park, the city of Detroit was slapped with a lawsuit. The ACLU accused the city of targeting homosexuals unconstitutionally. According to the group's press release, "Undercover officers would follow or approach men they perceived to be gay, make eye contact, and encourage the men to respond in a sexual manner." Those who offered such a response to the police officers' advances were arrested.

Under the pressure of the ACLU's lawsuit, the city of Detroit settled—agreeing to (1) stop conducting undercover stings to target homosexual "cruisers" (2) pay $170,000 in damages and attorneys fees, and (3) force its police officers to undergo sensitivity training for gay, lesbian, bisexual, and transgender issues.[42]

The ACLU has successfully fought similar police tactics in other states, including California and Maryland.

TRANSSEXUAL THERAPY AT TAXPAYER EXPENSE

All too often, the perverted agenda of a small minority has trampled the rights of the majority. Increasingly, unsuspecting taxpayers are forced to finance the ACLU's perversion.

In 1999, the ACLU filed a federal lawsuit against the Virginia Department of Corrections on behalf of a self-perceived transsexual prisoner, arguing that Virginia's taxpayers should be forced to fund his transgender hormone therapies.

Six years earlier, while imprisoned in Virginia's correctional facilities, Michael A. Stokes began receiving estrogen from his doctors to remedy his so-called "gender identity disorder." After two years of therapy, the state discovered this gross abuse of tax dollars and discontinued the funding.

Subsequently, Stokes made twenty reported attempts at self-castration and twice had to be airlifted to a nearby hospital. He even attempted to mail a chunk of his own flesh to Virginia's governor. Stokes blamed the state for his behavior, asserting that he was suffering from estrogen withdrawal, which led him to engage in self-mutilation.

Kent Willis, executive director of the ACLU of Virginia, also blamed the state—making the absurd claim that "barring hormone treatment was akin to withholding chemotherapy for cancer patients."[43]

To rational citizens, it is utterly ridiculous to compare a person's gender confusion to the gravity of undergoing chemotherapy, but this is reality to the ACLU!

In September 2004, after a five-year legal struggle, the Virginia Department of Corrections caved, amending its policy to allow for "the care of inmates with 'Gender Identity Disorder.'" Under the new policy, the taxpayers of Virginia are forced to fund hormone therapy for self-perceived transsexual criminals.

FOLLOWING SUIT IN WISCONSIN

Unfortunately, in the legal arena, one case can impact the entire national landscape, and every precedent set by the ACLU adds to the growing arsenal of tools that the organization's attorneys can use to bully other states into submission.

Using the momentum of the Virginia settlement, the ACLU filed a federal lawsuit against the Wisconsin Department of Corrections, challenging the constitutionality of a state statute that prohibited the use of taxpayer dollars to fund the hormone therapy and gender reassignment surgeries of state prisoners.

Larry Dupuis, an attorney representing the ACLU of Wisconsin, argued that this policy of denying prisoners taxpayer-funded hormone therapy and sex-change operations constituted a "cruel and unusual punishment." Dupuis claimed that sex change operations met the state's standard of "reasonable and necessary medical care."[44]

"If the state provides care that is deliberately indifferent to serious medical needs . . . that's unconstitutional," he concluded.

It is reprehensible to force taxpayers to fund elective surgeries to satisfy the desires of sexual deviants. Unfortunately, in January 2006, one federal judge sided with the ACLU and issued an injunction preventing Wisconsin from enforcing its law. In his preliminary decision, U.S. District Judge Charles N. Clevert,

Jr., overruled the will of the state legislature, declaring that "continuing the plaintiff's hormone treatments is more important than the saving of state and federal funds."[45]

Wisconsin state Rep. Scott Suder, the original sponsor of the statute barring such allocations, called the judge's decision "the height of judicial activism." Suder told reporters:

> To stop forcing taxpayers to pay for sex-change therapy for prisoners certainly is not cruel and unusual punishment. . . . I think it is absurd for anyone, especially a federal judge, to argue that sex-change therapy is somehow medicinal in nature. The so-called disorder the ACLU is referring to is not a medically necessary treatment. It is a choice! It is unfortunate that crazy groups like the ACLU think it is a good idea to give sex-change operations to prisoners.[46]

Indeed, the philosophy of the ACLU seems to affirm the idea that *all* people are entitled to engage in any behavior—so long as the behavior is not religious in nature—and the American taxpayer should foot the bill.

U.S. MILITARY V. HOMOSEXUAL AGENDA

This was made evident by the ACLU's campaign to undermine military recruiting on our nation's college campuses. In 2002, in an effort to support the homosexual agenda, Yale Law School instituted a campus-wide ban on military recruiters—demanding that the military rescind its "don't ask, don't tell" sexual orientation policy. In response, the U.S. Department of Defense invoked the Solomon Amendment (10 U.S.C. 983) and threatened to cut $350 million in annual funding from the Yale

University budget.[47]

In the midst of America's war on terrorism, the Forum for Academic and Institutional Rights (F.A.I.R.), an association of law schools, filed a lawsuit challenging the federal statute, which stipulates that the federal government may withdraw all funds from any university that prevents military recruiters from operating on campus.[48] According to the federal statute, all universities are entitled to promote anti-military viewpoints, but they may not bar the government's military recruiters while accepting the government's dollars.

The ACLU filed an *amicus* brief in support of the lawsuit. It contended that conditioning a school's funding on whether they allowed military recruiters violated the First Amendment and amounted to "compelled speech" and "viewpoint discrimination."[49]

However, in a unanimous 8-0 decision, U.S. Supreme Court Chief Justice John Roberts explained:

> Universities are free to decline the federal funds.
> . . . The Solomon Amendment neither limits what law schools may say nor requires them to say anything. . . . The Solomon Amendment regulates conduct, not speech. It affects what law schools must do—afford equal access to military recruiters—not what they may or may not say.[50]

FORCING THE GAY AGENDA ON AMERICAN CHILDREN

While fighting tooth and nail to deny equal access to military recruiters on college campuses, the ACLU has worked diligently to force rural public schools to organize student assemblies so that homosexual advocates can teach students and faculty all the latest propaganda of the homosexual agenda.

In 2003, the ACLU filed a lawsuit against the Boyd County (Ky.) Board of Education seeking to force the district to host "diversity training" seminars, where students would be taught to accept the homosexual lifestyle at taxpayers' expense. In the summer of 2004, as part of a settlement of that lawsuit, the district agreed to a new policy requiring all middle and high school students, staff, and teachers to attend "mandatory anti-harassment workshops."

When the children returned from summer break and were told of the scheduled seminar, parents began to file complaints. On the day of the workshops, in a mass show of protest, nearly one-third of all students skipped the program.

In response, James Esseks, the litigation director for the ACLU Lesbian and Gay Rights Project, roared, "Parents don't get to say, 'I don't want you to teach evolution or this, that, or whatever else.' If parents don't like it, they can home school; they can go to a private school; they can go to a religious school."[51] Apparently, the ACLU does not believe that families with traditional values have a place in determining the educational content for their own children.

The ACLU threatened to file another lawsuit unless the district agreed to enforce its "mandatory" attendance policy. At the urging of the ACLU—and in a direct assault on parental rights—the district announced that the newly adopted policy would not allow parents to opt their children out of the program—even if the program conflicted with a family's deeply held religious beliefs.[52]

Immediately, concerned Christian parents contacted the Alliance Defense Fund (ADF). Kevin Theriot, senior legal counsel for ADF, reviewed portions of the so-called "diversity training" program and concluded, "This mandatory 'diversity training' hardly teaches diversity. It not only puts a gag on students who disagree with homosexual behavior, it also actively attempts to change their moral beliefs."[53]

ADF attorneys urged the district to make exceptions for religious families, to no avail. On February 15, 2005, ADF filed a federal suit against the Boyd County Board of Education.[54] Not surprisingly, the ACLU volunteered its services to defend the school district's program.

On February 17, 2006, U.S. District Judge David L. Bunning issued his decision, siding with the ACLU. In a ruling that stripped parents of their right to determine the moral content of their children's education, Judge Bunning declared, "There is simply no basis for an opt-out."[55]

THE NEED FOR DILIGENCE

Only decades ago it would have been utterly inconceivable for a public school to force its students to endure a program in which homosexual activists presented a viewpoint principally designed to undermine deeply held religious convictions. Parents would not have tolerated it. Today, the courts have instructed parents that they no longer have a choice in the matter.

This is indicative of a far more serious condition. As Americans stand idly by, the ACLU is consistently overruling the people. From advancing the so-called "rights" of prostitution and homosexual sodomy, to undermining parental rights and forcing taxpayers to fund prisoner sex changes, the ACLU seems determined to thrust the nation down every conceivable road of sexual debauchery imaginable.

By twisting the law and dismissing the role of morality from the legislative table, the ACLU has vigorously opposed and actively litigated against a multitude of laws and programs designed to promote responsibility and sexual restraint.

Regrettably, the organization has experienced great success in these endeavors.

FIVE

Sexualizing America's Children

*Train up a child in the way he should go, and when he
is old he will not depart from it.*

— Proverbs 22:6

In this emerging culture of sexual anarchy, parents and children face daunting new challenges. Once upon a time, moms and dads were comfortable allowing their children to walk home from school or play outside without supervision. Today, with the decline of tight-knit neighborhoods and the rise of sexual predators, parents are hesitant to allow their children out of sight—and justifiably so.

Parents can find no peace of mind when dropping their children off at public schools either. Recent reports released by the federal government suggest that public school students are routinely subjected to far more than the ambiguous sex education lessons of yesteryear. As public school curricula grow increasingly infatuated with sex education, the incidence of sexual misconduct between teachers and students has skyrocketed. In June 2004, the U.S. Department of Education released an in-depth study focusing on the sexual misconduct of public school educators. The results were deplorable![1]

One survey, conducted with students in grades 8-11 (ages 13-17), discovered that nearly one out of every ten students (9.6

percent) had experienced "educator sexual misconduct that was unwanted."[2] Another Department of Education study claimed that "more than 4.5 million students are subject to sexual misconduct by an employee of a school sometime between kindergarten and 12th grade."[3]

Shamefully, these cases are far too often ignored by school districts—swept under the rug to avoid embarrassment. One study conducted in New York surveyed 225 cases of educator-student sexual misconduct in which an educator actually admitted to sexually abusing a student. Researchers were startled to discover that not one of the admitted abusers had been reported to the authorities, and only one percent lost their license to teach![4] Similar findings were made in other districts across the nation.

EMERGENCE OF THE PRO-PEDOPHILE AGENDA

Certainly, most Americans would consider the sexualization of children appalling, but there are a growing number of activists and academics seeking to legitimize the idea of sexually "liberated" children. Several major universities have employed outspoken professors, even department chairs, who openly support legalized pedophilia.[5] Cornell University has offered a class on pedophilia, "The Sexual Child." Accuracy in Academia investigated the course and reported, "The syllabus for 'The Sexual Child' reads like a veritable who's-who of pro-pedophilia academics and activists."[6]

In addition, groups like the American Psychological Association (APA) have also shown tendencies to sympathize with this agenda. In a 1998 edition of the *Psychological Bulletin,* the APA published "The Rind Report," calling for Congress to abandon negative terms like "molestation" when referring to the act of sexually abusing children. Instead, the APA encouraged the use of more "value-neutral" terms like "adult-child sex"—especially if the experience was what the APA labeled a "willing encounter with positive reactions."[7]

Of course, most Americans cannot conceive of a day when our country will mirror the pedophiliac licentiousness of the ancient Greeks. Then again, the vast majority of 1950s Americans would have never envisioned a day when America would allow its babies to be killed during delivery or recognize open homosexual relationships—much like the ancient Greeks.

The battle to defend the innocence of our children against the onslaught of sexual predators may be in its infant stages, but make no mistake about it, there are many people dedicated to tearing down what remains of society's safeguards for children.

Supporting a Reduced Age of Sexual Consent

Despicably, a number of ACLU attorneys have proposed significant reductions in the legal age for sexual consent—inching closer to legalized pedophilia.

In 1977, while serving as General Counsel for the ACLU, current Supreme Court Associate Justice Ruth Bader Ginsburg co-authored a report for the U.S. Commission on Civil Rights. In this report she argued that the United States legal code should be amended to read, "A person is guilty of an offense if he engages in a sexual act with another person, not his spouse, and . . . the other person is, in fact, less than 12 years old."[8]

Amazingly, this woman, who once suggested that 12-year-old children should have the legal capacity to consent and engage in sexual activity, was considered the most qualified person in America to serve on the High Court. Had Congress heeded the advice of the ACLU's former lead attorney, parents would be powerless to prevent grown men and women from preying on their sixth-grade sons and daughters.

ACLU Urges Sexual Rights for 13-Year-Olds

More recently, in the case of *Kansas v. Limon*, the ACLU filed a brief arguing that 13-year-old children should have a constitutional right to make their own decisions about sex.

In February 2000, Matthew Limon was convicted of the statutory rape of a mentally handicapped 14-year-old boy. Under the guidance of Kansas state law, Limon was sentenced to serve 17 years in prison. On November 15, 2001, the ACLU appealed his sentence, arguing that Kansas law had unfairly permitted the judge to impose a more severe penalty on Limon because his crime was homosexual in nature.

However, in its opening brief, the ACLU went far beyond the normal talking points of the homosexual agenda. The ACLU argued that all teenagers have the right to offer legal consent for sex. It further argued, "It is well established that teenagers . . . have a due process liberty interest in being free from state compulsion in personal decisions relating to . . . sexual intimacy."[9]

Kansas Attorney General Phill Kline was stunned that the ACLU dared to make such a bold assertion. He told Fox News' Bill O'Reilly:

> The ACLU states specifically in its brief that it is a constitutional right for any child age 13 and older to consent to have sex with anyone.[10] . . . It is absolutely a remarkable assault on the authority of the family. When your daughter walks out the door and says, "I'm going to meet my 40-year-old boyfriend," and you try to guide her and parent her and say, "No, that is not going to happen," and she holds up an ACLU card and says, "Call my attorney," we are living in a different type of America.[11]

PROTECTING PRO-PEDOPHILIA PROPAGANDA

Perhaps the most despicable case involving the ACLU and the pro-pedophile agenda occurred when the organization agreed to volunteer its services in defense of NAMBLA—the North American Man-Boy Love Association.

On October 1, 1997, Charles Jaynes (a NAMBLA member) and Salvatore Sicari drove through the streets of Cambridge, Massachusetts, with the intention of abducting 10-year-old Jeffrey Curley. As Jeffrey was walking his dog, the two men approached him, luring him into their car with the promise of a new bicycle. After Jeffrey was in the car, the men went to the Boston Public Library, where they accessed the NAMBLA website.

After leaving the library, the men attempted to sexually abuse Jeffrey in the car. Tragically, as Jeffrey fought off their sexual advances, the men gagged him with a gasoline-soaked rag— eventually suffocating him to death. These callous men proceeded to undress his corpse, later stuffing his naked body into a cement-filled Rubbermaid container and dumping it off the Great Works River Bridge in South Berwick, Maine.[12]

Police arrested Jaynes and Sicari the next evening. During their investigation, police discovered NAMBLA publications in Jaynes' car. They also searched Jaynes' apartment, where they discovered handwritten journals about seducing young boys. In one entry, Jaynes explained that discovering NAMBLA "was a turning point in discovery of myself . . . NAMBLA's *Bulletin* helped me to become aware of my own sexuality and acceptance of it."[13]

Subsequently, Jeffrey's parents filed a $200 million lawsuit against NAMBLA, arguing that the organization was partially responsible for spurring the deadly actions of Charles Jaynes.

Larry Frisoli, the Curley family attorney, pointed out

NAMBLA resources like *The Survival Manual: The Man's Guide to Staying Alive in Man-Boy Sexual Relationships.* Frisoli explained:

> Its chapters explain how to build relationships with children, how to gain the confidence of children's parents, where to go to have sex with children so as not to get caught. . . . There is advice, if one gets caught, on when to leave America and how to rip off credit card companies to get cash to finance your flight. It's pretty detailed.[14]

Incredibly, the ACLU of Massachusetts volunteered to defend NAMBLA against the Curleys' lawsuit. The ACLU claimed that it was "unconstitutional" to sue NAMBLA for the content of its resources. In its legal papers, the ACLU argued that even if the materials advocate illegal activity, "speech is not deprived of the protection of the First Amendment simply because it advocates an unlawful act."[15]

John Reinstein, legal director of the ACLU of Massachusetts, explained, "We contend that the First Amendment was intended to apply exactly to organizations like this."[16]

Either the ACLU is absolutely ignorant of American history, intentionally dishonest, or both.

Regardless, the ACLU has mastered the art of manipulating public opinion by using today's commonly accepted, but ill-defined, notion of tolerance. In an interview with CNN, ACLU attorney Harvey Silvergate tried to tap into this "tolerance," urging the CNN audience to agree that "there is room in this country for people who believe man-boy love is okay."[17]

The Curleys' lawsuit against NAMBLA was eventually dismissed because the NAMBLA organization had been established as an association—not a corporation. However, the Curley family pursued wrongful death lawsuits against several individual NAMBLA members, including the entire NAMBLA Steering Committee.[18]

RIGHTS OF PERVERTS TRUMP SAFETY OF KIDS

The ACLU is unapologetic in its efforts to defend child pornography and pro-pedophilia literature. This was evidenced again in 2002, as the ACLU joined the Free Speech Coalition in a lawsuit to strike down the Child Pornography Prevention Act of 1996—a law that prohibited the distribution and possession of child pornography. The ACLU and others argued that the law was unconstitutional.

Former acting Solicitor General Barbara D. Underwood insisted that all forms of child pornography should be outlawed. Underwood warned that virtual and computer-generated images of child sex could just as easily be "used by pedophiles and child sexual abusers to stimulate and whet their own sexual appetites."[19]

Indeed, clinical research and forensic pathology have proven that sexual images often trigger the demented appetites of child molesters and rapists. One study published in the *Journal of Sex Research* found that over one-third of child molesters and rapists had been driven to commit a sex crime after viewing pornography.[20] Adding to the urgency for such legislation were recent statistics showing that child pornography was the fastest growing of all online industries—generating billions of dollars each year.[21]

Nevertheless, the ACLU defended the industry—claiming it was irrelevant whether images of child pornography tempted sex offenders. In its *amicus* brief filed with the Supreme Court the ACLU argued, "The fact that such material 'might lead to deviant sexual behavior' is not sufficient to criminalize its possession."[22]

Translation: the sexual perversions of pedophiles are more important than the safety of children.

In the case of *Ashcroft v. Free Speech Coalition* (2002), the U.S. Supreme Court sided with the ACLU and struck down the federal statute. The Court declared that it was unconstitutional for Congress to prohibit virtual and computer-generated child pornography.[23]

Much like the phantom constitutional rights of abortion and sodomy, the Court had discovered a nonexistent constitutional right for sexual deviants to create and enjoy child porn—so long as the images of raped, molested, or sexualized children are computer-generated.

Justice Anthony Kennedy authored the majority opinion for the Court. Echoing the sentiments of the ACLU, the Court explained, "The mere tendency of speech [virtual child pornography] to encourage unlawful acts is not a sufficient reason for banning it."[24]

Ignoring common sense and documented social science, the Court concluded: "Without a significantly stronger, more direct connection, the Government may not prohibit speech on the ground that it may encourage pedophiles to engage in illegal conduct."

Justice Kennedy even argued that it would be unfair to punish filmmakers for creating videos that include child sex scenes "without inquiry into the work's redeeming value."

DEFENDING CHILD PORN AUTHOR

As with every Supreme Court ruling, this decision initiated a domino effect—slowly but undeniably changing the legal and moral landscape of America.

In 1998, Franklin County, Ohio, resident Brian Dalton was arrested for possessing child pornography—pictures of children engaged in sexual acts—which he had downloaded from the Internet. While searching his property, police also discovered a journal entry in which Dalton described the reportedly fictional rape of a ten-year-old girl. Dalton later admitted that the little girl was his cousin, whom he had molested when he was 15 years old.

Thus, in 2001, when police discovered another journal containing 14 handwritten pages describing the rape, torture, and caging of young children, authorities decided to charge Dalton with breaking a 1977 law that made it a crime to "create, reproduce, or publish any obscene material that has a minor as one of its participants."[25]

Dalton pled guilty at first to the charges, but later withdrew his guilty plea in order to challenge the constitutionality of the Ohio statute prohibiting obscene materials involving minors. Not surprisingly, the ACLU volunteered to represent Mr. Dalton.

In its appeal, the ACLU relied heavily upon the recent Supreme Court decision in *Ashcroft v. Free Speech Coalition*. The ACLU explained:

> The diary entries for which Dalton was convicted involved depictions of sex with fictitious minor children. . . . [The] Supreme Court held last year that imaginary depictions of child erotica cannot be criminalized because their creation "records no crime and creates no victim."[26]

On March 4, 2004, under guidance from the new precedent, the Franklin County Common Pleas Court sided with the ACLU and reversed the conviction—dismissing the charges against Dalton. Judge David Cain wrote, "The state is concerned that he may re-offend, but the judicial branch of government must resist the temptation to engage in preemptive strikes."[27]

FIGHTING FOR TEEN & PRE-TEEN NUDIST CAMPS

The ACLU has consistently failed to promote the safety of children, opting instead to hinder the ability of law enforcement officials to protect minors from sexually compromising situations. As for parental rights . . . it seems that the ACLU is only interested in defending parental rights when the parents are attempting to pervert their children.

In March 2004, the Virginia Legislature took action to shut down a nudist camp that had been designed for children ages 11-18—an obvious magnet for sexual predators. The Virginia Legislature passed a law prohibiting the state's health commissioner from issuing a license "to the owner or lessee of any hotel, summer camp or campground in this Commonwealth that maintains, or conducts as any part of its activities, a nudist camp for juveniles."[28]

Almost immediately, the ACLU filed a federal lawsuit on behalf of White Tail Park, arguing that parents have a constitutional right to send their children to nudist camps. Kent Willis, executive director of the ACLU of Virginia, likened a child's right to attend a nudist camp with a child's right to play baseball. He assured reporters that if the court affirmed the state's right to shut down such camps, it would mean that "legislators are now free to prevent children from swimming, playing baseball, or riding a bus."[29] Willis also claimed that teen nudist camps are "wholesome, beneficial summertime events for teens."[30]

On August 10, 2004, a federal judge ruled that the White Tail Park did not demonstrate adequate standing to challenge the constitutionality of the statute. Consequently, the ACLU appealed the decision to the 4th U.S. Circuit Court of Appeals. The ACLU argued:

> The plaintiffs ... each have suffered, and continue to suffer, a concrete and particularized injury as a result of the law. The plaintiff organizations are injured because they are unable to operate their 'nudist camp for juveniles' and thereby disseminate information and values to nudist youth.[31]

John Byrum, an attorney from the Virginia Department of Justice, reminded the appellate court that "there is no constitutional parental right to send your child to a juvenile nudist camp,"[32] but nothing is out of bounds for our modern judiciary.

A unanimous three-judge panel for the 4th U.S. Circuit Court chose to resurrect the ACLU's outlandish lawsuit. "[The plaintiff] contends that the statute encroached on its First Amendment right by reducing the size of the audience for its message of social nudism," wrote Judge William B. Traxler, Jr. "We think this is sufficient for purposes of standing."[33]

The fact that a federal court is willing to consider the merits of a case that involves adults who believe they should have the right to instruct naked 11-year-olds on the benefits of "social nudism" is beyond perversion.

DEFENDING THE DESIRES OF PEDOPHILES

While the ACLU fought to allow unchaperoned pre-teens to vacation at nudist camps, the organization was also fighting to overturn ordinances barring convicted sex offenders from venturing into locations frequented by children—like public parks and school zones.

In Lafayette, Indiana, a convicted child sex offender admitted visiting the city's public parks so that he could fantasize about having sex with the playing children. As a result, the city barred him from entering the parks. Lafayette Mayor Dave Heath told reporters, "Parents need to be able to send their kids to a park and know they're going to be safe—not being window shopped by a predator."[34]

This particular sexual predator had amassed a long rap sheet. In 1978, he was arrested for engaging in sexual acts with a young boy. In 1979, it happened again. In 1985, he was caught peeping into a woman's apartment. In 1986, he engaged in self-gratification in full view of five children. In 1988, he was charged with voyeurism for peeping into an apartment and also with indecent exposure for exposing himself outside a teenage boy's home. In 1991, he pled guilty to child molestation.[35] With such a track record, his fantasies in the park warranted great concern.

However, immediately after the city approved the ordinance, the Indiana Civil Liberties Union (a state chapter of the ACLU) came to his aid, filing a federal lawsuit on his behalf. Kenneth Falk, an attorney with the ICLU, admitted, "He had urges. He went into the park. He felt urges toward the kids." Even so, Falk concluded, "The idea that you could be punished for your thoughts seems to run really far from our view of our protected rights under the First Amendment."[36]

Initially, a three-judge panel of the Seventh U.S. Circuit Court of Appeals issued a 2-1 decision siding with the ICLU. In their ruling, Judges Ann Claire Williams and Diane P. Wood explained, "Presumably, untold numbers of Lafayette residents wander the city's parks every day, many of them potentially thinking offensive or objectionable thoughts. [This sexual predator] may not be punished for merely thinking perverted thoughts about children."[37]

Judge Kenneth F. Ripple wrote a fiery dissent:

Mr. Doe did not simply entertain thoughts. He had sexual urges directed toward children, and he took several steps toward gratifying those urges. He went to not one, but two parks in search of children at play, in order to achieve sexual gratification . . . and consequently became sexually aroused. In short, he engaged not only in thought, but in activity directed toward an illegal and very harmful end.[38]

Thankfully, the city of Lafayette appealed the panel's decision, and this disgraceful ruling was overturned. In an 8-3 decision by the full Seventh Circuit, the court explained that the ban was not intended to muzzle any particular thoughts. Rather, the court agreed, "The inescapable reality is that Mr. Doe did not simply entertain thoughts; he brought himself to the brink of committing child molestation."[39]

OPPOSING ORDINANCES TO PROTECT KIDS

Such cases are not out of the ACLU's ordinary purview. It has opposed numerous city, state, and federal laws aimed at protecting children from sexual predators.

In 2005, after a string of highly publicized child abductions in Florida, a number of communities approved ordinances prohibiting registered child sex offenders from living close to area schools, day care centers, or parks. The ACLU not only fought to prevent these measures from passing but threatened possible legal action against the many communities that already had such laws on the books. Alessandra Meetze, communications director for the ACLU of Florida, told reporters, "We have about forty of these ordinances that are now under review. . . . Sooner or later, the constitutionality of these ordinances will have to be tested in court."[40]

In July 2002, the Iowa legislature enacted a similar law prohibiting convicted sex offenders from living within 2,000 feet of a school or day care facility—a common sense approach to reducing the incidence of child sexual abuse. But almost immediately, the Iowa Civil Liberties Union (ICLU), an affiliate of the ACLU, filed a class-action lawsuit on behalf of all affected sex offenders, claiming that the law imposed an "unconstitutional punishment."

To begin with, U.S. District Judge Robert Pratt sided with the ICLU, but a three-judge federal appeals court panel overturned his ruling. On September 29, 2005, the ICLU announced that it had appealed the decision to the U.S. Supreme Court. Ben Stone, executive director for the ICLU, explained, "The ICLU urged the Justices to review the statute promptly, because towns and cities across the nation are quickly adopting laws and ordinances banning sex offenders from living in their jurisdictions."[41] No decision has been rendered.

Indeed, states across the country are passing laws to empower parents and protect children. To most Americans, this is welcome progress. To the ACLU, such precautionary measures to protect children are alarming. Mary Dixon, spokeswoman for the ACLU of Illinois, lamented, "It is troublesome that we're getting closer to outright banishment of sex offenders."[42]

The ACLU has consistently fought measures to toughen penalties for child sex offenders. On March 12, 2002, as the U.S. House was preparing to vote on legislation that would have imposed mandatory life sentences for criminals twice convicted of a "federal sex offense in which a minor is the victim," the ACLU sent letters of opposition to all members of the House. It read:

We are writing to ask you to oppose H.R. 2146,

the "Two Strikes You're Out Child Protection Act." This bill would impose a mandatory life sentence for any person convicted of certain federal sex offenses against a minor, if the person has a prior conviction for a sexual offense against a minor. This mandatory sentencing scheme raises grave civil liberties concerns.[43]

Two days later, despite the best efforts of the ACLU, the U.S. House voted 382-34 to pass the legislation. Unfortunately, the measure never received a simple up or down vote in the U.S. Senate.

CONTESTING SEX OFFENDER REGISTRIES

The organization has also opposed other simple, common sense measures to protect children—like establishing public sex offender registries.

In 2003, legislation was introduced in the Louisiana Senate that would have required convicted sex offenders enrolled or employed at institutions of post-secondary education to inform the school that they had been convicted of a sex crime. The ACLU of Louisiana opposed the measure, claiming that the establishment of sex offender registries constituted an excessive penalty and "only succeeds in ostracizing a sex offender to the margins of society."[44]

The organization issued a press release explaining, "The ACLU of Louisiana is opposed to the registration of sex offenders because it is an unfairly imposed penalty."

Perhaps the ACLU opts to ignore the high recidivism rate of pedophiles, or maybe its members fail to grasp the horrendous nature of child sexual abuse. After reviewing the statements of the ACLU, chances are that both are correct. In describing the crime of "felony carnal knowledge of a juvenile" (sex with a minor), the ACLU of Louisiana explained that these were "crimes for which the offenders serve no threat to society, and for which sex offender registration bestows a penalty far exceeding the crime."[45]

In other words, the ACLU considers sex offender registration to be a punishment that far exceeds the fair penalty for raping or molesting a child.

AMERICAN DILIGENCE: A MUST!

America's young people are drowning in the stormy seas of promiscuity, disease, heartbreak, and rampant sexual abuse. Our kids desperately need adults to step up to the plate and offer responsible, moral guidance; they need moral lifelines. Instead, our society (the entertainment industry, the courts, the public schools, etc.) continues to toss them heavy anchors of moral depravity.

As arrogant judges and unscrupulous ACLU lawyers ponder the constitutional "rights" of pedophiles, scores of children have been forsaken by a judicial system that has diligently protected the voracious perversions of sex offenders.

Americans must wake up to this growing epidemic of child sexual abuse!

Consider these statistics:

- There are more than 500,000 registered sex offenders in the United States.[46]
- The National Center for Missing and Exploited Children and the U.S. Justice Department conducted a joint study—finding that one in every five kids aged 10 to 17 had received an online sexual solicitation

from an adult in the previous year.[47]

- In a nationwide survey of high school students conducted by the CDC, roughly 9 percent reported that they had been forced into sexual encounters (11.9 percent of female students and 6.1 percent of male students).
- For female victims of sexual assault, 54 percent of all rapes occur before age 18, and 22 percent occur before age 12.
- For male victims of sexual assault, 75 percent of all rapes occur before age 18, and 48 percent of all rapes occur before age 12.[48]

The U.S. Department of Education reported:

For most children, being the victim of sexual misconduct does damage that lasts well into adulthood, and for most it is never fully repaired. Child sexual abuse targets lose trust in adults and authority figures, suffer physical ailments and lowered immune systems, and do less well in school. They often drop out of or avoid school. . . . Sexually abused children are more likely than children who are not sexually abused to be substance users as adults and to have difficulty forming intimate relationships.[49]

According to the American Psychological Association, "Child sexual abuse victims are more likely . . . to be involved in physically abusive relationships as adults,"[50] and the U.S. Justice Department reports that these victims face a dramatically increased likelihood of spending time in prison.[51]

If this nation is to preserve the sexual innocence of ourchildren . . . if we are to stop the onslaught of child sex abuse if . . . we are to protect our children from the lies of our decaying culture, then Americans must demand better from our legislators, our judges, our schools, and our pulpits.

The fact that America now suffers from a condition of moral bankruptcy is not solely an indictment against the likes of the ACLU; it is an indictment against the collective apathy of God's Church.

Jesus calls his disciples to defend and care for little children. "Whoever receives one little child like this in My name receives Me," Jesus taught. "Whoever causes one of these little ones who believe in Me to sin, it would be better for him if a millstone were hung around his neck, and he were drowned in the depth of the sea."[52]

If our nation is to avoid the shameless fate of ruined nations, Americans must not only demand a better society, we must become contributing members of a better society, a society that stands in fervent opposition to the absurd and reckless agenda of the ACLU, a society where a child's right to be safe trumps the perverted appetite of sexual predators.

We owe at least this much to the future generations of Americans!

SIX

Redefining Marriage and Family

*Therefore a man shall leave his father and mother and
be joined to his wife, and they shall become one flesh.*

— Genesis 2:24

Much has happened since God first ordained the institutions
of marriage and family. Empires have risen to glory, only to fade
into the history books. Mighty armies have destroyed their foes,
only to follow them to the grave. Kings and pharaohs have
constructed glorious temples to honor their gods, but these
structures now lie forsaken and crumbling beneath the elements
of creation. Without fail, the whimsical follies of man rise and fall.
Yet every civilization in history has recognized that the
institutions of marriage and family are essential pillars of society.

DESTROYING THE PILLARS

Amidst the decline of American sexual mores, our increasingly self-centered society has failed to understand the critical importance of protecting and preserving the family for future
generations. As a result, the decadent union of sexual chaos and
moral relativism has given birth to a perilous new trend that, if left
unchecked, could lead to the collapse of marriage and family
in America.

Marriage is under fire from all sides—plagued by divorce, co-habitation, premarital sex, adultery, and most recently, an attack on the very definition of marriage itself. In recognition of these societal ills, the *New York Times* suggested that "the United States is becoming a post-marital society."[1]

If marriage is indeed under attack in America, then no one is leading this assault more ferociously than the ACLU. Not only has the ACLU fought to eliminate laws governing divorce, fornication, and adultery, the organization has also been involved in numerous lawsuits seeking to legalize same-sex marriage, gay adoption, and even polygamy.

As early as 1919, ACLU founder Roger Baldwin was determined to redefine the role of both the church and the state in the affairs of marriage, once saying, "The present institution of marriage among us is a grim mockery of essential freedom."[2]

POSTER CHILD OF POST-MARITAL CULTURE

Looking to Scandinavia—where countries have swallowed many of these poisonous, post-modern notions that aim to redefine marriage and family—we see cultures that have all but forsaken these sacred institutions. As these societies have embraced counterfeit marriages, the value and importance of real marriage has lessened to such a degree that few bother to take that step anymore. Indeed, Scandinavian sociologists have noted that the common foundations for settling a family "have moved from marriage to parenthood."[3]

Dr. Stanley Kurtz, a research fellow at the Hoover Institution, with a doctorate in social anthropology from Harvard University, has studied the conditions of marriage and family throughout Scandinavia. In an article published in *The Weekly Standard*, he noted:

> Marriage is slowly dying in Scandinavia. A majority of children in Sweden and Norway are born out of wedlock. Sixty percent of first-born children in Denmark have unmarried parents. Not coincidentally, these countries have had something close to full gay marriage for a decade or more.[4]
>
> America's situation is not unlike Norway's in the early nineties, with religiosity relatively strong, the out-of-wedlock birthrate still relatively low (yet rising), and the public opposed to gay marriage. If, as in Norway, gay marriage were imposed here by a socially liberal cultural elite, it would likely speed us on the way toward the classic Nordic pattern of less frequent marriage, more frequent out-of-wedlock birth, and skyrocketing family dissolution.[5]

Marriage is the bedrock of civilization and the cornerstone of the family. When a society embraces counterfeit forms of marriage, it opens the door to the devaluation of the sanctity of both marriage and family. No intelligent society would ever allow or encourage its citizens to produce counterfeit currency, because a flood of fake currency would inevitably devalue the real thing in the eyes of its citizens. Likewise, if America embraces the various counterfeit forms of marriage, it sends a loud message to younger generations that marriage is nothing more than an outward declaration of attraction—not the sacred institution ordained by God to yield the fruits of family.

A number of countries in Western Europe are now learning this costly lesson.

After witnessing the negative repercussions in nations that embrace same-sex unions, even the French Parliament issued a report recommending that the government reject proposals to legalize same-sex marriage and homosexual adoption. The French *Parliamentary Report on the Family and the Rights of Children* urged government officials to affirm the true definitions of marriage and family, concluding, "The best interests of the child must prevail over adults' exercise of their liberty."[6] France got this one right!

America needs a resurgence of decency. We desperately need bold pastors and principled politicians to come to the aid of marriage and family. It is a travesty that so many elected officials and clergymen have failed to confront the issues plaguing marriage in America, opting to sit idly by as the nation dilutes the sanctity of marriage.

Consider its current trajectory in America:

- Each year, approximately one million children experience the divorce of their parents.
- Forty-three percent of first marriages dissolve within fifteen years.
- From 1990-2000, the number of cohabiting couples with children nearly doubled—rising from 891,000 in 1990 to roughly 1.7 million in 2000.
- From 1960 to 1995, the percentage of children living in single-parent homes tripled, rising from 9 percent to 27 percent.
- Today, nearly twenty million children live in single-parent homes.
- In 2000, 1.35 million births (one-third of all births) occurred out of wedlock.[7]
- And numerous states now offer some form of legal recognition to same-sex

relationships, including California, Connecticut, the District of Columbia, Hawaii, Maine, Massachusetts, New Jersey, and Vermont.[8]

FORSAKING FUTURE GENERATIONS

Tragically, rather than coming to the rescue of an already ailing institution, many judges and politicians now seem determined to deliver its death blow—by completely redefining marriage and undermining any remaining respect for "mom and dad" homes. Vermont, the first state to endorse same-sex civil unions, has already exhibited how homosexual unions make a mockery of marriage. The University of Vermont conducted a 2003 survey and found that only 34 percent of the state's gay men who were involved in self-described "committed relationships" believed that it was wrong to have sex outside of this primary relationship. Of homosexual men involved in state-sanctioned civil unions, only half felt that adulterous sexual relationships were wrong.[9]

A Dutch study, published in the May 2003 edition of the *AIDS Journal*, echoed these findings. It found that the average homosexual relationship only lasted 1.5 years and concluded that "men in homosexual relationships, on average, have eight partners a year outside those relationships."[10]

Anne Peplau, professor of psychology at the University of California, Los Angeles (UCLA), concurred. "There is clear evidence that gay men are less likely to have sexually exclusive relationships than other people," said Peplau, "but this is not typically harmful to their relationships because partners agree that it's acceptable."[11]

Though this sort of widespread promiscuity would undoubtedly make a mockery of marriage, today's judges and legislators seem determined to force the door of holy matrimony wide open for all people—with little regard for the sanctity of the institution. To say the least, things have changed in our great country. At one time, the U.S. Supreme Court issued unanimous decisions like *Murphy v. Ramsey* (1885):

> No legislation can be supposed more wholesome and necessary in the founding of a free, self-governing commonwealth . . . than that which seeks to establish it on the basis of the idea of the family, as consisting in and springing from the union for life of one man and one woman in the holy estate of matrimony.[12]

Our society must recapture this solemn respect for the sanctity of marriage. Unfortunately, many of our elected officials and the nation's judiciary are working against us.

PANDORA'S BOX OPENED IN MASSACHUSETTS

On November 18, 2003, in one of the most egregious court decisions in our nation's history, the Massachusetts Supreme Judicial Court issued a 4-3 decision striking down the state's ban on same-sex marriage and ordering the state legislature to codify the ruling into law. With one swing of the gavel, four judges plunged the nation into turmoil, usurping the role of the elected legislature and bucking millennia of moral tradition.

Not surprisingly, the ACLU led the way in calling for such a decision. In the case of *Goodridge v. Department of Public Health*, the organization filed an *amicus* brief urging the court to grant marriage licenses to seven homosexual couples.[13]

The court sided with the ACLU, arrogantly declaring:

> We are mindful that our decision marks a change

in the history of our marriage law. Many people hold deep-seated religious, moral, and ethical convictions that marriage should be limited to the union of one man and one woman . . . [but] our concern is with the Massachusetts Constitution.[14]

Nonsense! If these four judges were truly concerned with the Massachusetts Constitution, then they would have been well aware that Chapter III, Article 5, declares, "All causes of marriage, divorce, and alimony . . . shall be heard and determined by the governor and council, until the legislature shall, by law, make other provision."[15]

The court clearly overstepped its bounds. The Massachusetts Constitution charges the governor and the legislature with the responsibility of determining marital law. Several Christian legal groups urged the court to review its ruling. In its appeal, the Thomas More Law Center argued, "What happens with the legal institution of marriage should ultimately depend on the democratic processes outlined in the Commonwealth's Constitution rather than by judicial fiat."[16]

Regardless, the court refused to reverse itself—affirming its prior decision ordering the Massachusetts Legislature to amend the state's marital laws within 180 days.

In the wake of the *Goodridge* decision, the ACLU launched a nationwide campaign to challenge the constitutionality of marriage laws in numerous states, hoping that other ideologically-driven judges would overrule the will of the people and impose their own agendas. The ACLU filed lawsuits in California, Indiana, Maryland, Nebraska,[17] New York, Oregon, and Washington.[18]

AMERICAN VOTERS RESPOND

The *Goodridge* decision generated tremendous public outcry from citizens concerned over the future of marriage. Prior to the decision, only four states (Alaska, Hawaii, Nebraska, and Nevada) had explicitly prohibited same-sex marriage in their state constitutions. Within one year, states across the nation had mounted massive grassroots campaigns and petition drives to have the issue settled at the ballot box—allowing voters to determine whether to approve state constitutional amendments defining marriage as the union of one man and one woman.

Naturally, the ACLU stood in firm opposition to these efforts. The organization filed numerous lawsuits—in Arkansas,[19] Florida,[20] Georgia, Michigan, Tennessee,[21] and Utah[22]—hoping that activist judges would declare these proposed elections unconstitutional, thereby stripping Americans of their right to govern themselves.

Despite the best efforts of the ACLU, thirteen states approved marriage amendments by overwhelming margins in the fall of 2004. These states included Arkansas (75%), Georgia (77%), Kentucky (75%), Louisiana (78%), Michigan (59%), Mississippi (86%), Missouri (71%), Montana (66%), North Dakota (73%), Ohio (62%), Oklahoma (76%), Oregon (58%), and Utah (66%).[23]

In 2005, the states of Kansas (75%) and Texas (75%) followed suit. In 2006, Alabama (81%) approved an amendment, and six additional states (Idaho, South Carolina, South Dakota, Tennessee, Virginia, and Wisconsin) are expected to approve marriage amendments in November,[24] bringing the total of states from four in 2003 to twenty-six in 2006.

Despite this flurry of activity, many pro-family advocates warned that these efforts would not be sufficient to protect marriage. After all, state amendments can only protect marriage laws from state courts, but it would only take one federal judge to strike down a state's marriage amendment. The ACLU has already filed federal lawsuits aimed at doing just that.

Thus, a nationwide effort was launched to pass a federal marriage amendment.

OPPOSING THE FEDERAL MARRIAGE AMENDMENT

Senator Wayne Allard (CO) and Congresswoman Marilyn Musgrave (CO) introduced the Federal Marriage Amendment, later renamed the Marriage Protection Amendment, in 2004. The proposed amendment read:

> Marriage in the United States shall consist only of the union of a man and a woman. Neither this Constitution, nor the constitution of any State, shall be construed to require that marriage or the legal incidents thereof be conferred upon any union other than the union of a man and a woman.[25]

The ACLU vehemently opposed the measure, labeling the proposed amendment as a "mean-spirited proposal" that would be "harmful to children."[26]

Despite being flooded with letters, phone calls, e-mails, and millions of petitions pleading with them to support the Marriage Protection Amendment, both Houses of Congress failed to produce the two-thirds majorities necessary to approve a constitutional amendment.

FEDERAL JUDGE STRIKES STATE AMENDMENT

Subsequently, on May 12, 2005, the fears of pro-family

advocates were realized. U.S. District Judge Joseph F. Bataillon struck down Nebraska's state constitutional amendment, which had defined marriage as a contract "between a man and woman." The amendment had been approved by 70 percent of Nebraska voters, but the ACLU managed to find one federal judge willing to overrule them all.[27]

This lawsuit, originally filed by the ACLU and Lambda Legal in April 2003, contended that it was unconstitutional for Nebraska to deny marital benefits to same-sex couples. After filing its opening brief in the case, Sharon McGowan, a staff attorney for the ACLU, told reporters that the state amendment was nothing but "an extreme and sweeping attack on gay families . . . designed to punish gay people and completely block them from the political process."[28]

As usual, the ACLU's rhetoric was grossly exaggerated. In truth, the amendment simply codified the definition of marriage that has existed for millennia: "Only marriage between a man and woman shall be valid or recognized in Nebraska. The uniting of two persons of the same sex in a civil union, domestic partnership, or other similar same-sex relationship shall not be valid or recognized in Nebraska."

Judge Bataillon ruled that the amendment constituted "a denial of equal protections," adding that "any blanket prohibition on any type of legal recognition of a same-sex relationship not only denies the benefits of favorable legislation to these groups, it prohibits them from even asking for such benefits."[29] If the logic undergirding his decision is allowed to stand—with an exclusionary definition of marriage constituting a "denial of equal protections"—it would be utterly impossible for any government to maintain the criminalization of polygamous or incestuous marriage.

In an attempt to intimidate other states considering marriage amendments, Amy Miller, spokeswoman for the ACLU of

Nebraska, told reporters, "The judge was clear that states can't enact amendments that bar gay people from the democratic process."[30] These comments were completely unfounded, ignoring two important facts: (1) the "democratic process" was exactly what had determined that marriage should remain between a man and woman, and (2) homosexuals were allowed to participate in that election.

Disappointed by the decision, Dr. James Dobson, founder of Focus on the Family, reminded people:

> Last year when the Marriage Protection Amendment (MPA) was being debated in the U.S. Senate, some senators—including Nebraska's own Ben Nelson—used the excuse that the MPA was "not needed," and that the crucial matters MPA addresses could be handled at the state level. Apparently not![31]

The state of Nebraska appealed the decision to the Eighth U.S. Circuit Court of Appeals, where a three-judge panel eventually overturned Judge Bataillon's ruling. The court explained:

> The institution of marriage has always been, in our federal system, the predominant concern of state government. Laws limiting the state-recognized institution of marriage to heterosexual couples are rationally related to legitimate state interests and therefore do not violate the Constitution of the United States.[32]

A Legacy of Lawsuits in Washington

The assault against traditional marriage is nothing new for the ACLU. More than thirty years ago, in 1972, the organization filed a lawsuit against the state of Washington on behalf of two homosexuals (John Singer and Paul Barwick) who sought to marry.

In the case of *Singer v. Hara,* a Washington State appellate court ruled, "The denial of a marriage license to two people of the same sex does not constitute an abridgement of any constitutional rights." The court added, "Society . . . views marriage as the appropriate and desirable forum for procreation and the rearing of children."[33]

In 1998, the Washington State Legislature further solidified its marital laws, passing the Washington Defense of Marriage Act. This law defined marriage as "a civil contract between a male and a female"[34] and prohibited any marriage "when the parties are persons other than a male and a female."[35]

In early 2004, spurred by Massachusetts' *Goodridge* decision, the ACLU and Lambda Legal once again joined forces to strike down Washington's law—hoping to reverse the 1972 *Singer* precedent. Eight homosexual couples, represented by Lambda Legal, filed suit in King County, and eleven homosexual couples, represented by the ACLU, filed suit in Thurston County.

Both cases were successful! Individual judges thumbed their noses at the *Singer* precedent.

King County Superior Court Judge William L. Downing sided with Lambda Legal. He declared, "Americans have differing views as to what morality requires in the definition of marriage. It is not for our secular government to choose . . . sides in such a debate."[36] Ironically, the judge remained oblivious to the fact that he had just chosen sides in the debate.

One month later, in an ACLU lawsuit involving eleven

same-sex couples, Thurston County Superior Court Judge Richard D. Hicks issued a similar decision. Showing more regard for pop culture than the actual law, Judge Hicks explained that he was reversing the 1972 *Singer* precedent because "the community, and its values, has substantially changed from the times of *Singer*."[37]

At the core of his ruling, Judge Hicks contended that the state's expressed purpose for the law—"to encourage procreation and stable environments for children"—was irrational, because the state already permitted homosexual couples to adopt children. The judge then insinuated that the state legislature was unaware of "what a family really is."[38]

Though the role of a judge is to *interpret* the law—not to create new laws—Judge Hicks simply dismissed the collective will of Washington voters. Ironically, after explaining the reasons for his one-man edict, he arrogantly concluded by proclaiming, "This is the democracy of conscience." Apparently, in the mind of Judge Richard D. Hicks, democracies are governed by judges.

The state appealed the decision to the Washington Supreme Court, where the ACLU took the lead role in representing the homosexual couples.[39]

On July 26, 2006, the Washington Supreme Court issued its 5-4 decision, protecting real marriage and overturning the lower court decisions. The court declared:

> The legislature was entitled to believe that limiting marriage to opposite-sex couples furthers the State's legitimate interests in procreation and the well-being of children. It cannot be overemphasized that our state constitution provides for a representative democracy and that the people, who have consented to be governed, speak through their

elected representatives [rather than through judges].[40]

UNDERMINING THE DEFENSE OF MARRIAGE ACT

The ACLU has also fought to legalize transsexual marriage by twisting the intentions of the federal Defense of Marriage Act (DOMA) of 1996 which states, "The word 'marriage' means only a legal union between one man and one woman as husband and wife, and the word 'spouse' refers only to a person of the opposite sex who is a husband or a wife."[41]

In November 2002, Gia Teresa Lovo-Ciccone petitioned the U.S. Citizenship and Immigration Services board, asking that her new transsexual "husband" be recognized as her legitimate husband and granted citizenship. Initially the board refused, claiming that DOMA prohibited the federal recognition of any marriages besides those between a man and a woman. The plaintiff appealed the decision to the U.S. Department of Justice Board of Immigration Appeals.

On December 16, 2004, the ACLU filed a brief in support of the plaintiff's appeal. In an attempt to validate transsexual marriages, the ACLU argued, "A marriage between two people of the opposite sex is an opposite-sex marriage for purposes of . . . DOMA, irrespective of the fact that one member of the couple has undergone a sex reassignment surgery."[42]

Surprisingly, on May 18, 2005, the U.S. Department of Justice Board of Immigration Appeals issued an 8-page decision siding with the ACLU. The board declared, "The Defense of Marriage Act . . . does not preclude, for purposes of Federal law, recognition of a marriage involving a postoperative transsexual, where the marriage is considered by the State in which it was performed as one between two individuals of the opposite sex."[43]

FIGHTING FOR TRANSSEXUAL MARRIAGE IN KANSAS

The ACLU has fought for transsexual marriage at the state level, as well. In February 2004, a pre-operative transsexual, born Edward Gast, applied for a marriage license falsely claiming to be a female—in hopes that Leavenworth County (Kansas) officials would allow him to marry his same-sex partner, George Somers. He was granted a marriage license, but after the county was informed of his true gender, he was arrested for falsifying information on his application.[44]

The ACLU immediately came to his defense. Though his birth certificate states that his gender is male, the ACLU argued that physical gender at birth was irrelevant, because Gast had actually changed his legal name to "Sandy" and registered as a female on his driver's license.

On several occasions during the course of the trial, the county prosecutor rightly referred to Gast as "Mister" and "Sir." In response, Pedro Irigonegaray, the ACLU attorney who argued the case, exclaimed, "I think the inappropriateness of referring to Sandy as 'Mister' needs to come to an end. There is no need for that; Sandy is a woman."

After the case had been argued, Irigonegaray explained that he believed same-sex transsexual couples should be permitted to marry because "we come out of the same genetic soup."

Genetic soup—the ACLU's benchmark for marriage!

Thankfully, Frank Kohl, the Leavenworth County prosecuting attorney, was unwilling to accept the ACLU's distorted notion of gender. Kohl told reporters: "The change of driver's license, the change of name—even though they were done through legal channels—does not change gender. The gender you are born with is the gender you remain for life."[45]

In the case of *Kansas v. Gast*, Leavenworth County Judge Frederick Stewart ultimately protected marriage, but rendered two conflicting decisions. Judge Stewart ordered Gast to surrender his marriage license in order to prevent a same-sex marriage, but then ruled that Gast did not falsify his marriage application when he claimed that he was of the opposite sex.[46]

THE ACLU'S LONG HISTORY OF SUPPORTING BIGAMY

Given the ACLU's tendency to support anything outside of traditional values, it should come as no surprise that the organization has also been a long-time supporter of polygamous marriage. When U.S. Supreme Court Justice Ruth Bader Ginsburg served as the General Counsel for the ACLU, she co-wrote a report challenging the constitutionality of a federal statute prohibiting polygamy.

Ginsburg wrote that a statute criminalizing bigamy (48 USC §1461) "is of questionable constitutionality, since it appears to encroach impermissibly upon private relationships."[47]

PROMOTING POLYGAMY IN UTAH

In 1999, the ACLU reaffirmed its commitment to legalize polygamous marriages—announcing its support for an effort to overturn a 1935 Utah statute that criminalized such unions.

Claiming that anti-bigamy laws are nothing more than outdated attempts to legislate morality, Stephen Clark, legal director for the ACLU of Utah, stated:

> The bigamy statute, like sodomy statutes and like other anachronistic moralistic legislation, goes to the core of what the Supreme Court identifies as important fundamental privacy rights. . . . Talking to Utah's polygamists is like talking to gays and lesbians. So certainly, that kind of privacy

expectation is something the ACLU is committed to protecting.[48]

However, the ACLU faces rigid opposition in this effort. Not only do ninety percent of Utah adults support the current law, but the U.S. Supreme Court has affirmed laws prohibiting polygamous marriage on several occasions.[49]

Indeed, we are not the first generation forced to defend the integrity of marriage. In 1852, under the leadership of Brigham Young, the Mormon Church endorsed the concept of polygamy for its members—causing a tremendous uproar throughout the United States.[50]

By 1856—just four years later—the issue of polygamy had grown so politically charged that it was addressed in the first-ever official national platform of the Republican Party. The platform declared that it was "the imperative duty of Congress to prohibit, in the territories, those twin relics of barbarism—polygamy and slavery."[51]

During the latter half of the 1800s, opposition to the threat of polygamy intensified—leading the U.S. Supreme Court to consider the matter in several cases. A group of Mormons argued that the First Amendment's religious liberty clause allowed them to engage in polygamy. However, the Court upheld the traditional definition of marriage and refused to allow polygamous marriages.

THE CONCLUSIONS OF PRINCIPLED JUDGES

In the case of *United States v. Reynolds* (1878), the U.S. Supreme Court declared:

> It is impossible to believe that the constitutional guaranty of religious freedom was intended to

prohibit legislation in respect to this most important feature of social life. Marriage, while from its very nature a sacred obligation, is nevertheless, in most civilized nations, a civil contract, and usually regulated by law. Upon it society may be said to be built, and out of its fruits spring social relations and social obligations and duties, with which government is necessarily required to deal.[52]

In the case of *Davis v. Beason* (1890), the Court offered further explanation for why polygamous marriages should remain criminalized:

Bigamy and polygamy are crimes by the laws of all civilized and Christian countries. They are crimes by the laws of the United States, and they are crimes by the laws of Idaho. They tend to destroy the purity of the marriage relation, to disturb the peace of families, to degrade woman, and to debase man. Few crimes are more pernicious to the best interests of society, and receive more general or more deserved punishment. To extend exemption from punishment for such crimes would be to shock the moral judgment of the community.[53]

Abandoning the Natural Order

The ACLU wants more than to simply eradicate a meaningful definition of marriage. It wants to destroy the concept of family as well. This is evidenced by the organization's support for policies which allow homosexual couples to adopt children. In supporting such programs, the organization ignores a vast accumulation of evidence proving that children fare best in homes with both a mother and a father.

Indeed, studies have shown that having both a father and a mother in the home contributes directly to better school performance, reduced substance abuse, less crime and delinquency, fewer emotional and other behavioral problems, and a lowered risk of abuse or neglect.[54]

Advocates of "two mom" homes ignore mountains of evidence emphasizing the important role that a father plays in a child's life.

According to the National Fatherhood Initiative, children who live without a father figure are far more likely to (1) be victims of child abuse; (2) use drugs; (3) experience educational, health, emotional, and behavioral problems; (4) drop out of school; and (5) engage in criminal behaviors.[55] The U.S. Department of Health added, "Fatherless children are at dramatically greater risk of suicide."[56]

In light of this evidence, the U.S. Department of Health and Human Services concluded, "There is simply no substitute for the love, involvement, and commitment of a responsible father."[57]

Nonetheless, the ACLU opts to advance the homosexual agenda at the expense of American kids.

IGNORING THE BEST INTERESTS OF KIDS

Other studies have shown that growing up with homosexual parents can greatly influence the sexuality of a child. A study conducted by University of Southern California sociologists Judith Stacey and Timothy Biblarz revealed that children raised by homosexual couples "seem to grow up to be more open to homoerotic relations."[58] In fact, the study showed that 12 percent of girls raised in lesbian homes become active lesbians themselves—an increase of over 850 percent above the incidence of lesbianism (1.4 percent) in the population at large.[59]

So much for being born that way!

In response to these findings, Aimee Gelnaw, director of the pro-homosexual Family Pride Coalition, admitted that a child's social environment (not genetics) influences his or her sexual orientation. She stated, "Of course our kids are going to be different. They're growing up in a different social context."

Likewise, Kate Kendall, director of the National Center for Lesbian Rights, responded:

> If we're ashamed of that outcome, it means we're ashamed of ourselves. . . . There's only one response to a study that children raised by lesbian and gay parents may be somewhat more likely to reject notions of rigid sexual orientation—that response has to be elation.[60]

Despite the serious implications for children raised without parents of both sexes, the ACLU and many others remain determined to forsake the optimal interests of children, choosing instead to promote a concept that nature itself forbids—homosexual couples having children.

Children are hardwired to desire relationships with both a mother and a father. Thus, it is unfair and selfish to *intentionally* strip them of either relationship. Consider the following exchange between Diane Sawyer and outspoken gay adoption advocate, Rosie O'Donnell, on ABC's *Primetime Thursday*:

> Diane Sawyer: Would it break your heart if your son said, "I want a mommy *and* a daddy?"
> Rosie O'Donnell: He has said that. . . . Of course

he has. He's a six-year-old boy. He says, "I want to have a daddy." I said . . . "If you were to have a daddy, you wouldn't have me as a mommy, because I'm the kind of mommy who wants another mommy." You know, he understands that there are different types of people, that he grew up in another lady's tummy, that God looked inside and saw there was a mix-up, and that God brought him to me . . . He understands.[61]

The selfish desires of adults should never trump the best interests of innocent children. Sadly, in the case of homosexuals like O'Donnell, they often do. Nevertheless, the ACLU is determined to redefine the family—ignoring science, nature, and the best interests of children.

FIGHTING FOR GAY ADOPTION IN FLORIDA

In May 1999, the ACLU filed a federal lawsuit against the state of Florida on behalf of six homosexual couples seeking to strike down Florida's ban on homosexual adoption.[62]

U.S. District Judge James Lawrence King dismissed the ACLU's lawsuit, but the organization appealed Judge King's decision to the 11th U.S. Circuit Court of Appeals, asking the court to overrule the representative will of the voters. While failing to address the studies that have shown that children are better off living with both a mom and a dad, the ACLU's brief did explain that "morality" and "the views of others" were not adequate reasons to uphold the law.[63]

Howard Simon, executive director for the ACLU of Florida, went a step further, saying that the state law was passed due to the "irrational prejudices of state legislators."[64]

After nearly two years, the 11th U.S. Circuit Court of Appeals reached its decision. In a rare and refreshing act of judicial restraint, the appellate court affirmed the Florida state law, which is the only complete prohibition on homosexual adoption remaining in the United States.

In a decision respectful of both states' rights and representative government, the court declared:

> The State of Florida has made the determination that it is not in the best interests of its displaced children to be adopted by individuals who "engage in current, voluntary homosexual activity," and we have found nothing in the Constitution that forbids this policy judgment. Thus, any argument that the Florida legislature was misguided in its decision is one of legislative policy, not constitutional law. The legislature is the proper forum for this debate, and we do not sit as a superlegislature "to award by judicial decree what was not achievable by political consensus."[65]

Unsurprisingly, the ACLU appealed this decision all the way to the U.S. Supreme Court. On January 10, 2005, the High Court rejected the appeal.[66]

This decision, coupled with mounting nationwide efforts to protect true marriage, has reenergized voters to protect children from circumstances in which the child's best interests are not the foremost concern. According to USA Today, "Efforts to ban gays and lesbians from adopting children are emerging across the USA... Steps to pass laws or secure November ballot initiatives are underway in at least 16 states."[67]

DESTROYING THE NUCLEAR FAMILY

The ACLU's quest to redefine the traditional family unit goes beyond same-sex marriage and gay adoption. The ACLU actively promotes the notion that live-in, homosexual partners deserve parental rights over their partner's biological children—even after the couple has separated!

On June 1, 2002, Christina Smarr and Tina Burch were heading home, when Tina fell asleep at the wheel and swerved into oncoming traffic. Tragically, the couple was involved in a head-on collision, killing Christina and leaving her two-year-old son an orphan.[68]

Following the accident, Christina's parents sought custody of their grandson, but they were viciously opposed by Tina, her supposed lesbian partner. A West Virginia family court initially awarded custody to Tina, but this decision was reversed by a state appellate court, which granted custody to the grandparents.

Burch then filed an appeal with the West Virginia Supreme Court of Appeals, demanding custody of her deceased partner's child. Callously ignoring the best interests of the then five-year-old boy, the ACLU filed an *amicus* brief in support of Burch's lawsuit. The brief argued that a lesbian partner should enjoy custodial rights to a child . . . even over the claims of the child's own grandparents.

Incredibly, on June 17, 2005, the West Virginia Supreme Court of Appeals revoked custody from the boy's grandparents, declaring that the parental rights of an unrelated lesbian woman trumped the rights of the boy's maternal grandparents. The court declared that the lesbian partner was entitled to custody because she was the boy's "psychological parent."[69]

Andrew Schneider, executive director of the ACLU of West Virginia, praised the court's decision, saying, "The court, in its wisdom and compassion, has recognized Tina Burch for what she is: the surviving parent of a little boy who has already lost *one of his mothers.*"[70]

Stephen M. Crampton, chief counsel for the American Family Association Center for Law and Policy, responded, "This court has once again demonstrated the lethal effects of judicial activism on the nuclear family, which is the cornerstone of our civilization."

In a similar case, the ACLU filed an *amicus* brief with a Washington state court, asking the judge to establish parental rights for any lesbian who assumes motherly roles while dating another woman with children. In this particular case, two lesbians had broken up and, on absolutely no legal grounds, the former girlfriend began demanding parental and visitation rights—in order to visit her former partner's biological child.

Initially, a lower court ruled that the lesbian woman could not exercise parental rights over a child without biological or legal ties. However, upon appeal, the Washington Court of Appeals sided with the ACLU, ruling that a lesbian partner who assumes the obligations of parenthood, with the consent of a biological parent, automatically becomes what the court called a "de facto parent."

Leslie Cooper, a staff attorney with the ACLU, exclaimed, "This is wonderful news for gay parents and their children. The court recognized that being a parent is not just about blood ties," adding that gay partners cannot be denied parental rights "simply because that parent doesn't have a biological connection."[71] Of course, Cooper failed to acknowledge that this ruling could undermine the rights of all biological parents who feel that previous boyfriends or girlfriends should stay away from his or her children.

As society continues to tolerate the deterioration of the family unit and dismiss the traditional roles of moms and dads, the ACLU and activist judges will continue to reshape the family unit into a hodgepodge of loosely bound "de facto" and "psychological" homosexual guardians.

A LEGACY AT RISK

The turmoil surrounding marriage and family is threatening the future of American culture. As our nation is confronted by the agenda of the ACLU, we must work diligently to ensure that wrong-headed notions of liberty and tolerance do not trump the sacred institutions that have served as the bedrock of civilized societies for thousands of years.

In the late nineteenth century, America staved off the push for legalized polygamy. Today, Americans are confronted with an ACLU agenda that seeks to normalize same-sex marriage, polygamy, homosexual adoption, assumed custodial rights for non-biological and unmarried partners, and numerous other assaults to the sacred institution of marriage. This will no doubt require tremendous endurance on the part of pro-family advocates, but it is a battle worth fighting.

Sixteen years after the 1890 *Davis* decision outlawing polygamy, America's governing officials had remained steadfast in their resolve to defend the institutions of marriage and family. In 1906, as the battles to fend off polygamy were still of paramount concern, President Theodore Roosevelt delivered his State of the Union address, instructing Congress to remain ever-vigilant:

> Surely, there is nothing so vitally essential to the welfare of the nation, nothing around which the nation should so bend itself to throw every safeguard, as the home life of the average citizen. When home ties are loosened; when men and women cease to regard a worthy family life— with all its duties fully performed and all its

responsibilities lived up to—as the life best worth living, then evil days for the commonwealth are at hand.[72]

Once again, America rests at a pivotal point in the history of marriage. Many of our elected leaders no longer believe that the institution—as it has existed for millennia of human history—is worth defending, leaving the electorate to answer a key question: Will our nation come to the defense of marriage and family, or will our apathy unfairly thrust our future generations into an era when "mom and dad" households are merely something mentioned in the history books?

Aided by the vigilance of concerned citizens and principled politicians, marriage and family have survived the attacks of the past two centuries. Today, more than ever, the American family is in desperate need of advocates who are willing to speak the truth in love for the sake of future generations, lest we thrust our children into a society that has forsaken any firm devotion to our most sacred institution.

SEVEN

Promoting Obscenity

Finally, brethren, whatever things are true, whatever things
are noble, whatever things are just, whatever things are
pure, whatever things are lovely, whatever things are
of good report, if there is any virtue and if there is
anything praiseworthy—meditate on these things.

– Philippians 4:8

In today's increasingly crude culture, parents are charged with the tremendous task of sheltering the hearts and minds of their little ones. A parent's responsibility is no longer quite as simple as merely changing the channel. Instead, parents are challenged with guiding and counseling a generation that is bombarded incessantly with sex, vulgarity, and violence via television shows, movies, songs, radio programs, magazines, books, school curricula, the Internet, billboards, and virtually every other form of mass communication.

Unfortunately, as parents struggle to protect their children from the inescapable vulgarity of modern culture, the ACLU is advancing philosophies teaching that children should be allowed to "decide for themselves whether porn is a good or bad thing."[1] As our culture confronts the countless tragedies born of the sexual revolution, the ACLU continues its passionate quest to flood society with all forms of perversion—from legalized public sex acts and unbridled online pornography to unrestrained nudity and rampant indecency on the public airwaves.

The challenges for parents seem to grow exponentially as technology evolves and the media plays an increasing role in the lives of young people. In March 2005, the Kaiser Family Foundation (KFF) conducted a study investigating the role of the media in the lives of children between ages 8 and 18. The study discovered that kids spend an average of 6 hours and 21 minutes in front of some form of media each day (television, Internet, video games, etc.)—more than 40 hours each week![2]

A stunning article published in the journal, *Pediatrics*, reported that by the time the average adolescent graduates from high school, he or she will have spent 15,000 hours in front of a television, compared with just 12,000 hours in a classroom.[3] The television has become like a foul-mouthed, perverted babysitter—one that no parent would ever deliberately hire.

Considering that media outlets consume such a disproportionate amount of time in the lives of our children, it seems logical to assume that most parents have established rules and safeguards to protect their kids. However, the KFF study found that when it comes to media exposure, most children have absolutely no parental guidance or restrictions.

As of 2005, 68 percent of the nation's children had a television set in their own bedrooms, and 31 percent had a computer in their rooms—most with completely unsupervised access to the Internet.[4] Among students in grades 7-12, only 13 percent had any restrictions on what kind of television shows they were allowed to watch, while the majority of them had absolutely no rules for television. Despite the growing threat of online sexual predators and the pervasiveness of Internet pornography, only 23 percent of the students said that their parents had imposed any restrictions on what they are allowed to do online.[5]

In other words, it seems that many in this generation have been abandoned to fend for themselves.

In a culture where so many parents fail to understand the

importance of guarding the hearts and minds of young children, where most pastors cower from addressing the moral issues of the day, and where entertainment industry executives are determined to push the envelope—our governing officials must stand in the gap to stave off the media's mounting aspiration to saturate our culture with increasingly sexual, vulgar, and violent content.

LIVING UNDER THE INFLUENCE

For years, media executives refused to admit their programs exerted influence over the behavior of young people. Social research has proven them wrong. Considering that the media industry collected over $141 billion in advertising revenues in 2004,[6] it would be wholly disingenuous to claim that this multi-billion dollar industry is completely ineffective when it comes to influencing personal behavior.

Emerging evidence now confirms the link between media content and child behavior. In 2001, the American Academy of Pediatrics (AAP) released a report concluding that television has a "powerful influence on adolescents' sexual attitudes, values, and beliefs."[7] In 2004, the Rand Corporation confirmed these findings, revealing that teens who watch significant amounts of television with sexual content are twice as likely to engage in sexual intercourse as those who do not.[8]

Despite the proven effects of such programming, the media continues to aggressively drench viewers with a torrent of images depicting inconsequential and gratuitous sexual encounters. In 2001, the AAP warned, "The average American adolescent will view nearly 14,000 sexual references each year." Yet barely one percent of these references will be accompanied by a message on self-control, abstinence, or the risks of pregnancy and STDs.[9]

What's more, if 14,000 sexual references each year were not

enough for American families to endure, the Kaiser Family Foundation reports that the number of sexual scenes on television is on the rise—nearly doubling between 1998 and 2005.[10]

Kevin Martin, chairman of the Federal Communications Commission (FCC), has acknowledged a dramatic increase in parental outcry concerning broadcast indecency. "The number of complaints received by the commission has risen year after year," he wrote in March 2006. "They have grown from hundreds to hundreds of thousands, and the number of programs that trigger these complaints continues to increase as well."[11]

"WARDROBE MALFUNCTION" LIGHTS FIRESTORM

The number of annual complaints to the FCC has escalated dramatically since the 2004 Super Bowl controversy. On February 1, 2004, roughly 89 million people gathered around television sets across the country to watch the National Football League's championship game—an event that was marred by an MTV-sponsored halftime show. Only four days prior to the Super Bowl, MTV had advised viewers to expect "shocking moments,"[12] and it delivered. At the conclusion of the halftime show, as pop star Justin Timberlake sang, "I'm gonna have you naked by the end of this song," parents were shocked when Timberlake ripped off a portion of Janet Jackson's tight leather costume, revealing her right breast.[13]

Indecency was not limited to the halftime show. Throughout the broadcast, CBS treated families to a litany of trashy displays including striptease performers, gyrating transvestites, simulated lesbian sex, and a song instructing people to "take off all your clothes." The commercial breaks weren't much better, featuring erectile dysfunction drugs, foul-mouthed kids, a talking monkey soliciting sex from a woman, and other racy commercials.[14]

One day later, then-FCC Chairman Michael Powell issued

a statement:

> I am outraged at what I saw during the halftime
> show of the Super Bowl. Like millions of Amer-
> icans, my family and I gathered around the tele-
> vision for a celebration. Instead, that celebration
> was tainted by a classless, crass, and deplorable
> stunt. Our nation's children, parents, and
> citizens deserve better.[15]

In response, the ACLU slammed Powell and the FCC for
getting involved in the matter. Marvin Johnson, legislative
counsel for the ACLU, told reporters, "It is not the
government's business to decide what is and is not decent. That
is up to the individual, the parents, and the viewer to make the
decision."[16]

In the days that followed, parents did make the decision.
Incensed with CBS, parents flooded the FCC with more than
200,000 complaints in just five days.[17]

As a result, over the ACLU's objections, the FCC voted
unanimously to fine twenty CBS affiliates the maximum
penalty, a total of $550,000, the largest penalty ever handed
down by the FCC for indecency. Even so, FCC Commissioner
Jonathan S. Adelstein admitted, "I find today's remedy totally
inadequate. After all the bold talk, it's a slap on the wrist that can
be paid with just seven and a half seconds of Super Bowl
ad time."[18]

OPPOSING EFFORTS TO CLEAN UP TV

The FCC Commissioners were not alone in calling for higher
indecency fines. Sixty-three percent of parents support increased
regulations and fines to reduce the amount of sexual and violent

content on television during the hours when children are most likely to be watching.[19]

Nevertheless, as Congress began to debate legislation to increase caps on FCC fines, the ACLU launched a lobbying blitz to defeat the measure. Perhaps threatened by the possible resurgence of decency, the ACLU mockingly reminded Congressmen that "society has changed drastically since the days when a husband and wife could not even be shown in the same bed."[20]

In a letter urging members of the U.S. House to vote against the Broadcast Decency Enforcement Act, the ACLU declared, "The bill would dramatically increase fines for obscene, indecent, or profane broadcasts, sending a widening chill into the atmosphere of free expression."

After months of debate and stall tactics, both houses of Congress passed the Broadcast Decency Enforcement Act with overwhelming support—increasing the FCC's maximum fine for broadcast indecency ten-fold, from $32,500 to $325,000. Tony Perkins, president of the Family Research Council, lauded, "The era of 'slap on the wrist' [fines] has ended. . . . The message is simple: clean up or pay up!"[21]

Though the bill passed, the ACLU was undoubtedly relieved Congress failed to spell out any particular decency violations. In fact, when similar legislation was introduced in the previous congressional session, the ACLU admitted, "The legislation could have been much worse. It could have . . . spelled out the 'eight dirty words,' in graphic detail, that would have imposed instant fines for their utterance on television."[22]

DEFENDING THE "DIRTY WORDS"

To the ACLU, it would be tragic to live in a world where broadcast networks were not permitted to indiscriminately spew the "eight dirty words" during primetime programs. In fact, the ACLU has lobbied the FCC to approve use of the "f-word" on broadcast television.

This issue entered the national spotlight after the 2003 Golden Globe Awards, at which an overexcited recipient exclaimed, "This is really, really, f***ing brilliant." Because it was a live broadcast, the network failed to bleep the word. As a result, tens of thousands of parents phoned the FCC with complaints. The FCC was forced to make a determination: Should FCC decency standards prohibit the use of this word on broadcast television?

Most Americans support such decency standards to shield children from obscenity—but not the ACLU. The organization joined a handful of media conglomerates in a petition to the FCC, warning the commissioners that any efforts to punish networks for airing such language would only "chill free speech" and constitute "an unconstitutional expansion of the government's intrusion into broadcast content."[23]

In a preliminary decision that stunned many parents, the FCC Enforcement Bureau sided with the ACLU. David Solomon, chief of the enforcement bureau, acknowledged that the language used at the Golden Globes "may be crude and offensive" but concluded, "The use of specific words, including expletives or other 'four-letter words' *does not* render material obscene."[24]

Thankfully, the FCC overruled the enforcement bureau's decision,[25] explaining:

> The 'f-word' is one of the most vulgar, graphic and explicit descriptions of sexual activity in the English language. Its use invariably invokes a coarse sexual image. The fact that the use of this word may have been unintentional is irrelevant.

It still has the same effect of exposing children to indecent language.[26]

Sadly, the media giants (ABC, CBS, NBC, and Fox) refused to accept these common sense decency standards and filed a federal lawsuit—asking a judge to create a constitutional right to use the "f-word" during all hours of programming.[27] As of this printing, the case is pending.

PROMOTING PROFANITY IN THE MARKETPLACE

The ACLU is dedicated to the right to use profanity on more than just our airwaves. In 1995, the Colorado Liquor Enforcement Division refused to approve a label for Flying Dog Brewery. The company wanted approval for a beer label: "Good Beer, No S—t." Though this language would be displayed for all eyes to see, the ACLU filed a lawsuit on behalf of the brewery, claiming that the agency's decision violated the company's First Amendment rights.

In March 1999, Judge John W. Coughlin ruled against the ACLU, writing:

> This Court feels that the government has every right to protect against vulgarity and to protect against what is unfit to be seen in public. It is unseemly and indecent to use the word s—t in public. The fact that it is often used does not change the fact that it is still vulgar and indecent to use the word.[28]

Though the ACLU lost its case in federal court, the company's profane labels were eventually approved for business. Rather than reapplying to the state agency, the company submitted its request to the federal Bureau of Alcohol, Tobacco, and Firearms and managed to receive federal approval to use the word on its labels.[29] Unfortunately, this quick bureaucratic decision could provide a foothold for the ACLU to push for additional profanity-laced products on the market.

SUPPORTING OBSCENE EXPRESSIONS OF RELIGION

Graphic sex on the movie screen and profanities blasted throughout primetime or plastered on the side of beer cans is not sufficient for the ACLU. It is seeking to bring unrestrained obscenity into the public realm.

On August 14, 2001, the ACLU filed a lawsuit on behalf of Daria Fand against the city of Honolulu, Hawaii, after city officials refused to display her painting—featuring a crucified naked woman—in the Honolulu City Hall during the city's tribute to women. City administrators explained that the painting was inappropriate for children.

Brent White, legal director for the ACLU of Hawaii, strongly disagreed. "The city banned this piece because they thought it was controversial and might offend certain individuals," he told reporters. "This censorship of Fand's artwork is, in itself, offensive. It also violated her First Amendment rights in a clear manner." Fand claimed that the painting was barred "due to the subjective evaluation of a few officials catering to a hyper-conservative religious mindset."[30]

On March 6, 2002, the city of Honolulu settled the lawsuit, agreeing to display Fand's painting in City Hall for sixteen days and to pay the ACLU $5,000 in attorneys' fees. "This is certainly a vindication of the principle that the government cannot censor art or speech based upon its content," said White. "The city deprived Ms. Fand of her constitutional rights and all of us of the opportunity to view the work of a fine artist."[31]

While the ACLU rushes off to court every time an adult complains about a Ten Commandments display in public, the organization finds nothing objectionable about the prospect of young children being exposed to a painting of a crucified naked woman inside the Honolulu City Hall.

The ACLU is obviously not interested in protecting children.

BACKING PUBLIC NUDITY

In 2003, a group of nudist anti-war protesters petitioned the state of Florida to protest and enter Palm Beach County's John D. MacArthur Beach State Park for a photo shoot in which naked protesters planned to lie down in the shape of a peace sign.

Park officials refused, explaining that the state "has a significant interest in keeping the entire park open to all visitors [including children] during operating hours." The state's letter concluded, "You are, of course, free to conduct your activities, absent the nudity."

As could be expected, the ACLU came to their aid and filed a federal lawsuit, arguing that the state of Florida had infringed upon the right of nudists to express their opinion—ignoring the rights of families to avoid such a spectacle in a public park. Randall Marshall, legal director for the ACLU of Florida, argued, "For these demonstrators, nudity is an essential part of their political expression."[32]

Incredibly, a federal judge sided with the ACLU and issued an injunction, prohibiting state officials from interfering with the nudists' public protest. With obvious ideological motivations (and little legal basis) behind his decision, U.S. District Judge Donald M. Middlebrooks wrote, "The value of freedom is found not only in the larger issues of life, but also in the fanciful and strange. Events like Fantasy Fest in Key West and Mango Strut in

Miami may not be to everyone's taste, but they add a spice of life in South Florida that, on the most part, we enjoy."[33]

Typical of the modern judiciary, this judge failed to understand the importance of shielding the hearts and minds of children. Once again, the moral welfare of America's families was sacrificed on the altar of extreme hedonism and licentiousness.

FIGHTING FOR PORN IN PUBLIC LIBRARIES

At every turn, the ACLU seems determined to destroy our societal safeguards. In December 2000, Congress enacted the Children's Internet Protection Act (CIPA)—a federal statute requiring all federally-funded public libraries to install pornography filters on computers to shield young children from online pornography.[34] Well aware of the dangers posed by on-line pornography, the U.S. Senate passed the measure, 95-3, with overwhelming bipartisan support.[35]

The ACLU mounted a legal campaign to overturn the collective will of the people and ensure that taxpayers would be forced to foot the bill for providing public access to pornography with no regard for children. Filing a lawsuit on behalf of the Multnomah County, Oregon, Public Library System, the ACLU took the issue all the way to the U.S. Supreme Court. In its first pretrial brief, the ACLU argued that the statute should be struck down—lamenting that it "prevents adults from access to protected speech [pornography] in the name of protecting children."[36]

Thankfully, the U.S. Supreme Court issued a 6-2 decision in the case of *United States v. American Library Association*, allowing Congress to base federal funding on whether pornography filters were installed in public libraries. In the June 2003 decision, then-Chief Justice William Rehnquist wrote, "Congress has wide latitude to attach conditions to the receipt of federal assistance in order to further its policy objectives."

"Its objectives—of restricting access to obscenity, child pornography, and material that is comparably harmful to minors—are 'legitimate' and indeed often 'compelling,'" continued Rehnquist. "To the extent that libraries wish to offer unfiltered access, they are free to do so without federal assistance."[37]

This seems to be a recurring dilemma for the ACLU—promoting unrestricted access to pornographic material versus protecting children. Sadly, the ACLU has consistently failed to side with the children.

TARGETING TEENS WITH TRASH

The ACLU not only opposes the installation of pornography filters in public libraries to protect children, it has actually fought to *force* a state-funded library to promote a sexually provocative website *designed* for teenagers.

In South Dakota, for example, Governor Mike Rounds ordered the state's publicly-funded library website to remove an offensive link from its homepage. This particular link directed users to a Planned Parenthood website (teenwire.com), but Governor Rounds argued that the website's content was far too vulgar and graphic for the state library to endorse as a link for children.

In addition to its vulgarity, the website embraces a reckless and amoral worldview, teaching kids that "the definition of virginity leaves lots of room for interpretation."[38] Rather than promoting the indisputable benefits of abstinence, the website advises teens, "Everyone has different values about sexual experience. What's right for one person may not be right for another. But in any case, having lots of experience doesn't make someone a 'slut.'"[39]

With troubling ease, Teenwire plows into disturbing discussions, like whether "swallowing sperm makes you fat."[40] The debauched website also offers information on the nutritional value of semen,[41] how to best perform oral sex,[42] and how to "enjoy anal sex,"[43] along with vivid descriptions of what happens to semen after two people engage in sodomy.[44]

Who could possibly fault Governor Rounds for shielding teens from such perverted content? The ACLU. That's who!

Immediately after the governor announced plans to remove the link, the ACLU announced public opposition to his efforts. Jennifer Ring, director of the ACLU of the Dakotas, said, "We are investigating what appears on the surface to be a case of censorship. The government has opened a public forum by including links to websites. When government opens a forum, it can regulate it in terms of time, place, and manner, but not in terms of content."[45]

Dale Bertsch, a spokesman for Governor Rounds' office, rejected the ACLU's accusations of censorship. "We're not infringing on anyone's First Amendment rights to free speech," he said. "The state has ownership of that website. Nobody has an inherent right to have the content of their website linked from the state site."

Governor Rounds stood his ground, and the ACLU's threats never materialized.

OPPOSING ONLINE PROTECTIONS FOR MINORS

As the Internet continues to grow exponentially as a medium of mass information and communication, it has also torn down the barriers to pornography. In days past, customers would have to endure the shame of walking into an X-rated video store or paying a neighborhood clerk for a pornographic magazine. Today, shocking images of gross sexual immorality and utter degradation are just a click away.

In 1998, in an effort to shield children from the rapidly growing presence of online pornography, the U.S. Congress passed the Child Online Protection Act (COPA). The federal statute sought "to require persons, who are engaged in the business of distributing . . . material that is harmful to minors, to restrict access to such material by minors."

Simply put, the law sought to make it illegal for people to recklessly or willfully disseminate obscene material to minors via the Internet. Those guilty of violating this law could be fined up to $50,000 and imprisoned for six months. With the dawn of Internet technology, this law appeared absolutely necessary. After all, if liquor distributors and convenience store clerks are responsible for checking the ages of customers when selling alcohol or pornographic magazines, then online pornographers should not face any less scrutiny.

The ACLU disagreed and immediately flew into action to protect the porn industry, demanding that COPA be struck down. The organization filed a federal lawsuit and eventually took the case all the way to the U.S. Supreme Court. In its brief to the High Court, the ACLU argued, "The government may not justify the suppression of constitutionally-protected speech [pornography] under the guise of protecting children."[46]

Instead, the ACLU promoted a legal rationale that would allow pornographers to bombard America's families with obscene images—blindly relying on parents to sort it out on their own. Ann Beeson, the associate legal director of the ACLU who argued the case in front of the Supreme Court, told *The Washington Post*: "We should provide our children with values that let them decide for themselves whether porn is a good or bad thing."[47]

Do American citizens really want naïve elementary and middle school students with no substantive parental guidance to determine whether pornography is a good thing or a bad thing? This seems patently unfair to an already oversexualized generation. The ACLU's philosophy may appeal to advocates of less intrusive government, but it absolutely ignores the tragic fact that tens of millions of children are raised in homes with no substantive parental involvement.

Unfortunately, a closely divided Court took the side of the ACLU and the pornographers. In the case of *Ashcroft v. ACLU*, the U.S. Supreme Court issued a 5-4 decision overruling Congress and the American people.

In the dissenting opinion, Justice Stephen Breyer lamented that the Court's decision ignored the fact that the law had only imposed "minor burdens on some protected material—burdens that adults wishing to view the material may overcome at modest cost," while also noting that the law "significantly helps to achieve a compelling congressional goal, protecting children from exposure to commercial pornography."[48]

FIGHTING FOR PUBLIC SEX ACTS IN OREGON

If the ACLU has its way, pornography and obscenity will be unavoidable. Apart from magazines, television, and the Internet, the ACLU is advancing an agenda to ensure that virtually every imaginable act of sexual debauchery will be permissible—even in public venues.

Just how far is this group willing to go?

In November 2003, the ACLU of Oregon submitted an *amicus* brief to the Oregon Supreme Court in support of a lawsuit seeking to strike down a state statute that banned public displays of live sex acts.[49] The common sense statute in question (Oregon Revised Statute 167.062) stated, "It is unlawful for any person to knowingly engage in sadomasochistic abuse or sexual conduct in a live public show . . . [and] it is unlawful for any person to knowingly direct, manage, finance or present a live public show in which the participants engage in sadomasochistic abuse or sexual conduct."[50]

The ACLU argued that this statute's prohibition of public sex acts violated Section 8 of the Oregon Constitution, which guarantees that "no law shall be passed restraining the free expression of opinion." In an attempt to stretch the clear intention of the state constitution, the ACLU argued that live public displays of sexual intercourse conveyed an "opinion."

Among its many reasons for supporting the legalization of public sex acts, the ACLU warned Oregonians that this law could bring negative repercussions by "prohibit[ing] people in a play, or in a ballet, or in a musical from engaging in sexual conduct during the performance."

Certainly, most Americans would roll their eyes at the utter foolishness of such an argument, but—in an egregious ruling—the Supreme Court of Oregon issued a 5-1 decision siding with the ACLU and creating a constitutional right to engage in public sex.

The court declared that a citizen's right to freely express an opinion "precludes prosecution under ORS 167.062 for directing a live public show in which performers engage in certain sexual conduct."[51] These five arrogant judges—obviously consumed by postmodern relativism—made a blatant effort to portray all decency codes as archaic, arguing that modern statutes forbidding public sex acts were comparable to "examples of eighteenth and nineteenth century laws."

The Oregon court concluded that the values of our Founders are irrelevant. Thus, in Oregon's modern "enlightened" culture, bars and restaurants can allow couples to engage in public sex shows—so long as they don't light a cigarette afterwards. Smoking a cigarette in public buildings is one "opinion" that remains illegal in the state of Oregon.[52]

Noting the ACLU's blatant double standard for free speech, Bill O'Reilly, host of Fox News' *The O'Reilly Factor*, quipped, "The ACLU is bullish on public displays of sex, but bearish on public displays of the baby Jesus."[53] Indeed, it seems that the only "opinions" worth protecting to the ACLU are those that mirror its own agenda.

Public sex in. Baby Jesus out.

PUBLICLY FUNDED PORN FOR PRISONERS

There are no bounds for the ACLU's defense of smut. In July 2006, the ACLU filed a class-action lawsuit against the Indiana prison system on behalf of more than 20,000 prisoners. The lawsuit claimed that an Indiana law barring prisoners from receiving pornographic materials (e.g., *Playboy*, *Hustler*, and *Penthouse*) violates the Constitution.[54]

In its brief, the ACLU argued, "The policy is written so broadly that it includes within its prohibitions such things as personal letters between prisoners and loved ones and much of the world's great literature and art."

Jeremy Tedesco, an attorney with the Alliance Defense Fund, responded, "The ACLU is hard at work trying to destroy American values once again. They want to tear down crosses. They want to keep religion out of the public square. But they want to make sure prisoners have access to pornography."[55] As of this book's printing, the case was pending.

ABANDONING THE BEST TRADITIONS OF LAW

The modern judiciary no longer seems interested in protecting society from the devastating impacts of obscenity. This is a significant reversal from previous decades. In the case of *Barnes v. Glen Theatre* (1991), the U.S. Supreme Court ruled that anti-obscenity laws may be "justified, despite its incidental limitations on some expressive activity," because the Court recognized that there was a "substantial governmental interest in protecting societal order and morality."[56]

In the case of *Paris Adult Theatre v. Slaton* (1973), the High Court declared, "There are legitimate state interests at stake in stemming the tide of commercialized obscenity. . . . There is a 'right of the Nation and of the States to maintain a decent society.'"[57]

Sadly, in the absence of this motivation, the disturbing ideological platform of the ACLU has prevailed, and the hedonistic desires of a selfish, oversexed culture consistently trump the best interests of its most vulnerable citizens.

Contrary to popular claims, pornography is not a victimless industry. Ted Bundy, one of the most infamous serial murderers and rapists in American history, once explained that pornography played a huge role in shaping his carnal mind. In an interview with Dr. James Dobson, Bundy confessed:

> I've lived in prison for a long time now, and I've met a lot of men who were motivated to commit violence like me. And without exception, every one of them was deeply involved in pornography—without exception . . . without exception—deeply influenced and consumed by an addiction to pornography.[58]

The Great Cost of Indecency

The consequences of America's sex-drenched culture are not mere statistics on a page. The cost of obscenity and pornography is measured one broken heart at a time . . . one broken home at a time . . . and all too often, one emotionally broken victim of sexual abuse at a time.

Sadly, despite the mounting evidence of the dangers associated with the various forms of public obscenity, the ACLU remains its most avid defender. Indeed, the ACLU has plowed the path to eliminate all responsibility and moral restraint in the media, in the community, and in public policy. The organization actively opposes any attempt to remove one of the greatest toxins plaguing American culture—a toxin that poisons minds, destroys marriages, endangers children, and degrades its subjects. These are the rotten fruits of the ACLU!

EIGHT

Promoting the Culture of Death

*You formed my inward parts; You covered me in my
mother's womb. I will praise You, for I am fearfully
and wonderfully made; marvelous are Your works,
and that my soul knows very well.*

— *Psalm 139:13-14*

In virtually all facets of its agenda, the ACLU seems determined to abandon Western civilization's noblest truths and traditions—only to regress to the pre-Christian worldview of unbridled decadence and callous barbarism.

Ancient Greco-Roman cultures failed to recognize the beauty of marriage, the importance of family, the dignity of sex, or the sanctity of human life. Instead, they embraced a variety of depraved lifestyles—from sexualizing young children and honoring homosexuality, to reveling in obscenity and the slaughter of their most vulnerable citizens.

This archaic philosophy should sound familiar; it is faithfully promoted by the modern-day antics of the ACLU.

During the pre-Christian reign of the Roman Empire, citizens placed little or no value on the sanctity of human life, a hollow perspective which ushered in the abominable practices of abortion and euthanasia. Under the tradition of *paterfamilias*, if a Roman citizen opted not to care for his newborn baby, the baby would be abandoned—forsaken to die from exposure to the elements.

As Christian ethics spread through the Empire—changing the course of Western civilization—such practices were increasingly viewed as abhorrent and were finally banned by Emperor Justinian.[1]

The Justinian Code offered protection to society's most vulnerable members, declaring:

> Those who expose children, possibly hoping they would die, and those who use the potions of the abortionist, are subject to the full penalty of the law—both civil and ecclesiastical—for murder. Should exposure occur, the finder of the child is to see that he is baptized and that he is treated with Christian care and compassion. They may be then adopted as *ad scriptitiorum*—even as we ourselves have been adopted into the kingdom of grace.[2]

SLIDING BACKWARD INTO BARBARISM

Unfortunately, the ACLU and its pro-abortion allies seem determined to push America back into that dark era when parents chose to murder their own children and abandon the blessings of parenthood for no reason other than personal convenience.

Abortion is now the most commonly performed surgical procedure in America.[3] To understand the scope of its impact on America, imagine if the entire populations of Arizona, Arkansas, Colorado, Idaho, Iowa, Kansas, Minnesota, Missouri, Montana, Nebraska, Nevada, New Mexico, North Dakota, Oregon, South Dakota, Utah, and Wyoming were completely wiped out with no survivors! Such a tragedy would still fall short of the staggering death toll credited to America's abortion clinics since the controversial *Roe v. Wade* decision.[4]

The pro-abortion Alan Guttmacher Institute estimates that approximately 47 million unborn babies were killed between 1973 and 2005,[5] and the ACLU seems proud of this! On its website, the organization boasts, "The ACLU was the first national organization to argue for abortion rights before the Supreme Court and has been the principal defender of those rights since 1973."[6]

In fact, former ACLU President Norman Dorsen served on the team of lawyers representing "*Jane Roe*" in the landmark case that opened the door for legalized abortion-on-demand in America.[7]

THE ERRANT FOUNDATIONS FOR *ROE V. WADE*

On January 22, 1973, in the case of *Roe v. Wade*, the U.S. Supreme Court struck down a Texas statute that prohibited abortion, essentially legalizing the procedure throughout the United States. Rather than attempting to ground its decision in the actual text of the Constitution, the Court was forced to use stretched reasoning to justify creating a "right" to abortion.

The Court even drew part of its justification from the barbaric practices of Greek and Roman cultures. "Abortion was practiced in Greek times as well as in the Roman era, and . . . it was resorted to without scruple," explained Justice Harry Blackmun in the Court's majority opinion. "Greek and Roman law afforded little protection to the unborn."[8]

Incredibly, after exalting the "scruples" of ancient pagans, the High Court then shunned the role of religion, traditional morals, and family values in modern jurisprudence, explaining:

One's religious training, one's attitudes toward

life and family and their values, and the moral standards one establishes and seeks to observe, are all likely to influence and to color one's thinking and conclusions about abortion. . . . Our task, of course, is to resolve the issue by Constitutional measurement, free of emotion and of predilection.[9]

Morality certainly played no role in the Court's decision, but to argue that *Roe* was resolved with "constitutional measurement" is disingenuous at best! In fact, the fundamental basis for *Roe* centered on the so-called "right of privacy"—a phrase never mentioned in the Constitution.

Much like the oft-cited, but nonexistent "wall of separation between church and state," the Court created this constitutional provision out of thin air! In his decision, Justice Blackmun even admitted that "the Constitution does not explicitly mention any right of privacy," before concluding that "the right of personal privacy includes the abortion decision."[10]

EVEN PRO-ABORTION LEGAL SCHOLARS REJECT *ROE*

Decades later, society remains bitterly divided on the issue of abortion, but most legal scholars will admit that there are tremendous problems with *Roe*. Many of the abortion industry's most prominent legal minds have openly admitted that *Roe* was wrongly decided.

Supreme Court Justice Ruth Bader Ginsburg, an uncompromising advocate of legalized abortion who once served as general counsel for the ACLU, has described *Roe* as "heavy-handed judicial intervention" that is "difficult to justify."[11]

Alan Dershowitz, a well-known pro-abortion Harvard law professor, has labeled *Roe* an example of "judicial activism."[12]

Edward Lazarus, who clerked for Justice Harry Blackmun (*Roe's* author), has called his own mentor's decision a "jurisprudential nightmare" that "required an analytical leap with little support in history or precedent."[13] Lazarus also stated, "As a matter of constitutional interpretation and judicial method, *Roe* borders on the indefensible. I say this as someone utterly committed to the right to choose . . . and as someone who loved *Roe's* author like a grandfather."[14]

Nevertheless, with one ideologically driven swing of the gavel, America's once "unalienable right to life" was compromised, thrusting our nation into an intense culture war in which more than 47 million unborn babies have been slaughtered. Sadly, the ACLU is vigorously devoted to the perpetuation of this tragedy.

EMERGING SCIENCE IS ON THE SIDE OF LIFE

As medical technology develops, the justifications offered by the pro-abortion crowd are consistently disproved. For years, abortion advocates claimed that abortion procedures remove little more than excess tissue or a clump of cells. With the help of science, this argument can now be summarily rejected.

The majority of surgical abortions take place between the seventh and tenth week of pregnancy.[15] By the seventh week, unborn babies have developed a steady heartbeat, arms, legs, eyes, and lips. At this stage of pregnancy, brain waves are measurable, the baby moves around, and the beginnings of every single internal structure are present and need only time to develop.[16]

In addition, science has shattered the erroneous argument that an unborn baby is merely a part of the mother's body. To the contrary, every unborn baby has a unique DNA (the blueprint for life), his or her own blood type, and half of the time he or she has a different gender than the mother.

Much like a toddler, an unborn baby is completely depend-ent upon the compassion and care of another for survival. The two primary distinctions between an unborn baby and a toddler are developmental maturity and location. Neither characteristic should serve as a basis for disqualifying a human baby from enjoying the right to life. No legal scholar could seriously argue that a five-year-old has a greater right to life than a two-year-old because of greater developmental progress. Nor should anyone claim that a baby born prematurely in the seventh month of pregnancy has a greater right to life than an unborn baby comfortably nestled in the womb during the eighth or ninth month of pregnancy.

Sadly, our society now sanctions a procedure that denies unborn babies their God-given right to life, simply because adults do not want to be bothered by the responsibilities of parenthood.

The late Mother Teresa once wisely declared:

> America needs no words from me to see how your decision in *Roe v. Wade* has deformed a great nation. The so-called right to abortion has pitted mothers against their children and women against men. It has portrayed the greatest of gifts—a child—as a competitor, an intrusion, and an inconvenience.[17]

OPPOSING INFORMED CONSENT FOR WOMEN

The truth is that abortion not only destroys unborn human life, it scars women. Numerous studies have shown that post-abortive women suffer an increased risk of depression, substance abuse, alcohol abuse, suicide, infertility, premature delivery, ectopic pregnancy, miscarriages, stillbirths, sexual dys-function, cervical cancer, ovarian cancer, and breast cancer.[18]

Not surprisingly, you won't find this kind of information in any ACLU brochure. In fact, the organization actively opposes state laws that require abortionists to inform women of the potential risks associated with abortion—even though such information would be certified by the state. The ACLU would rather trust abortion doctors.

"Mandatory anti-choice lectures do not give women accurate or meaningful medical information," the ACLU claims. "Rather, women are typically read a list of possible but very rare complications from the abortion procedure."[19]

The ACLU admits that complications are "possible." This begs the question: If the ACLU is such a champion of women's rights and the so-called "right to choose," why is the organization so rabidly committed to opposing legislation that would require abortionists to inform women about the "possible complications?"

The ACLU claims it opposes such laws because they only "make a woman's very personal decision even more difficult" and might "discourage the procedure."[20]

There is no other surgical procedure where a doctor would ever be permitted to withhold its possible side-effects or risks simply because the ugly facts could possibly "discourage the procedure" or make a decision "more difficult." Seeking to deny women essential medical information concerning abortion is reprehensible.

The web of deception surrounding the abortion industry is more common than some would like to think. In March 2005, the South Dakota Legislature approved the creation of a commission to study abortion. Nine months later, the commission released its findings:

> We received and reviewed the testimony of more than 1,940 women who have had abortions. . . .

Women were not told the truth about abortion, were misled into thinking that nothing but 'tissue' was being removed, and relate that they would not have had an abortion if they were told the truth.[21]

Unfortunately, while the ACLU bills itself as a champion for women's rights, the organization is fighting to perpetuate the very set of circumstances that has wrought tragedy in the lives of countless women.

TRAMPLING PARENTAL RIGHTS

If the scourge of abortion leaves such deep physical, mental, and emotional scars on the most mature of women, then one can only imagine how much worse the wounds must be for a confused and desperate teenager. With this in mind, dozens of state legislatures have passed laws requiring abortionists to involve a child's parents before performing an abortion on their minor daughter.

The ACLU and other pro-abortion organizations have mounted a nationwide legal campaign aimed at striking down laws requiring parental involvement in the abortion decision. The ACLU naively contends that teens should be free from any compulsion to involve their parents.[22]

Thankfully, most Americans do not accept the ACLU's laissez-faire philosophy of parenting. In fact, a November 2005 Gallup poll found that the vast majority of Americans not only support laws requiring parental *notification*, but 69 percent of Americans would support legislation that requires parental *consent* before a minor's abortion.[23]

As of June 2006, 44 states had approved laws requiring either parental consent or notification before a doctor could perform an abortion on a minor. Due to a flood of lawsuits, only 35 of these laws are in effect.[24]

The state of Florida has seen its share of legal battles on this issue. The Florida Legislature twice passed statutes requiring parental involvement in abortion decisions. Both laws were struck down by the Florida Supreme Court. In 1989, the state court struck down a law that required parental consent, and in 2003, it struck down a law requiring parental notification.[25]

Howard Simon, executive director of the ACLU of Florida, told his supporters that teens should be trusted to make these decisions on their own. "Most teens voluntarily involve their parents in their decisions," he said, "but those who don't, often have very good reasons for not doing so."[26]

The state of Florida requires parental involvement when a minor gets a tattoo[27] or body piercing,[28] sees an R-rated movie, skips school,[29] or receives any other form of medical attention.[30] Yet the ACLU believes that teens should be free to choose whether to inform parents of an invasive surgical procedure which takes the life of another human being. Most Floridians would consider it reckless and cruel to cast such an enormous weight upon a confused and desperate teenager without involving her parents.

Nevertheless, on July 10, 2003, in a disastrously worded opinion, the Florida Supreme Court agreed with the trial court that the Florida law requiring parental notification constituted

> a direct and significant intrusion on a minor's right of privacy because, as the title of the Act implies, a minor would be required to disclose . . . to her parents . . . one of the most intimate aspects of her private life.[31]

The Court insisted that its decision did nothing to impair

parental rights:

> [O]ur decision today in no way interferes with a
> parent's right to *participate* in the decisionmak-
> ing process or a minor's right to *consult* with her
> parents.[32]

Florida residents were rightfully outraged. In the coming months, the state legislature approved a ballot initiative, allowing the voters to determine the issue once and for all. In November 2004, 65 percent of Florida voters approved an amendment to the state constitution allowing the state to require parental notification before a doctor could perform an abortion on a minor.[33]

After losing its battle to block the parental notification law in the courts, the ACLU of Florida remains unwilling to honor the spirit of the law. In December 2005, the organization launched the PATH Project, which hosts a website offering advice to children on how they can manipulate the judicial system . . . "so you don't have to tell a parent."[34]

Susan Derwin, director of the PATH Project, stated,

> Many of these young women—for a variety of
> reasons—are unable to tell their parent or
> guardian that they want to have an abortion. The
> PATH Project trains attorneys to assist these
> teens with judicial bypass orders and helps match
> up teens with attorneys.[35]

DEFENDING DRUG ABUSE FOR PREGNANT WOMEN

The ACLU refuses to offer *any* rights to unborn babies—even when a mother plans to carry the baby to term. In a stance that reveals the ACLU's mindless devotion to dehumanizing the unborn, the organization defends women who expose their child to illegal drugs in utero.

On January 13, 2005, Kelly Lynn Cruz gave birth to a son, who was delivered with considerable amounts of cocaine in his bloodstream. Ms. Cruz was subsequently charged and convicted of reckless endangerment, which the Maryland criminal code defines as any illegal behavior that may bring harm to another "person."

According to the American Pregnancy Association:

> Babies born to mothers who use cocaine throughout their pregnancy may . . . have a smaller head and their growth hindered. . . . [They] may be born dependent and suffer from withdrawal symptoms such as tremors, sleeplessness, muscle spasms, and difficulties feeding. Some experts believe that learning difficulties may result as the child gets older. Defects of the genitals, kidneys, and brain are also possible.[36]

With no regard for the health of the child, the ACLU challenged the conviction, claiming that by attaching the rights of a person to an unborn baby, the state acted in a manner that was both "unprecedented and illegal."[37] In its legal brief with the court, the organization contended, "The crime of reckless endangerment of another does not apply to the context of pregnancy."[38]

On August 3, 2006, the Court of Special Appeals of Maryland sided with the ACLU, overturning the conviction. In response, David Rocah, a staff attorney for the ACLU, stated:

> The ACLU of Maryland is heartened that the

high court agrees that prosecuting drug-dependent pregnant women is not what the state of Maryland considers good policy. We believe that using criminal law to regulate a pregnant woman's conduct on the theory that it might harm a fetus or her newborn child is counterproductive, illegal, and, ultimately bad for children and society.[39]

In a similar case, the ACLU came to the defense of two Texas women who had also ingested large quantities of a controlled substance while pregnant.

The ACLU contended that pregnant women who harm their unborn babies by ingesting illegal drugs should not be held accountable for their babies' resulting injuries. Disregarding the long-lasting effects of illegal drug use on a baby's future health, the ACLU callously asserted that—like abortion—a pregnant woman's decision to ingest illegal drugs should be viewed as "personal decisions as to what one does with his or her own body."[40]

State prosecutors disagreed, charging the women with the crime of "delivering a controlled substance to a child."[41] In a brief filed with Texas' 7th Circuit Court of Appeals, the ACLU argued, "The term 'child' should not be construed to include fetuses. . . . The term 'child' as used in [the Texas statute] can only rationally be construed to mean *human beings who are born*."[42]

Tragically, a unanimous Texas appellate court sided with the ACLU and reversed the convictions.[43]

DEFENDING THE SLAUGHTER OF PARTIALLY BORN BABIES

As despicable as these actions are, perhaps no other action reveals the ACLU's heartless devotion to abortion more than its vehement defense of the partial-birth abortion procedure. *The Los Angeles Times* described partial-birth abortion in these terms:

> The procedure requires a physician to extract a fetus, feet first, from the womb and through the birth canal until all but its head is exposed. Then the tips of surgical scissors are thrust into the base of the fetus' skull, and a suction catheter is inserted through the opening and the brain is removed.[44]

Once the brain is sucked out, the skull collapses and the dead baby's body is discarded.

Dr. D. James Kennedy, president and founder of Coral Ridge Ministries, explains:

> At present, it would be considered murder in America to put to death a just-birthed baby. So to avoid the charge of murder, the partial-birth abortion procedure extracts a living infant from the mother, except for the head, which remains *in utero*. By killing the child before it is completely birthed, the doctor is performing a legal abortion, not an illegal murder.[45]

In the 1990s, as the graphic details of this inhumane procedure emerged, Americans were appalled. Consequently, Congress twice passed legislation banning the gruesome procedure, but President Bill Clinton vetoed the proposed bans on both occasions.[46]

Left with no alternative, several state legislatures passed laws to prohibit the partial-birth abortion procedure. As a result, the

ACLU flooded the nation with lawsuits aimed at striking them down. The ACLU's website brags, "We have successfully challenged bans in Alaska, Idaho, Illinois, Kentucky, Michigan, Montana, New Jersey, and Rhode Island, notably winning the first case in the nation to invalidate a ban."[47]

HIGH COURT UPHOLDS BARBARIC PROCEDURE

Given the lack of consistent guidance from state and federal courts, the U.S. Supreme Court finally entered the fray— agreeing to consider the constitutionality of a Nebraska law banning partial-birth abortion.

The ACLU was on hand to file a brief in support of the abortion industry. In its brief, the ACLU dismissed the state's legislative motivations as mere "reflections of repugnance" and accused Nebraska lawmakers of "dramatizing the ugliness of abortions."[48]

"Every method of abortion will be outrageous to some and at least unsettling to most," the ACLU admitted. "If that alone were sufficient to support bans on various procedures, a woman's right to obtain a safe and legal abortion would soon vanish."[49]

Translation: If Americans truly understood the gruesome details of what happens to unborn babies during any type of abortion (i.e. mutilation, dismemberment, decapitation, burning skin in saline solution, etc.), they would not have the stomach for any abortion procedure. True enough.

Tragically, on June 28, 2000, in the case of *Stenberg v. Carhart*, the U.S. Supreme Court issued a 5-4 decision siding with the ACLU and striking down Nebraska's partial-birth abortion ban. With a contemptible disregard for the fate of thousands of babies who would suffer as a result of the Court's ruling, Justice Stephen Breyer declared that it was unconstitutional for a state to place "an undue burden upon a woman's right to make an abortion decision."[50]

In his dissenting opinion, Justice Antonin Scalia blasted the Court for usurping a state's right to govern itself:

> The method of killing a human child . . . proscribed by this statute is so horrible that the most clinical description of it evokes a shudder of revulsion. . . . The Court should return this matter to the people—where the Constitution, by its silence on the subject, left it—and let *them* decide, State by State, whether this practice should be allowed.[51]

A RENEWED CALL FOR A FEDERAL BAN

In the following years, public outcry continued at a fevered pitch. A January 2003 Gallup poll revealed that seventy percent of Americans supported a federal ban on partial-birth abortion.[52] Shortly thereafter, by a nearly 2-1 margin, Congress voted once again to approve a federal ban on partial-birth abortions (with an exception to save the life of the mother).

On November 5, 2003, President George W. Bush signed into law the Partial Birth Abortion Ban Act of 2003. "For years, a terrible form of violence has been directed against children who are inches from birth, while the law looked the other way," he said. "At last, the American people and our government have confronted the violence and come to the defense of the innocent child."[53]

Five days before the President could sign this legislation into law, the ACLU had already filed papers asking a federal judge in New York to issue a temporary injunction that would prevent the Justice Department from enforcing the law.[54]

Within one day of President Bush's signing ceremony,

federal judges in Nebraska, New York and San Francisco did exactly that.[55] The law would not be enforced until its constitutionality was settled in the courts. Subsequently, the ACLU filed a lawsuit in New York, Planned Parenthood filed a lawsuit in San Francisco, and the Center for Reproductive Rights filed a lawsuit in Nebraska.

In the months that followed, these courts conducted trials and collected shocking testimony on the brutal details of partial-birth abortion. One abortion doctor testified that babies often display "spontaneous movements" and "respiratory activity." Another abortionist spoke of how babies' feet would continue to kick "until the skull was crushed."[56] One clinic employee submitted an affidavit that recounted watching the "fingers of the baby opening and closing" just before the baby was killed.[57] Dr. Kanwaljeet Anand, a pediatrician from the University of Arkansas, testified that babies endure "severe and excruciating" pain during a partial-birth abortion.[58]

The testimony was heartbreaking! President Bush was right: "The best case against partial-birth abortion is a simple description of what happens and to whom it happens."[59]

FEDERAL COURTS SIDE WITH THE ABORTIONISTS

The forces of death proved to be quite skillful at choosing sympathetic courts for rulings on this matter. Despite the abundance of chilling testimony, each of the three federal judges issued decisions striking down the federal ban on partial birth abortion.

In New York, U.S. District Judge Richard Casey sided with the ACLU. Judge Casey noted that the partial-birth abortion procedure was a "gruesome, brutal, barbaric, and uncivilized medical procedure." He even admitted that there was "credible evidence that [partial-birth abortion procedures] subject fetuses to severe pain."[60]

Nevertheless, Judge Casey and two other federal judges declared the ban unconstitutional, claiming that it was (1) an "undue burden" on a woman's right to choose abortion, (2) "unconstitutionally vague," and (3) lacking an exception for the preservation of the mother's health.

Actually, Congress did make an exception to save a mother's *life*. U.S. Solicitor General Paul Clement took issue in a legal brief with the judges' findings. He noted that Congress determined, "following nine years of hearings and debates, that partial-birth abortion is never necessary to preserve a mother's health."[61]

The U.S. Government appealed the decisions through the federal appellate courts to no avail. In February 2006, the U.S. Supreme Court announced plans to once again consider the constitutionality of a partial-birth abortion ban.[62] With the resignation of Justice Sandra Day O'Connor (who ruled against the Nebraska ban in 2000) and the additions of Chief Justice John Roberts and Associate Justice Samuel Alito, many legal scholars are optimistically expecting a 5-4 decision that will uphold the federal ban on partial-birth abortion once and for all.

FIGHTING FOR TAXPAYER-FUNDED INFANTICIDE

Despicably, the ACLU is not only intent on ensuring that all methods of abortion remain legal in all circumstances, it has launched legal battles to ensure that taxpayers are forced to fund such lethal procedures.

After *Roe v. Wade*, tax dollars were used to fund the abortions of all women on Medicaid. In 1977, U.S. Rep. Henry Hyde championed legislation (the Hyde Amendment) to prohibit federal funds from being used to finance abortions—unless the mother's life was endangered. Immediately after this legislation was enacted, pro-abortion advocates filed federal lawsuits challenging its constitutionality. Not surprisingly, the lower courts declared the law unconstitutional.

The case was then appealed to the U.S. Supreme Court. In a 5-4 ruling in the case of *Harris v. McCrae* (1980), the U.S. Supreme Court overturned the lower courts and upheld the statute's constitutionality.[63] Though the ACLU acknowledges the Court's decision, it continues to advocate that "the Hyde Amendment and other bans should be repealed."[64]

In December 2003, the ACLU Reproductive Freedom Project filed a motion in a Georgia state court asking Judge M. Gino Brogdon to issue an immediate injunction to prohibit enforcement of a law that prohibits the state Medicaid program from funding abortions.[65]

Georgia's Medicaid program already covered abortions for low-income women in special cases (rape, incest, or when doctors felt that the procedure was necessary to save the mother's life). The ACLU argued that taxpayer funds should be used to cover all abortions for women enrolled in Medicaid. The organization argued that by denying abortions for low-income women, the state was violating women's rights of "privacy" and equal protection.

In its motion, the ACLU argued:

> The state's Medicaid program not only reflects, but perpetuates, a limited role for women. . . . Motherhood—particularly when unplanned, unwanted, and unaffordable—dramatically curtails a woman's educational opportunities, economic prospects, and self-determination.[66]

Using this shallow and misguided logic, the ACLU argued that Georgia taxpayers should be forced to bear the financial burden associated with ending the lives of unborn children.

PROMOTING THE CULTURE OF DEATH

The ACLU contended that the Georgia State Constitution required taxpayers to fund "medically necessary" abortions. The phrase "medically necessary" is vague and misleading; mental anxiety over a pregnancy could feasibly qualify a woman for a "medically necessary" abortion.

Mark Daniel, Georgia's Medicaid director, noted that if the state Medicaid program were to cover all abortions deemed "medically necessary," the taxpayers would be forced to finance the deaths of roughly 8,000 unborn children at a cost to Georgia taxpayers of $5.1 million annually.[67]

Regardless, the ACLU and other pro-abortion organizations have spearheaded efforts to repeal such bans in several states. Already, a number of state courts and legislatures have required taxpayers to fund these so-called "medically necessary" abortions in Arizona, Alaska, California, Connecticut, Hawaii, Illinois, Indiana, Massachusetts, Minnesota, Montana, New Jersey, New Mexico, New York, Oregon, Vermont, and Washington.[68]

The ACLU will no doubt continue to push the abortion agenda to force all taxpaying Americans—pro-life and pro-abortion alike—to finance the murder of unborn babies.

PUSHING AMERICA TOWARD EUTHANASIA

Decades ago, the late Francis Schaeffer warned that opening the door to abortion would be followed by other equally horrid attacks on the sanctity of human life:

> This lowering of the view of human life may begin with talking about extreme cases in regard to abortion, but it flows on to infanticide and on to all of human life being open to arbitrary, pragmatic judgments of what human life is worthy to be lived—including your human life when you

become a burden to society.[69]

Schaeffer warned that an acceptance of abortion would inevitably lead to a general disregard for all human life. History has proven him right. Just three decades after the legalization of abortion-on-demand, society is now grappling with concerns over cloning, medical experimentation on human embryos, euthanasia, and physician-assisted suicide.

The devaluation of human life in American courtrooms—coupled with mounting deficits, a burgeoning national debt, and an increasingly strained Social Security program—leaves one to wonder when and if our nation will resort to euthanasia as an answer to the various strains imposed by an enormous Baby Boom generation now entering its retirement years.

Already, the ACLU is leading the charge to ensure that doctors can help society's most vulnerable members kill themselves "with dignity." Steven R. Shapiro, national legal director for the ACLU, is an outspoken advocate for physician-assisted suicide:

> Each of us should have the right to die. The exercise of this right is as central to personal autonomy and bodily integrity as rights safeguarded by this Court's decisions relating to marriage, family relationships, procreation, contraception, child rearing, and the refusal or termination of life-saving medical treatment.[70]

Of course the ACLU's philosophy flies in the face of our nation's best traditions and the most fundamental of medical ethics. The American Medical Association Code of Ethics declares, "Physician-assisted suicide is fundamentally incompatible with the physician's role as healer, would be difficult or impossible to control, and would pose serious societal risks. ...

Patients should not be abandoned once it is determined that cure is impossible."[71]

Likewise, C. Everett Koop, former U.S. Surgeon General, warned:

> We must be wary of those who are too willing to end the lives of the elderly and the ill. . . . If we ever decide that a poor quality of life justifies ending that life, we have taken a step down a slippery slope that places all of us in danger. . . . As I have said many times, medicine cannot be both our healer and our killer.[72]

Nevertheless, the issue has been stirring in American courts for years.

In the case of *Washington v. Glucksberg* (1997), the U.S. Supreme Court considered the constitutionality of Washington state's Natural Death Act of 1979—a state law banning physician-assisted suicide.[73] The High Court voted unanimously to uphold the Washington statute.

Former Chief Justice William Rehnquist authored the Court's opinion:

> We begin, as we do in all due-process cases, by examining our Nation's history, legal traditions, and practices. In almost every State—indeed, in almost every western democracy—it is a crime to assist a suicide. The States' assisted-suicide bans are not innovations. Rather, they are long-standing expressions of the States' commitment to the protection and preservation of all human life. . . . Indeed, opposition to and condemnation of suicide—and, therefore, of assisting sui-

cide—are consistent and enduring themes of our philosophical, legal, and cultural heritages."[74]

Unfortunately, this ruling did not close the book on physician-assisted suicide in America.

FIGHTING FOR ASSISTED SUICIDE IN OREGON

Only three years prior to the *Glucksberg* decision, Oregon had enacted its Death With Dignity Act—the first law of its kind allowing physicians to assist patients in committing suicide. In 2001, former Attorney General John Ashcroft declared, "Assisting suicide is not a 'legitimate medical purpose' . . . [and] prescribing, dispensing, or administering federally controlled substances to assist suicide violates the Controlled Substances Act [CSA]." Under this directive, Ashcroft vowed to revoke the medical license of any physician who took part in assisting a suicide.[75]

Consequently, the state of Oregon filed a federal lawsuit against the Justice Department, claiming that the CSA should not be construed to prohibit a state from allowing physician-assisted suicide. Both a district court and the Ninth U.S. Circuit Court of Appeals struck down Ashcroft's directive, and in 2005, the U.S. Justice Department appealed the lower court ruling to the Supreme Court.

In an *amicus* brief filed with the Court, the ACLU declared, "We believe that the individuals eligible for the Death with Dignity Act have a liberty, privacy, and dignity right to physician-assisted suicide."[76] Tellingly, Charles Hinkle, an attorney with the ACLU of Oregon, admitted that the organization harbored concerns that any decision concerning physician-assisted suicide "could have a spillover effect on abortion, gay rights, and women's issues."[77]

On January 17, 2006, the U.S. Supreme Court issued a 6-3 decision, affirming the lower court rulings and essentially securing the right of Oregon physicians to assist in the suicides of their patients. Writing for the majority, Justice Anthony Kennedy explained that the national government had acted unconstitutionally by barring the dispensation of controlled substances for assisted suicide.

In his dissenting opinion, Justice Scalia (joined by Justices Thomas and Roberts) pointed out:

> Virtually every medical authority from Hippocrates to the current American Medical Association (AMA) confirms that assisting suicide has seldom or never been viewed as a form of "prevention, cure, or alleviation of disease," and (even more so) that assisting suicide is not a "legitimate" branch of that "science and art.". . . If the term "*legitimate* medical purpose" has any meaning, it surely excludes the prescription of drugs to produce death.[78]

FOLLOWING IN DANGEROUS FOOTSTEPS

As the ACLU fights to promote a culture of death, the organization is walking down a path that history has proven disastrous. By describing physician-assisted suicide as a merciful act of dignity and compassion, the ACLU is subtly—and perhaps unintentionally—promoting the notion that a sickly life is not worth living. It teaches that the most dignified and compassionate act society can offer an incurable patient is assistance with suicide. This is not the first time a government has allowed its doctors to be involved in mercy killings.

In October 1939, Adolf Hitler initiated the T-4 program to

eliminate "life unworthy of life." In a fateful memo, Hitler wrote, "Reich Leader Bouhler and Dr. Brandt are charged with the responsibility of enlarging the authority of certain physicians, designated by name, so that patients who, on the basis of human judgment, are considered incurable, can be granted a mercy death."

Under the direction of these two men, roughly 80,000 people suffered "mercy deaths."[79]

Thomas Jefferson once wrote, "The care of human life and happiness and not their destruction is the first and only legitimate object of good government."[80] As heirs to the tremendous blessings that have been bestowed upon America, we must take care to ensure that the right to life applies to all Americans— whether unborn, infirm, elderly, or destitute.

History has shown that when a society no longer considers life an unalienable right from our Creator, and citizens measure the value of human life based on the whims of what the Führer once called "human judgment," mankind will invariably suffer the same dark and devastating fates that befell ancient Greece, the Roman Empire, and Nazi Germany.

NINE

Impeding America's War on Terror

When He avenges blood, He remembers them; He does not forget the cry of the humble. Have mercy on me, O Lord! Consider my trouble from those who hate me, You who lift me up from the gates of death, that I may tell of all Your praise in the gates of the daughter of Zion. I will rejoice in Your salvation. The nations have sunk down in the pit which they made; in the net which they hid, their own foot is caught.

– Psalm 9:12-15

On top of its appalling social agenda, the American Civil Liberties Union has an unswerving track record of undermining national security. In particular, the ACLU has positioned itself against the security interests of Americans in the global war on terrorism.

This is consistent with the worst traditions of the ACLU. After all, it was the ACLU's founder, Roger Baldwin, who once admitted, "I am for socialism, disarmament, and ultimately for abolishing the state itself."[1] The organization's recent actions seem to indicate a continuing devotion to its founder's objective—"abolishing the state."

First, Americans must understand the perilous history and modern trajectory of the radical Islamic movement to understand the gravity of the ACLU's treachery. This international cancer was not born on September 11, 2001. Rather, the recent escalation of Islamic terrorism is the result of decades of Western complacency and willful ignorance—allowing a dangerous ideology to spread and intensify.

UNDERSTANDING THE THREAT

On November 4, 1979, Iranian terrorists led by the powerful Ayatollah Khomeini, seized the U.S. Embassy in Tehran, taking 66 American hostages and the international spotlight. Khomeini sought to inspire militant Muslims to advance the agenda of Islamic dominance through terror. In January 1980, *Time* magazine recognized his enormous influence, naming him "*Time*'s Man of the Year" and warning, "The revolution that [Khomeini] led to triumph threatens to upset the world balance of power more than any political event since Hitler's conquest of Europe."[2]

Khomeini, beloved by millions of fellow Muslims, despised the suggestion that Islam was a "religion of peace"—as often claimed today. Instead, he championed international jihad against the West, particularly the United States. In one speech Khomeini explained, "All those who study jihad will understand why Islam wants to conquer the world. . . . Those who know nothing about Islam pretend that Islam counsels against war. They are witless!"[3]

Khomeini fanned the flames of radical Islam, and subsequent decades are littered with hundreds of terrorist acts. The September 11 attacks on American soil were merely the zenith of decades of hate.

On the morning of September 11, 2001, millions of Americans huddled around their television sets—stunned with disbelief as the World Trade Center towers fell and clouds of smoke and ash barreled through the streets of New York City.

Watching plumes of smoke rise from the collapsed walls of the Pentagon, Americans realized that our seemingly impenetrable borders were no longer sufficient protection against the maniacal hatred of radical Islam. In an address to Congress and the American people, President Bush declared, "Our nation has been put on notice: We are not immune from attack."[4]

As America grieved the loss of its countrymen, we were collectively appalled and infuriated by televised images of Middle Eastern men, women, and children dancing and cheering in their streets. Indeed, the hijackers had struck the Pentagon, the nerve center of our national defense; the terrorists erased two iconic 110-story buildings from the skyline of Manhattan; they destroyed four commercial airliners; and in one ghastly moment, turned the world's spotlight on the insanity of radical Islam and unchecked terror.

For radical Muslims, the September 11 tragedy was their greatest trophy of aggression against the West. It was certainly not their first. The U.S. Department of State has recorded hundreds of terrorist attacks involving Muslim militants. The following twenty examples demonstrate the consistency of their hatred for the West:

> **November 4, 1979** – Iranian radicals seize the U.S. Embassy in Tehran and take 66 American diplomats hostage.
>
> **April 18, 1983** – The terrorist group Islamic Jihad bombs the U.S. Embassy in Beirut, Lebanon, killing 63 people and injuring 120 others.
>
> **October 23, 1983** – Islamic Jihad bombs the U.S. Marine barracks and a French compound in Beirut simultaneously, killing 242 American and 58 French troops.

March 16, 1984 – Islamic Jihad kidnaps, tortures, and later kills Beirut's CIA station chief, Lt. Colonel William Buckley.

June 14, 1985 – Muslim terrorists hijack TWA Flight 847 and murder a U.S. Navy sailor.

October 7, 1985 – Four Palestinian Liberation Front terrorists hijack the Italian cruise liner *Achille Lauro*, taking its 700 passengers hostage and killing one U.S. passenger.

March 30, 1986 – A Palestinian terror organization detonates a bomb aboard TWA Flight 840, killing four U.S. citizens.

April 5, 1986 – Two U.S. soldiers are killed and 79 others wounded, when Libyan terrorists bomb a Berlin discotheque.

February 17, 1988 – U.S. Marine Corps Lt. Colonel William Higgins is kidnapped and murdered by the Iranian-backed Hezbollah ("the party of God").

April 14, 1988 – The Organization of Jihad Brigades detonates a car bomb in Naples, Italy, killing one U.S. sailor.

June 28, 1988 – U.S. Defense Attaché Captain William Nordeen, of the U.S. Embassy in Greece, is killed when a car bomb detonates outside his home in Athens.

December 21, 1988 – Pan American Airlines Flight 103 is blown up over Lockerbie, Scotland, by a bomb believed to have been placed on the aircraft by Libyan terrorists. All 259 passengers are killed.

September 19, 1989 – UTA Flight 772 is blown up over the Sahara Desert during a flight to Paris. All 170 passengers are killed.

February 26, 1993 – Islamic terrorists detonate a car bomb in the underground garage of New York City's World Trade Center. The bomb kills six people.

August 25, 1995 – December 25, 2003 – Islamic terrorists conduct at least 17 separate bombings aboard crowded Israeli buses or at bus stops, killing more than 150 people.

June 25, 1996 – A fuel truck carrying a bomb explodes outside the U.S. military's Khobar Towers housing facility in Dhahran, Saudi Arabia, killing 19 U.S. military personnel.

August 7, 1998 – Muslim terrorists bomb the U.S. Embassy in Nairobi, Kenya, killing 12 U.S. citizens, 32 Foreign Service Nationals, and 247 Kenyans.

August 7, 1998 – Muslim terrorists bomb the U.S. Embassy in Dar es Salaam, Tanzania, killing seven Foreign Service Nationals and three Tanzanians.

October 12, 2000 – Muslim terrorists detonate a small dinghy filled with explosives as it drifts alongside the *USS Cole*, killing 17 sailors and injuring 39 others.[5]

The terrorist attacks of September 11 were not aberrations from an otherwise peaceful trend. They were the culmination of more than 20 years of hatred and violence. This undisputed and lengthy history of terrorism not only justified a military response, it required it.

Recognizing this, the U.S. Senate voted 98-0 and the U.S. House voted 420-1 to approve a resolution authorizing

President Bush to "use all necessary and appropriate force against those nations, organizations, or persons he determines planned, authorized, committed, or aided the terrorist attacks" or "harbored such organizations or persons, in order to prevent any future acts of international terrorism against the United States by such nations, organizations or persons."[6]

Despite this remarkable expression of solidarity, the ACLU emerged immediately as a treacherous antagonist to U.S. efforts to fight the war on terror.

ACLU Fights Measure to Halt Terrorists' Funding

Only weeks after the tragedy, Congress acted to dismantle the financial infrastructure supporting known terrorist organizations. On October 3, 2001, U.S. Rep. Michael Oxley (OH) introduced the "Financial Anti-Terrorism Act of 2001," seeking to freeze all accounts directly linked to the "financing of terrorism."

The need for such legislation was deemed so vital to national security that it passed the U.S. House on a vote of 412-1.[7] Almost the entire Congress recognized that this legislation's passage was imperative. Still, on the day before the vote was scheduled, the ACLU delivered letters of opposition to all members of Congress.

"We urge you to oppose the 'Financial Anti-Terrorism Act of 2001,'" the letter began. Why? One portion of the bill made it a federal crime to conceal large amounts of "illegally obtained" cash (over $10,000) while traveling. In a desperate and shameful attempt to justify its stance, the ACLU played the race card. The letter argued, "This provision may impact, disproportionately, people of color and immigrants . . . [because] these groups of people often have a more difficult time getting access to sources of credit and bank accounts and so use cash transactions more frequently than do others."[8]

The organization wanted U.S. Congressmen to believe that the "Financial Anti-Terrorism Act of 2001" was discriminatory because it might force impoverished minorities without access to bank accounts to conceal more than $10,000 in cash. Since when do impoverished people carry more than $10,000 cash? Even though the law only criminalized the concealment of such funds "if the money was illegally obtained," the ACLU attempted to use race to compromise national security.

Thankfully, the ACLU's efforts to sabotage the law were unsuccessful, and provisions of the "Financial Anti-Terrorism Act of 2001" were incorporated and enacted under the Patriot Act.[9]

ACLU OFFERS FREE COUNSEL TO SUSPECTED TERRORISTS

Later in the war, the ACLU actually volunteered its legal services to represent suspected terrorists!

In 2004, the U.S. Supreme Court heard arguments from several alleged "illegal enemy combatants," including two cases involving U.S. citizens (Yaser Esam Hamdi and Jose Padilla)[10] and one case involving 14 foreign "illegal enemy combatants."[11] The ACLU filed *amicus* briefs on behalf of the suspected terrorists in each case,[12] arguing that all "enemy combatants" captured during a time of war should have access to American courtrooms—regardless of their citizenship.

The Pentagon contended that "enemy combatants" should face military tribunals—the standard procedure in all previous international wars. U.S. Solicitor General Theodore Olson, whose wife, Barbara Olson, was killed on September 11, when Flight 77 crashed into the Pentagon,[13] reminded the Supreme Court Justices that the plaintiffs were requesting a "jurisdiction that is not authorized by Congress, does not arise from the Constitution, [and] has never been exercised by this Court."[14]

Though the U.S. Constitution does not extend rights to non-citizen enemy combatants, judicial restraint did not prevent the modern Court from creating this new right out of thin air. In several split decisions, the U.S. Supreme Court ruled that all "enemy combatants"—regardless of citizenship—were entitled to petition U.S. courts.

Seeming more interested in embarrassing the United States than protecting anyone's liberties, Robert Shapiro, the legal director of the ACLU, immediately celebrated the rulings as a "strong repudiation of the administration."[15]

DESTROYING AMERICA'S INTERNATIONAL REPUTATION

In January 2004, the ACLU continued its efforts to tarnish America's international reputation by filing an official complaint with the United Nations against the United States, accusing the U.S. of illegally arresting and deporting suspected terrorists. In its complaint, the ACLU argued: "The detention of petitioners and other September 11 detainees was arbitrary because . . . September 11 detainees were arrested pursuant to a policy . . . that had a disproportionate effect on Muslim men from South Asian and Middle Eastern countries."[16]

Of course the ACLU conveniently ignored the fact that all nineteen September 11 hijackers were Muslim men from Middle Eastern countries![17] Apparently, the ACLU would prefer that America's Homeland Security agents spend their time targeting Buddhist monks or Irish nuns.

Such clear disdain for common sense security policies leaves only two possible motives for the ACLU's actions: either the ACLU is driven by utter naiveté or by malicious animosity. After filing the complaint with the U.N., ACLU Executive Director Anthony Romero cleared up any confusion, declaring, "With today's action, we are sending a strong message of solidarity to advocates in other countries who have decried the impact of U.S. policies."[18]

Subsequently, the United Nations Human Rights Committee—comprised of nations like Cuba, Saudi Arabia, and China (all notorious for human rights abuses)—investigated U.S. policies. Unsurprisingly, several members spoke against the U.S. policies. Ann Beeson, director of the ACLU's human rights program, responded quickly: "The U.S. should be ashamed of itself."[19]

The American Heritage Dictionary defines "treason" as a "violation of allegiance toward one's country or sovereign, especially the betrayal of one's country by . . . consciously and purposely acting to aid its enemies."[20] The actions of the ACLU might rightly be construed as treasonous!

INFLAMING THE ENEMY

Consider the ACLU's actions following the Abu Ghraib prisoner abuse scandal. Immediately after reports of the scandal had spread worldwide, U.S. officials went before the United Nations Security Council, proclaiming that the U.S. "stood with the rest of the world in shock and disgust."

"President Bush strongly condemned those acts," the Council recorded, "and had apologized and made clear that those responsible would be held accountable."[21]

Indeed, the U.S. Department of Defense swung into action immediately, conducting a full scale investigation, which resulted in the removal of 17 soldiers from duty. Seven soldiers were charged with dereliction of duty, maltreatment, aggravated assault and battery, and were sent to prison.[22]

Even though the U.S. military had taken firm action to punish this behavior and deter its future occurrence, the ACLU seemed determined to rub salt in America's open wounds. Thus, when the U.S. Department of Defense refused to release additional photos and videos taken at Abu Ghraib, fearing that additional exposure would fuel anti-American sentiment in the Middle East through networks like Al Jazeera, the ACLU filed a federal lawsuit seeking to force the government to release the photos. The organization also issued press releases, using the scandal to accuse American soldiers of "systematic and widespread abuse of detainees."[23]

U.S. District Judge Alvin Hellerstein ordered the U.S. Department of Defense to release an additional 74 photos and three videos from the Abu Ghraib prison,[24] even after admitting that "there is a risk that the enemy will seize upon the publicity of the photographs and seek to use such publicity as a pretext for enlistments and violent acts."[25]

Like a kid in a candy store, the ACLU rushed to review the additional evidence and subsequently issued a press release calling the images "ugly and shocking." Then, with no new evidence to support its claims, the organization leveled additional charges against the U.S. military, claiming our soldiers were responsible for "widespread abuse of detainees . . . in Iraq, Afghanistan, and Guantanamo Bay."[26]

THE POT CALLING THE KETTLE BLACK

Interestingly, the ACLU has not always opposed the abuse of prisoners and detainees. While the U.S. government condemns the abuse of prisoners, the same cannot be said for ACLU founder, Roger Nash Baldwin.

In 1934, as communism was emerging in the Soviet Union, Roger Baldwin (an unflagging enthusiast for communism) wrote an article arguing that brutality against Soviet prisoners was an acceptable consequence of advancing communism.

Baldwin, who enjoyed his freedoms as a United States citizen, was often criticized for lending his support to the totalitarian Soviet government—a regime led by Joseph Stalin that would be remembered as one of the most brutally oppressive dictatorships in history.[27]

To defend his reckless support for the abuse of prisoners under Stalin, Baldwin wrote an article entitled, "Freedom in the U.S.A. and the U.S.S.R." He began his article by repeating a question often posed to him: "How can you consistently support the right of free agitation in capitalist countries when you defend a dictatorship that tolerates no agitation against its rule?"

His answer?

> I saw in the Soviet Union many opponents of the regime. I visited a dozen prisons—the political sections among them. I saw considerable of the work of the OGPU [secret police]. I heard a good many stories of severity, even of brutality, and many of them from the victims. While I sympathized with personal distress I just could not bring myself to get excited over the suppression of opposition when I stacked it up against what I saw of fresh vigorous expressions of free living by workers and peasants all over the land. And further, *no champion of a socialist society could fail to see that some suppression was necessary to achieve it. It could not all be done by persuasion.*[28]

In other words, the brutal abuse of prisoners was acceptable, so long as it furthered the cause of communism.

Despite such statements and Baldwin's candid commitment to "abolishing the state," he was awarded the Presidential Medal of Freedom—the highest award bestowed upon an American civilian—by President Jimmy Carter in 1981.[29]

Opposing Common Sense Precautions

The ACLU not only seems determined to undermine America's global relationships, but—even worse—the organization has worked vigorously to subvert several common sense security precautions on American soil.

On July 22, 2005, just fifteen days after Islamic terrorists detonated multiple bombs on London's transit system, killing 52 people and injuring 700 others,[30] New York City officials initiated a policy requiring transit authorities to conduct random bag searches on the roughly 4.5 million passengers entering the city's subways each day.[31]

Within two weeks, the New York Civil Liberties Union (an affiliate of the ACLU) had filed a federal lawsuit, asking a judge to prevent the police from conducting the searches on New York's public transportation system. "This NYPD bag search policy is unprecedented, unlawful, and ineffective," claimed Donna Lieberman, Executive Director of the NYCLU. In a press release, the organization demanded that the NYPD policy be declared unconstitutional because it "creates the potential for impermissible racial profiling."[32]

Yet again, the ACLU was playing the race card. Unfortunately, New York City Mayor Michael Bloomberg took the bait and issued a directive forbidding any use of racial profiling during the subway search procedures. "You cannot predict what a terrorist looks like," Bloomberg told reporters.[33]

Howard Safir, former New York City Police Commissioner, responded on MSNBC's *Hardball*, stating, "I do not consider this racial profiling. This is terrorist profiling. We know what the nineteen hijackers looked like on 9/11. We know what the London hijackers looked like. We know what the embassy bombers looked like in Africa. We know what the *Cole* bombers looked like."[34]

Though Mayor Bloomberg cowered from the NYCLU, U.S. District Judge Richard Berman refused to accept their arguments, upholding the constitutionality of the random bag search policy. In his decision, Judge Berman declared, "The need for implementing counter-terrorism measures is indisputable, pressing, ongoing, and evolving."[35]

MAKING AIRLINES LESS SAFE

This did not deter the ACLU from continuing its campaign against other common sense national security policies. It launched an aggressive campaign against national transportation safety standards in American airports—particularly the Transportation Security Administration's (TSA) Secure Flight program. The Secure Flight program requires airport screeners to compare names of ticket purchasers to the No-Fly List compiled by the FBI (Federal Bureau of Investigation) Terrorist Screening Center to ensure that airlines are not allowing known or suspected terrorists to board commercial flights.

According to the FBI, any person considered a "potential threat to U.S. civil aviation" is on the national No-Fly List. In an effort to challenge this policy, the ACLU filed a federal lawsuit against both the TSA and the FBI—demanding access to all names on the No-Fly List.

Initially, the agencies refused to share the information with the ACLU, arguing that the list contained information sensitive to national security. The FBI and TSA feared the List would assist terrorist networks in planning their operations, encouraging them to find terrorist recruits who had not yet been flagged. Unfortunately, U.S. District Judge Charles Breyer sided with the ACLU, ruling that the government's reason was not sufficient for withholding these names.

In addition, the FBI and TSA were forced to pay the ACLU

$200,000 in attorneys' fees and court costs.[36] Essentially, the American taxpayers were forced to compensate the ACLU for its successful efforts to subvert national security.

Within weeks of gaining access to the list, the ACLU was hard at work, searching for ways to topple the Secure Flight program. ACLU Legislative Counsel Timothy D. Sparapani was invited to testify before the Senate Committee on Transportation, where he urged senators to discontinue the program.

His reasoning?

Sparapani argued that the policy was unfair, because "the names most likely to be on the No Fly and Selectee Lists that will be utilized for Secure Flight are likely to be those of Muslims or people of Arab or Middle Eastern descent."[37]

At every turn, the ACLU attempts to undermine national security by ignoring common sense and exploiting the racial hypersensitivity of American politicians—as if U.S. counterterrorism officials are deviously ignoring scores of covert Amish terrorists to unfairly target Muslim men of Arab or Middle Eastern descent.

FIGHTING THE DEFUNDING OF TERRORISM

The ACLU has even defended charitable funding for organizations suspected of terrorism.

On November 10, 2004, the ACLU filed a federal lawsuit to force the government's Office of Personnel Management (OPM) to amend its policy concerning the operation of its charitable program (the Combined Federal Campaign). Each year, the Combined Federal Campaign (CFC) allows federal employees to donate a portion of their paychecks to a multitude of approved charities.

In 2003, over 1.4 million federal employees participated in this program, contributing over $248 million to the program's listed charities.

In response to the war on terrorism, the OPM initiated a policy in 2004 to check all recipients of the program's charity against a government watch-list, to ensure that none of the charitable dollars went to organizations with suspected ties to terrorism. Under this policy, if a charity wanted to be eligible for funds, they were required to make a simple pledge: "The organization in this application does not knowingly employ individuals or contribute funds to organizations found on the following terrorist related lists promulgated by the U.S. government, the United Nations, or the European Union."

To reasonable people, such a policy seems vital in the modern era. The ACLU lobbied for its repeal, and the OPM cowered from these threats, revising its policy to satisfy the ACLU. The revised policy statement declared, "Effective for 2006 and subsequent campaigns, OPM does not mandate that applicants check the Specially Designated Nationals List or the Terrorist Exclusion List."

ACLU executive director Anthony Romero hailed the decision, comparing the OPM policy to anti-communist blacklists. "Watch list requirements and other misguided policies of today remind us of the now-discredited anti-communist list checking of the early 1950s. It is no more justified now than it was then."

Not surprisingly, the ACLU had a vested interest in ensuring that all organizations remained eligible for CFC funding. In its own press release, the ACLU admitted that "CFC contributions earmarked for the ACLU typically totaled about $500,000 per year."[38]

GIVING THE ADVANTAGE TO THE ENEMY

In 2005, the ACLU filed a complaint against the National

Security Agency (NSA) for wiretapping international phone calls between U.S. residents and suspected terrorists. Though the need for such procedures is self-evident, the ACLU has remained dogged in its efforts to dismantle existing U.S. policies to gather foreign intelligence—even when the policy is designed to target phone calls with suspected terrorists.

In its official complaint, filed with a federal court in Michigan, the ACLU admitted, "Some of the plaintiffs, in connection with scholarship, journalism, or legal representation, communicate with people whom the United States government believes or believed to be terrorist suspects or to be associated with terrorist organizations."

Nevertheless, the ACLU argued that it is of inviolable importance to protect a journalist's privacy when engaged in conversations with "terrorist suspects."

In its complaint, the ACLU went on to argue that the NSA wiretapping policy should be declared unconstitutional because it "impinges on [a reporter's] ability to communicate freely and candidly with [suspected terrorists] to the detriment of his effectiveness as an investigative journalist."[39]

In other words, if a *Washington Post* reporter sets up an impromptu telephone interview with Osama bin Laden without giving the U.S. government ample time to obtain a warrant, the ACLU would argue that the NSA must sit idly by and ignore an opportunity to gather pertinent intelligence concerning our national security or the whereabouts of known terrorists.

Members of the Senate Judiciary Committee grilled U.S. Attorney General Alberto Gonzales about the wiretapping program, forcing him to answer questions about the limitations of the administration's powers. In response, Gonzales reminded the senators and the American people: "It is not simply a coincidence the United States has not been hit again since 9/11. . . . [I]t is because of tools like the terrorist surveillance program."[40]

The Attorney General called these wiretapping programs "indispensable" to the defense of our nation, and most Americans seem to agree. According to a survey conducted by Rasmussen Reports, "Sixty-four percent of Americans believe the National Security Agency (NSA) should be allowed to intercept telephone conversations between terrorism suspects in other countries and people living in the United States."[41]

On August 17, 2006, U.S. District Judge Anna Diggs Taylor sided with the ACLU, striking down the wiretapping program. As of this printing, the case is under appeal.

CONTINUED DILIGENCE IS NEEDED

The efforts of the ACLU mentioned in this chapter are merely the tip of a very dangerous iceberg. Already, the ACLU has challenged scores of U.S. policies meant to defend Americans from the hatred and violence of radical Islam, and sadly, the ACLU continues its campaign to hinder America's efforts to guard against terrorism.

As the ACLU labors to weaken our national security policies, Americans must remain alert, recognizing the unyielding menace posed by radical Islam. Though American soil has remained safe from terrorist attacks since September 11, the terrorists' desire to destroy the West has not faltered. Indeed, the mounting hostility between an increasingly secular Europe and a rising population of fundamentalist Muslims requires that Americans remain steadfast in the defense of our interests, both at home and abroad.

Speaking on Al Jazeera, an Arab satellite network, Libyan leader Moammar Gadhafi told fellow Muslims, "There are signs that Allah will grant Islam victory in Europe. . . . The 50 million Muslims of Europe will turn it into a Muslim continent within a few decades."[42]

Given such broad ambition, America will ignore the escalation of international Islamic violence to its own peril. The tension between free nations and the Islamic world is unsustainable.

- On March 11, 2004, ten bombs were detonated at three crowded train stations in Madrid, Spain, killing 190 people and injuring 1,240 others.[43]
- In November 2004, Dutch director Theo Van Gogh was killed after making a film exposing violence against women in Islamic cultures.[44]
- In July 2005, 52 people were killed and more than 700 wounded when Islamic militants detonated a series of bombs in London, England.[45]
- Iranian President Mahmoud Ahmadinejad promised to pursue weapons of mass destruction and called for the nation of Israel to be "wiped off of the map."[46]
- In November 2005, France was forced to institute a national state of emergency after twenty days of riots at the hands of militant Muslims resulted in multiple deaths, nearly 9,000 torched cars, and 2,888 arrests.[47]
- In February 2006, the Islamic world was set ablaze with fury—months after a small Danish newspaper published cartoons characterizing Mohammed as a promoter of violence. In response, the Islamic world erupted into violence. In Tehran, Iran, protesters pelted the Danish embassy with petroleum bombs. In the Gaza Strip,

Muslims stormed into European buildings. In Damascus, Syria, the Danish and Norwegian embassies were torched. In Kabul, Afghanistan, four people were killed during massive protests. In Beirut, Lebanon, thousands of Muslim protesters set fire to the Danish embassy.[48]

- Subsequently, a coalition of 57 Muslim nations urged the United Nations to vigorously oppose any speech that might "damage the image of a peaceful Islam."[49]

As the ACLU ignores these international developments and focuses on dismantling America's national security programs, Americans must remain ever-vigilant in the defense of our nation and the rich legacy of liberty that has been paid for with the blood of many patriots.

TEN

Looting the American Taxpayers

"In you they have made light of father and mother.... In you are men who slander to cause bloodshed ... in your midst they commit lewdness.... In you they take bribes to shed blood; you take usury and increase; you have made profit from your neighbors by extortion, and have forgotten Me," says the Lord GOD.

— Ezekiel 22:7a, 9, 12

It is difficult to deny the ACLU's overall effectiveness in redefining the cultural landscape of America. The latter part of the twentieth century witnessed a tremendous deterioration of societal values, largely facilitated by the organization.

As more and more Americans have begun to link the two, the ACLU is now the object of an unprecedented degree of public ill favor. Still, along with this newfound notoriety, the organization has experienced great institutional success. Its website boasts:

> We have grown from that roomful of civil libertarians to more than 500,000 members. The ACLU today is the nation's largest public interest law firm, with a 50-state network of staffed, autonomous affiliate offices. We appear before

the United States Supreme Court more than any other organization, except the U.S. Department of Justice. About 100 ACLU staff attorneys collaborate with about 2,000 volunteer attorneys in handling close to 6,000 cases annually.[1]

The ACLU exerts tremendous influence on American public policy and continues to grow stronger. In 2005, the ACLU Foundation recorded revenues in excess of $58 million and assets totaling over $196 million.[2]

The organization shows few signs of weakening. Indeed, with assistance from America's wayward judiciary, the ACLU continues to enlarge its financial war chest and successfully impose its will on a reluctant American population—from its efforts to rid the nation of all vestiges of Christianity and its actions to undermine the war on terror, to its advocacy for unrestricted access to abortion and the legalization of same-sex marriage.

Most Americans would never dream of donating their hard-earned money to an organization with such a despicable agenda, yet, unbeknownst to most citizens, the ACLU has been dipping its hand into the pockets of American taxpayers for decades.

Though the ACLU claims, "We do not receive any government funding,"[3] a review of the facts reveals this statement to be unequivocally false and misleading. In fact, the ACLU has used America's judiciary to collect millions from taxpayers.

With one swing of the gavel, judges can raid the public treasury and fund the ACLU. In some cases, the judiciary has sunk even lower—manipulating the system to divert public funds directly into the organization's bank account.

In one egregious abuse of the public trust, the Florida Supreme Court—under the umbrella of the Florida Bar Foundation (FBF)—helped funnel more than $615,000 to the

ACLU of Florida.

The FBF was established in 1956 by the Florida Supreme Court to provide legal assistance to the poor. In 1981, in an effort to increase the Foundation's funding, Florida's High Court created the nation's first IOTA (interest on trust account) program. The IOTA program requires all the money that changes hands via an attorney (i.e. home purchases, lawsuit awards, probate accounts, divorce settlements, etc.) to be temporarily deposited into a pooled interest-bearing account.

The 2004 annual report of the FBF reported that as of June 2004, there was an average balance of $3.6 billion in this account, generating tremendous interest, which in turn funds the Foundation. In the twenty years prior, this publicly funded foundation had distributed more than $175 million to various groups.[4] The Articles of Incorporation for the FBF require that all such grants are to be "specifically approved from time to time by the Supreme Court of Florida."[5]

Incredibly, between 1990 and 1997, under the guise of the FBF program, the Florida Supreme Court approved more than $600,000 in grants to help establish and pay the salary of a full-time legal director for the ACLU of Florida.[6] The FBF's financial records reveal the following grants:

$15,000 – March 21, 1986
$10,000 – March 22, 1990
$105,000 – November 30, 1990
$95,000 – March 20, 1992
$75,000 – March 19, 1993
$85,000 – March 18, 1994
$85,000 – March 17, 1995
$95,500 – March 22, 1996
$50,000 – June 27, 1997

Unquestionably, the Florida Supreme Court took advantage of hundreds of thousands of unsuspecting Floridians who never would have imagined that their monies were being used to generate funding for the ACLU. However, with assistance from the Florida high court, the organization has developed a massive financial war chest, enabling it to consistently oppose Florida voters. The ACLU of Florida has fought measures including:

- An informed consent law requiring abortionists to inform women of risks;[7]
- Mandatory parental notification laws for teens seeking abortions;[8]
- The state's ban on taxpayer-funded abortions;[9]
- The state's ban on same-sex marriage;[10]
- The state's ban on homosexual adoption;[11]
- Florida's proposed school voucher program;[12]
- A Ten Commandments monument in Polk County, Florida;[13]
- School prayer in Jacksonville, Florida;[14]
- and Bible curricula in Lee and Dade County schools.[15]

Due to the deceptive tactics of the Florida Supreme Court, Florida Christians (including this author) have helped finance the ACLU.

SEEING GREEN BEHIND THE GAVEL

For far too long, the ACLU has been permitted to exploit the nation's courtrooms.

In 1871, Congress passed a law (42 U.S.C. 1983) declaring

that any government entity found responsible for violating the rights of a citizen "shall be liable to the party injured in an action at law." This opened the door for plaintiffs to collect damages when a court deemed that they had suffered a "deprivation of any rights."[16]

More than a century later, Congress approved The Civil Rights Attorney's Fees Awards Act of 1976 (42 U.S.C. 1988), allowing the plaintiff's lawyers to collect fees from these lawsuits. The law declared, "The court, in its discretion, may allow the prevailing party . . . a reasonable attorney's fee as part of the costs."[17]

As the statute's name suggests, the law was originally intended to deter civil rights injustices against minorities by ensuring that indigent victims of civil rights violations would have access to skilled and often expensive counsel. The ACLU has manipulated the law to profit from cases involving religious displays, public prayer, abortion laws, the homosexual agenda, restrictions on pornography, and any other case in which an activist judge happens to rule that the ACLU's plaintiff suffered a deprivation of rights.

Rees Lloyd, a civil rights attorney who once worked for the ACLU, points out that the organization should not be entitled to collect attorneys' fees, because it does not allow its attorneys to keep the awarded money. In sworn testimony before a congressional committee, Lloyd explained, "As a former ACLU attorney, I know to a certainty that the ACLU's litigation is carried out by staff attorneys or by *pro bono* attorneys who are, in fact, precluded from receiving fees under the ACLU's own policies."[18]

These taxpayer-funded judgments do not reimburse volunteer attorneys for their time and effort. Instead, taxpayer dollars are funneled directly into the deep coffers of an already wealthy organization.

"The ACLU has perverted, distorted, and exploited the Civil

231

Rights Act," said Lloyd.[19]

As a result, it uses the threat of costly litigation as a tool to intimidate state and local governments into surrendering their common values. In his testimony, Lloyd warned Congress that this provision of the Civil Rights Act "is having a chilling effect on the exercise of fundamental First Amendment rights,"[20] due to the ACLU's abuse of it.

Mat Staver, president and founder of Liberty Counsel, has defended dozens of communities against the legal assaults of the ACLU. He echoed Lloyd's concerns, warning Congress: "The threat of attorneys' fees and damages has been wielded like a bully club to beat local government officials into submission, even when church-state claims are outrageous and frivolous.[21] They don't want to risk having to pay the ACLU's attorneys' fees.[22]

EXAMPLES OF ACLU TAXPAYER ABUSE

When the ACLU claims it does not receive "any government funding," Americans should be well aware that there is ample evidence to the contrary. Indeed, the ACLU has accumulated tremendous profits, with assistance from the nation's third branch of government—the judiciary. Consider the following:

> **$37,037 – Loudoun County (Virginia)** – On April 1, 1999, U.S. District Judge Leonie M. Brinkema ordered Loudoun County Public Library to pay more than $37,000 to the ACLU, after it successfully blocked the county from installing pornography filters in its public libraries.[23]
>
> **$18,000 – London (Ohio)** – In October 1999, the ACLU of Ohio was awarded $18,000 in attorneys' fees, after suing the London City School

District for allowing high school football coaches to pray with athletes.[24]

$121,500 – Kentucky – On July 25, 2000, U.S. District Judge Joseph Hood ordered the state of Kentucky to remove a Ten Commandments monument from the grounds of the Kentucky state capitol building.[25] In addition, Judge Hood ordered the state to pay $121,500 in attorneys' fees to the ACLU.[26]

$52,000 – Seattle (Washington) – In February 2001, the city of Seattle, Washington, was ordered to pay $52,000 in attorneys' fees to the ACLU, after the organization successfully defended a student's "right" to mock an assistant principal. The student had created online parodies in which the school administrator was portrayed sodomizing Homer Simpson and appearing in Viagra commercials.[27]

$299,500 – Kentucky – In 2001, the ACLU was awarded more than $299,500, after suing to overturn Kentucky abortion regulations.[28]

$63,000 – U.S. Congress – In 2002, American taxpayers were forced to pay the ACLU more than $63,000 for its legal efforts to remove a World War I Memorial Cross from the Mojave National Preserve.[29] In a letter to the National Parks Service, the ACLU threatened, "If we do go forward with a lawsuit, a court not only would order the government to remove the cross, but it also likely would assess damages against those . . . who knew about the cross and yet did nothing about it."[30]

$230,000 – San Diego (California) – In June

2002, the Ninth U.S. Circuit Court of Appeals ordered the city of San Diego to remove a Cross from the top of the Mount Soledad Korean War memorial. The city of San Diego settled the lawsuit, agreeing to pay $230,000 in legal costs and attorneys' fees to the ACLU and a private resident.[31]

$275,000 – Pittsburgh (Pennsylvania) – Also in June 2002, after a Pennsylvania appellate court struck down an anti-profanity ordinance, the Pittsburgh Police Department was forced to shell out $275,000 to the ACLU in order to settle 32 different complaints involving arrests that had been made under an ordinance prohibiting the use of profanity in public.[32]

$110,000 – Multnomah County (Oregon) – In July 2002, Multnomah County Circuit Court Judge Ellen Rosenblum awarded the ACLU nearly $110,000 in attorneys' fees after the organization sued the county school district for allowing the Boy Scouts of America to recruit on public school campuses. The Boy Scouts were deemed a discriminatory organization.[33]

$170,000 – Detroit (Michigan) – On July 23, 2002, under threat of a lawsuit, the Detroit Police Department agreed to rescind a policy aimed at preventing homosexuals from having sex in public parks. The ACLU was paid $170,000 in damages and attorneys' fees.[34]

$549,430 – Alabama – On November 18, 2002, U.S. District Judge Myron Thompson ruled against Alabama Chief Justice Roy Moore, ordering the state of Alabama to remove a Ten

Commandments monument from the rotunda of the Alabama Supreme Court building. In addition, the state was ordered to pay nearly $550,000 in attorneys' fees and court costs to be split between the ACLU, Americans United for Separation of Church and State, and the Southern Poverty Law Center.[35]

$75,000 – Pasco (Washington) – In March 2003, the city of Pasco, Washington, was forced to pay $75,000 to the ACLU, after the organization sued the city for covering a mural of a naked woman on the side of its City Hall building.[36]

$25,000 – Pulaski County (Arkansas) – In July 2003, the ACLU was awarded $25,000, after suing an Arkansas county school district for informing the parents of a 14-year-old student that the child was living an openly gay lifestyle at school.[37]

$940,000 – San Diego (California) – On July 31, 2004, U.S. District Judge Napoleon Jones, Jr., issued a decision nullifying a lease between the Boy Scouts of America and the city of San Diego. The federal judge explained that the Boy Scouts constituted a religious organization, because it requires kids to pledge an oath to God and to live a "morally straight" life. The judge claimed it was unconstitutional for the city to enter into such a contract with a religious organization.[38] In the subsequent months, the ACLU and the city of San Diego settled the lawsuit for a total of $940,000, with $790,000 given to the ACLU as attorneys' fees.[39]

$36,810 – Houston (Texas) – In August 2004, U.S. District Judge Sim Lake ordered officials in Harris County to remove a Bible display from the grounds of the county courthouse. Judge Lake also ordered the county to pay $36,810 in attorneys' fees to the ACLU.[40]

$135,000 – Cobb County (Georgia) – In January 2005, U.S. District Judge Clarence Cooper ordered Cobb County to pay $135,000 to the ACLU, after the organization sued to have advisory labels removed from the county's biology textbooks. The stickers simply informed students that "evolution is a theory, not a fact." The Eleventh U.S. Circuit Court of Appeals later reversed this decision.[41]

$156,960 – Nebraska – In May 2005, U.S. District Judge Joseph F. Bataillon struck down the Nebraska marriage amendment, which was approved by 70 percent of Nebraska voters, and awarded the ACLU nearly $157,000. The award was held in abeyance during the appeals process. Tim Butz, executive director of the ACLU of Nebraska, told reporters, "We expect the state to cut us a check, but not just yet."[42] In July 2006, the Eighth U.S. Circuit Court of Appeals overturned Judge Bataillon's ruling.[43]

$150,000 – Barrow County (Georgia) – In July 2005, U.S. District Judge William C. O'Kelley ordered Barrow County, Georgia, to remove a Ten Commandments plaque from its county courthouse. The county was ordered to pay $150,000 to the ACLU.[44]

$74,462 – Habersham County (Georgia) –

On November 17, 2005, the county was ordered to pay $74,462 to the ACLU for its lawsuit to remove a Ten Commandments display from the Habersham County Courthouse.[45]
$1,000,000 – Dover County (Pennsylvania) – On December 20, 2005, U.S. District Judge John E. Jones ruled that the Dover Area School District acted unconstitutionally by incorporating intelligent design into its biology curriculum. The judge initially awarded the ACLU and others more than $2 million in attorneys' fees.[46] This amount was later reduced to $1 million.[47]

These examples are only the tip of the iceberg.

With the assistance of activist judges, the ACLU is enabled to wage a persistent and effective campaign to overrule the values of states and local communities throughout the nation. Despicably, activist judges often add insult to injury—forcing these overruled voters to finance the very organization that has undermined their representative voice in government.

The Importance of Disciplined Judges

These shenanigans only reinforce the importance of appointing fair-minded judges who will not use the court's authority to advance personal agendas. America needs its judges to exercise consistent constitutional discipline. When the High Court abandons the text of the Constitution to inject personal ideology into its decisions, it muddies the law with whimsical opinions. As a result, state and local governments lose any sure footing in regard to constitutional guidelines, and they are made increasingly vulnerable to the inconsistent discretion of judges.

To illustrate, one needs only to understand the widespread

fallout that can be caused by an irrational court decision. For example, in the months after the U.S. Supreme Court struck down the Nebraska ban on partial-birth abortion, dozens of states with similar laws were made vulnerable to a flood of lawsuits from the ACLU and others. Armed with this hotly contested High Court precedent, the ACLU filed numerous lawsuits to strike down similar late-term abortion bans.

The flawed guidance in the Supreme Court's 5-4 decision enabled the ACLU and others to win a flurry of lawsuits, through which they collected financial awards estimated to be worth roughly $6 million. The financial fallout of this one Supreme Court case impacted thirty different states.[48] Consequently, these states were punished for exercising their right to self-government and banning a barbaric procedure.

SHIFTING CONSTITUTION OR SHIFTING COURTS?

To further demonstrate the dangers of judicial inconsistency, examine the confusion generated by various court decisions concerning the public display of the Ten Commandments.

In 1973, the Tenth Circuit Court of Appeals declared that a Ten Commandments monument in front of the Salt Lake County (Utah) Courthouse was constitutional.[49] In 2002, the same appellate court ruled that a Ten Commandments display in Ogden, Utah, was unconstitutional.[50]

In 1980, the U.S. Supreme Court issued a 5-4 decision, declaring that a Kentucky law requiring the Ten Commandments to be posted in all public school classrooms was unconstitutional.[51] On December 20, 2005, the Sixth U.S. Circuit Court of Appeals ruled that a Ten Commandments display at the Mercer County (Kentucky) Courthouse was well within the bounds of the Constitution.[52]

In 1999, U.S. District Judge Allen Sharp ruled that a Ten

Commandments plaque in front of the Elkhart (Indiana) City Hall did not violate the U.S. Constitution.[53] One year later, the Seventh U.S. Circuit Court of Appeals decided that the display was unconstitutional.[54]

In March 2002, U.S. District Judge Stewart Dalzell ordered Chester County, Pennsylvania, officials to remove a Ten Commandments display from the county courthouse.[55] One year later, a three-judge panel from the Third Circuit Court of Appeals overturned Judge Dalzell, declaring that the Chester County Ten Commandments display was constitutional.[56]

In May 2003, the Eleventh U.S. Circuit Court of Appeals upheld the official seal of Richmond County, Georgia, which included a depiction of the Ten Commandments.[57] Two months later, the same appellate court ruled that Alabama Chief Justice Roy Moore acted unconstitutionally by displaying the Ten Commandments in the rotunda of the Alabama Supreme Court building.[58]

Then, on June 27, 2005, the U.S. Supreme Court issued two conflicting 5-4 decisions concerning the public display of the Ten Commandments. In *McCreary County v. ACLU*, the Court declared that Ten Commandments displays at two Kentucky courthouses were unconstitutional. On the very same day, in the case of *Van Orden v. Perry*, the High Court upheld the constitutionality of a Ten Commandments display at the Texas State Capitol building.[59]

How could anyone honestly expect local government officials to navigate these murky waters safely?

Testifying before Congress, Mat Staver, president of Liberty Counsel, explained, "If the Justices of the Supreme Court are conflicted over the meaning of the Establishment Clause, then it is particularly inappropriate to punish government officials with the threat of attorneys' fees and costs for a mere misstep in this constitutional minefield."[60]

Efforts to Defund the ACLU

In an effort to remedy this abuse of American taxpayers, U.S. Rep. John Hostettler and Sen. Sam Brownback introduced the Public Expression of Religion Act (PERA).

The proposed legislation, which would amend the Civil Rights Act, was proposed "to eliminate the chilling effect on the constitutionally protected expression of religion by State and local officials that results from the threat that potential litigants may seek damages and attorneys' fees."[61]

If approved, this legislation would specify that "remedies with respect to a claim . . . where the deprivation consists of a violation of a prohibition in the Constitution against the establishment of religion shall be limited to injunctive relief." In other words, if PERA is passed, the ACLU could no longer collect attorneys' fees from lawsuits attacking Ten Commandments displays, nativity scenes, the Pledge of Allegiance, the national motto, war memorials, or any other case that involves the so-called "wall of separation between church and state."

Sen. Sam Brownback explained, "Congress's intent in passing the fee-shifting statute in 1976 was to prevent racial injustice and discrimination. Thirty years later, these laws are being used simply to purge religious faith—and symbols of any faith—from our society at taxpayer expense."[62]

In a speech delivered to a group of American Legion veterans, Rep. Hostettler explained that this bill is necessary to hinder the efforts of those who are seeking to "enrich themselves at the expense of the Constitution."[63]

According to Hostettler:

> This bill is designed to give public officials a chance in this fight. Because of PERA, our fellow patriots will not have to face financial ruin to de-

fend their real right to freedom of speech under our Constitution. . . . The Public Expression of Religion Act will restore legal balance in this country, and it will protect us from being the victims of this assault on our religious liberties.[64]

On February 17, 2006, after watching the ACLU profit from two separate cases involving the removal of crosses from war memorials, the American Legion distributed a letter encouraging three million veterans to support PERA. The letter stated:

There is a clear need to close a loophole in existing law that allows groups to raid taxpayers' pocketbooks in pursuit of their private agendas. . . . The very threat of such fees has made elected bodies, large and small, surrender to the demands of special interest groups to secularly cleanse the public square. . . . The American Legion Family cannot "safeguard and transmit to posterity" American values if we stand back and allow the symbols of our American heritage, established by our Founding Fathers, to be banned from the public square and effectively wiped from our history, our collective consciousness, and our national character.[65]

As of August 2006, this legislation had not yet been allowed a simple up or down vote in either house of Congress.

Restoring the Public Trust
In September 2005, Coral Ridge Ministries presented Rep. Hostettler with more than 165,000 petitions in support of PERA. Immediately after this delivery, Dr. D. James Kennedy

declared, "For decades, the ACLU has pursued a ceaseless, uncompromising campaign to rid the American public landscape of every acknowledgement of God. We need a 'Public Expression of Religion Act' which will stop the flow of tax dollars into the ACLU's bank account."[66]

In an open letter to the ACLU, Dr. Kennedy, joined by tens of thousands of Americans, pledged to "stand in direct opposition to your anti-Christian, anti-family, anti-virtue intimidation, propagandizing, and litigating...."[67]

Indeed, if no check is placed on the ACLU, judges will simply continue to enable this destructive organization to profit from the very people whom they are seeking to undermine. Tens of millions of unsuspecting American taxpayers—many of whom abhor the indefensible work of the ACLU—have been forced to fund its campaigns, which are wholly committed to the abolition of common decency and America's religious heritage.

As the ACLU and modern courts distort the Constitution and dismiss the wisdom of our Founding Fathers, the precious dream of American liberty is decaying into a perverse licentiousness where rights are determined by the government, rather than given from God. History proves that when the liberties of men are conditioned upon the whims of human judgment, the population is ripe for the oppressive bonds of tyranny.

Americans must not sit idly by and trust that someone else is fighting the battles for them. The battle to preserve the precious blessings of liberty will not be solved by legislation or court decisions. Rather, just as the foundation of American liberty was laid in our nation's churches, the battle for the future of America will be won or lost in its pulpits and pews.

If the Church remains apathetic and unengaged in American life, its inaction will no doubt be rewarded with the government and culture that it has rightly deserved.

ELEVEN

Ten Ways to Combat the ACLU

[I]f My people who are called by My name will humble themselves, and pray and seek My face, and turn from their wicked ways, then I will hear from heaven, and will forgive their sin and heal their land.

— II Chronicles 7:14

In this oft-cited passage of Scripture, God declares that the redemption of nations begins in the hearts and minds of His people, the Church. This challenge is not dictated to the unbelieving masses. Rather, God's promise of healing is based on the premise that *His* people are to humble *themselves*, pray, seek His face, and turn from *their own* wicked ways.

In a society where the actions of the Church too often mirror those of the world, it is no surprise that American culture is in a state of decay. Jesus called upon His Church to be "the salt and light of the world."[1] Just as salt was once rubbed into open wounds to prevent infection, so are Christians called to disinfect the wounds of a rotting culture with the healing sting of truth.

Jesus warned that "if the salt loses its flavor . . . it is then good for nothing but to be thrown out and trampled underfoot by men."[2]

Has the Church in America become so complacent that it

has lost its salty flavor? If we are sincere about combating organizations like the ACLU and saving America's future generations from the trajectory set by our own apathy, then change must begin within the hearts, minds, and actions of God's people.

PRAY

George Washington once declared, "It is the duty of all nations to acknowledge the Providence of Almighty God, to obey His will, to be grateful for His benefits, and to humbly implore His protection and favor."[3]

As our nation confronts numerous issues and controversies—from the fight to defend traditional marriage and common decency, to the war on terror and the defense of the unborn—it is imperative for Christians to pray for America's governing officials. Pray that they would be convicted to seek after righteousness and reject the folly of the ACLU.

We must also pray for the ACLU and its members. In His Sermon on the Mount, Jesus taught, "You have heard that it was said, 'You shall love your neighbor and hate your enemy.' But I say to you, love your enemies, bless those who curse you, do good to those who hate you, and pray for those who spitefully use you and persecute you."[4]

EVANGELIZE

The Apostle Paul warns us that the message and teachings of Christ will be "foolishness" to an unbelieving world.[5] To many, it is foolish to believe that Almighty God created man in His own image and loves us so much that He humbled Himself, became a man, and died on a Cross to endure the wrath reserved for our sins—a wrath we deserved—to redeem us in the sight of God.

To the world, Christianity is foolishness, but Jesus promised,

"He who believes in the Son has everlasting life; and he who does not believe the Son shall not see life, but the wrath of God abides on him."[6] This explains why—at the end of the Gospel of Matthew—Jesus commissions his followers to go and make disciples of all nations.[7]

A Christian who evangelizes is demonstrating his recognition that the significant issues we face as a nation cannot be changed—unless God first changes the hearts of the people. The power of God unto salvation is also the power of God to instill virtue into any society. His disciples are those who have caught a glimpse of the immeasurable love of Christ, and in return want to please God wholly!

Be an Example to Others

The spiritual vitality of the Church in early America did not occur in a vacuum. Rather, it was fostered by the earnest desires of godly men and women pursuing the will of God. Jesus instructed his followers, "Let your light so shine before men, that they may see your good works and glorify your Father in heaven."[8]

In a fallen world continually pushing the envelope of immorality, it is easy to tell people what they ought to do, but the greatest sermons of our lives are delivered by the examples we set. When a fallen world looks to the life of a believer and notices something extraordinary (e.g., joy, peace, selflessness, humility, longsuffering)—they will want to know why.

Educate Friends About the ACLU

The primary objective of this book was to educate the reader concerning the actions and involvements of the ACLU. Much of its content—if not all—may have surprised and possibly shocked you. Now think about the average person. It is easy to understand why so many people are in the dark about the ACLU's true agenda. On the surface, the American Civil Liberties Union sounds like an organization concerned for America's well-being.

Shed a little light on the subject. Tell them about some of the ACLU's cases, or give them a copy of this book. As Americans are made aware of the organization's destructive agenda, the ACLU will become increasingly marginalized in our culture. The organization will lose its credibility in our nation's courtrooms, legislatures, and town councils.

EQUIP CHILDREN WITH A CHRISTIAN WORLDVIEW

In spite of what many politicians and elites want you to believe, the responsibility of educating our children does not fall primarily on the shoulders of the government. That is doubly the case for Christians, who are tasked with bringing up children in the training and admonition of the Lord.[9]

Christians are called to raise their children to view all things through the lens of a Christian worldview. C.S. Lewis once stated, "I believe in Christianity as I believe that the sun has risen: not only because I see it, but because by it I see everything else."[10] We must take heed to raise our children with the benefit of observing everything under the light of God's Word.

VOTE FOR GODLY LEADERS

John Jay, America's first U.S. Supreme Court Chief Justice, once said, "Providence has given to our people the choice of their rulers, and it is the duty, as well as the privilege and interest of our Christian nation, to select and prefer Christians for their rulers."[11]

In today's culture, it may seem rare that godly men ever seek elected office, but when they do they should be able to count on the support of fellow Christians. The book of Exodus offers good instruction for selecting rulers: "[Y]ou shall select from all the people able men, such as fear God, men of truth, hating covetousness; and place such over them to be rulers."[12]

The Proverbs declare, "When the righteous are in authority, the people rejoice; but when a wicked man rules, the people groan."[13] We live in a *self-governing* republic. How can we honestly expect godly and righteous people to reach positions of authority, if God's people choose not to participate in elections?

SUPPORT MORAL LEGISLATION

Stay abreast of legislation pending at the national, state, and local levels. Where legislation exists to promote a godly, virtuous society, Christians should seek to mobilize grassroots support so that such legislation becomes law. Call, write, and visit your legislators, encouraging them to support moral policies.

By visiting the Center for Reclaiming America for Christ's website (www.reclaimamerica.org), you can become an informed citizen. Join the Center's E-Army and receive regular updates on the pressing issues of the day. Encourage your pastor to endorse "issues awareness" groups in your local church.

SUPPORT CONFIRMATION OF DISCIPLINED JUDGES

It is easy to complain about the tyrannical nature of modern activist courts, but if we fail to seek the confirmation of constitutionally principled judges who renounce the notion that the Constitution is a "living document" that "evolves" with the culture, then we have lost our right to complain. Contact the President and your senators and urge them to appoint and confirm principled judges who will honor the text of the Constitution and the intent of its framers.

Do you know lawyers who, if they became judges, would faithfully interpret the laws of the land rather than creating new ones? Encourage them to seek judicial seats. As we have seen time and again, judges need not sit on the U.S. Supreme Court to have an impact on society.

Support Christian Ministries

There are a myriad of worthy Christian ministries working tirelessly to impact our culture for Christ. As the body of Christ has differing parts with different emphases, so, too, do these ministries. Some may focus on the Cultural Mandate—the need for Christians to promote virtue in government and media. Others may seek to evangelize the lost. Still other ministries may seek to bring comprehensive theological understanding to believers.

Many are worthy of support. Beyond tithing to your local church, seek ways to support these faithful ministries with your time, talent, and treasure.

Be Aware of Christian Legal Groups

There are many Christian legal groups dedicated to protecting your right to religious expression in America—groups like the Alliance Defense Fund, co-founded by Dr. D. James Kennedy; the American Center for Law & Justice; Liberty Counsel; the Rutherford Institute; and the Thomas More Law Center.

Become familiar with their work and share their resources with your local elected officials. Do not hesitate to contact them if you ever find yourself in a situation where your religious liberties are threatened.

Alliance Defense Fund
1-800-TELL-ADF
www.alliancedefensefund.org

American Center for Law & Justice
1-757-226-2489
www.aclj.org

Liberty Counsel
1-800-671-1776
www.lc.org

Rutherford Institute
1-434-978-3888
www.rutherford.org

Thomas More Law Center
1-734-827-2001
www.thomasmore.org

CONCLUDING THOUGHTS

The financial and legal success of the ACLU is not merely an indictment against the wickedness of one organization. Rather, the deterioration of American society is an indictment against the apathy of God's Church. We, as Christians, must take seriously our roles, set forth by Christ, to be salt and light in this world. If America is to recapture the Christian values that defined previous generations, it will not be legislated by Congress or decreed by the courts; it will begin in the hearts and minds of God's Church.

C.S. Lewis once stated, "If you read history you will find that the Christians who did most for the present world were precisely those who thought most of the next. It is since Christians have largely ceased to think of the other world that they have become so ineffective in this one."[14]

If we are sincere in our prayer—that God's will would be done on earth as it is in Heaven—then we must recognize that such a cultural transformation will begin only when the people of God humble themselves, pray, seek His face, and turn from their own wicked ways. It begins with the Church!

It begins with you!

Endnotes

Introduction

1   William J. Federer, *America's God and Country: Encyclopedia of Quotations*, FAME Publishing, Inc.; Coppell, Texas, 1994, p. 23.
2   Ronald Reagan, "California and the Problem of Government Growth," January 5, 1967. http://www.reagansheritage.org/html/reagan01_05_67.shtml
3   George Washington's Farewell Address, September 1796. http://usinfo.state.gov/usa/infousa/facts/democrac/49.htm
4   "About Us," The American Civil Liberties Union, January 2006. http://www.aclu.org/about/index.html
5   David Barton, "Solving the Pledge of Allegiance Controversy," WallBuilders, 2003. http://www.wallbuilders.com/resources/search/detail.php?ResourceID=67
6   Amy Fagan, "Senate Targets Abortion Method," *The Washington Times*, October 22, 2003. http://www.washtimes.com/national/20031021-112742-9765r.htm
7   "Ten Commandments Judge Removed From Office," *CNN*, November 14, 2003. http://www.cnn.com/2003/LAW/11/13/moore.tencommandments/
8   Dana Blanton, "Majority OK With Public Nativity Scenes," *Fox News*, June 18, 2004. http://www.foxnews.com/story/0,2933,105272,00.html
9   Dana Blanton, "Majority Opposes Same-Sex Marriage," *Fox News*, June 14, 2004. http://www.foxnews.com/story/0,2933,103756,00.html
10 Janet Gilmore, "Youths More Conservative Than Their Elders on Issues Involving Religion and Abortion, New UC Berkeley Survey Reveals," University of California–Berkeley, September 24, 2002. www.berkeley.edu/news/media/releases/2002/09/24_youth.html
11 Elizabeth Armet, "Poll Analysis: Americans Lean More Conservative on Social Issues," *Los Angeles Times*, June 18, 2000. http://www.latimes.com/news/custom/timespoll/la-000618abortpoll-442pa2an,0,6427319.htmlstory?coll=la-news-times_poll
12 "2001 Religion and Public Life Survey," The Pew Research Center, March 18, 2001. http://people-press.org/reports/print.php3?PageID=118
13 "Poll: Americans back abortion limits," *CNN*, November 27, 2005. http://www.cnn.com/2005/US/11/27/abortion.poll/
14 "Abortion and Rights of Terror Suspects Top Court Issues," Pew Research Center, August 3, 2005. http://people-press.org/reports/display.php3?ReportID=253
15 "Vast Majority in U.S. Support 'Under God,'" *CNN*, June 30, 2002. http://archives.cnn.com/2002/US/06/29/poll.pledge/
16 "Nearly Two-thirds of U.S. Adults Believe Human Beings Were Created by God," Harris Poll, July 6, 2005. http://www.harrisinteractive.com/harris_poll/index.asp?PID=581
17 "Poll: Parents Want Feds To Tame TV," *CBS News*, September 23, 2004. http://www.cbsnews.com/stories/2004/09/23/entertainment/main645195.shtml
18 Steve Bonta, "Liberty and the Chains of Virtue," *The New American*, August 14, 2000. http://www.thenewamerican.com/tna/2000/08-14-2000/vo16no17_liberty.htm
19 David Barton, *Original Intent* (p. 22), WallBuilder Press, Aledo, Texas; 2000, p. 22.
20 John C. Eastman, "The 'Undercount' Fallacy," The Claremont Institute, December 11, 2000. http://www.claremont.org/projects/jurisprudence/001211eastman.html.
21 Alexander Hamilton, "The Federalist No. 78," *The Federalist Papers*, June 14, 1788.

http://www.constitution.org/fed/federa78.htm

22   "ACLU Campaign Finance Reform Fact Sheet," ACLU News Release, February 12, 2002.
     http://www.aclu.org/freespeech/cfr/11047leg20020212.html

23   "ACLU of New Jersey Defends Property Owner Against Government Seizure of Land to
     Give to Religious School," ACLU News Release, October 18, 2005.
     http://www.aclu.org/religion/govtfunding/21232prs20051018.html

24   "ACLU's Defense of Religious Liberty," ACLU News Release, March 2, 2005.
     http://www.aclu.org/religion/tencomm/16254res20050302.html

25   David Barton, *Original Intent*, p. 338.

26   Isaiah 5:20-21, New King James Version.

27   Plato, *The Republic*: Second Edition, Translated by Allan Bloom, 561[c] through 564[a],
     The Perseus Book Group, 1991.

Chapter One

1   Francis A. Schaeffer, *How Should We Then Live?* Fleming H. Revell, Old Tappan, N.J.,
     1976, p. 145.

2   D. James Kennedy, Ph.D., *Today's Conflict, Tomorrow's Crisis*, Coral Ridge Ministries,
     Fort Lauderdale, Florida, 2000, p.72.

3   Alexander Hamilton, *The Papers of Alexander Hamilton*, "The Farmer Refuted," edited
     by Harold C. Syrett et al. 26 vols. New York and London, Columbia University Press,
     1961-79.
     http://press-pubs.uchicago.edu/founders/documents/v1ch3s5.html

4   Benjamin Franklin, *The Autobiography of Benjamin Franklin*, March 1791, Ch. 10.
     http://www.earlyamerica.com/lives/franklin/chapt10/

5   David Barton, *Original Intent*, WallBuilder Press, Aledo, Texas, 2000, p. 157.

6   Statement of D. James Kennedy, Ph.D., Testimony Before the Subcommittee on
     Oversight of the House Committee on Ways and Means," May 14, 2002.
     http://waysandmeans.house.gov/Legacy/oversite/107cong/5-14-02/5-14kenn.htm

7   "Milestones: A Short History of Princeton University," *Princeton University Handbook*,
     June 2005. http://www.princeton.edu/hr/handbook/history.htm

8   Brad Simmons, "The Christian Right: Mixing Politics and Religion," *Princeton Tory*,
     September 2003.

9   David Barton, "God: Missing in Action from American History," WallBuilders, June
     2005. http://www.wallbuilders.com/resources/search/detail.php?ResourceID=121

10   "Religion and the Founding of the American Republic," Library of Congress, October
     27, 2003. http://www.loc.gov/exhibits/religion/rel04.html

11   "The Paris Peace Treaty of 1783," University of Oklahoma Law School, 2006.
     http://www.law.ou.edu/ushistory/paris.shtml

12   David Barton, "A New Acquisition," WallBuilders, Spring 1999.
     http://www.wallbuilders.com/resources/search/detail.php?ResourceID=45

13   "Members of the Supreme Court of the United States," U.S. Supreme Court, 2006.
     http://www.supremecourtus.gov/about/members.pdf

14   James McClellan, *Joseph Story and the American Constitution*, University of Oklahoma
     Press, January 1971, p. 119.

15   David Barton, *Original Intent*, pp. 29-30.

16   *Runkel v. Winemiller*, Maryland Supreme Court, 1803.

17   *People v. Ruggles*, New York Supreme Court, 1811.

18   *Updegraph v. Commonwealth*, Pennsylvania Supreme Court, 1824.

19   *Vidal v. Girard's Executors*, 43 U.S. 127, Supreme Court of the United States, January
     1844. www.facstaff.bucknell.edu/mazur/courses/documents/vidal.html

20   *Davis v. Beason*, 133 U.S. 333, Supreme Court of the United States, 1889.
     http://caselaw.lp.findlaw.com/cgi-bin/getcase.pl?court=US&vol=133&invol=333

21 *U.S. v. Church of the Holy Trinity*, 143 U.S. 457, Supreme Court of the United States, 1892.
22 *U.S. v. McIntosh*, Supreme Court of the United States, 1931.
23 "Judiciary Reorganization Bill of 1937," *Wikipedia*, July 10, 2006. http://en.wikipedia.org/wiki/Court_packing
24 "Members of the Supreme Court of the United States," Supreme Court of the United States, 2006. http://www.supremecourtus.gov/about/members.pdf
25 Debbie Elliot, "A Life of Justice: Hugo Black of Alabama," National Public Radio: *All Things Considered*, September 11, 2005. http://www.npr.org/templates/story/story.php?storyId=4828849
26 *Everson v. Board of Education*, 330 U.S. 1, U.S. Supreme Court, February 10, 1947. http://caselaw.lp.findlaw.com/cgi-bin/getcase.pl?court=US&vol= 330&invol=1
27 "Church and State: Religion in Our Public Schools," ACLU Briefing Paper, Summer 1999. http://www.aclu.org/FilesPDFs/church_state99.pdf
28 "Jefferson's Letter to the Danbury Baptists," Library of Congress, January 1, 1802. http://www.loc.gov/loc/lcib/9806/danpre.html
29 Michael Gaynor, "The U.S. Supreme Court Arbitrarily Took Separation of Church and State Much Too Far," Renew America, July 19, 2005. http://www.renewamerica.us/columns/gaynor/050719
30 "Church and State: Religion in Our Public Schools," ACLU Briefing Paper, Summer 1999. http://www.aclu.org/FilesPDFs/church_state99.pdf
31 Phil Kent, "Rein in the ACLU," *The Washington Times*, December 14, 2004. http://www.washtimes.com/op-ed/20041213-084741-7322r.htm
32 *Lemon v. Kurtzman*, 403 U.S. 602, Supreme Court of the United States, June 28, 1971. http://caselaw.lp.findlaw.com/scripts/getcase.pl?court=US&vol=403&invol=602
33 "*Engel v. Vitale*," *Thompson Gale Legal Encyclopedia*, Answers.com, 2006. http://www.answers.com/topic/engel-v-vitale
34 "List of Court Cases Involving the American Civil Liberties Union," *Wikipedia: The Free Encyclopedia*, July 18, 2006. http://en.wikipedia.org/wiki/List_of_ACLU_Cases
35 "ACLU: 100 Greatest Hits," ACLU of San Diego Resource, 2005. http://www.aclusandiego.org/100_greatest_hits/
36 "List of Court Cases Involving the American Civil Liberties Union," *Wikipedia: The Free Encyclopedia*, July 18, 2006. http://en.wikipedia.org/wiki/List_of_ACLU_Cases
37 *Edwards v. Aguillard*, 482 U.S. 578, Supreme Court of the United States, June 19, 1987. http://caselaw.lp.findlaw.com/scripts/getcase.pl?navby=CASE &court=US&vol=482&page=578
38 *Allegheny County v. ACLU*, 492 U.S. 573, Supreme Court of the United States, July 3, 1989. http://caselaw.lp.findlaw.com/scripts/getcase.pl?navby=CASE&court=US&vol=492&page=573
39 *Lee v. Weisman*, 505 U.S. 577, Supreme Court of the United States, June 24, 1992. http://caselaw.lp.findlaw.com/cgi-bin/getcase.pl?court=us&vol =505&invol=577
40 *Locke v. Davey*, No. 02-1315, ACLU Amicus Brief, July 17, 2003. http://www.aclu.org/FilesPDFs/davey.pdf
41 *Wallace v. Jaffree*, 472 U.S. 38, U.S. Supreme Court, Rehnquist Dissenting Opinion, June 4, 1985. http://caselaw.lp.findlaw.com/scripts/getcase.pl?court=US&vol= 472&invol=38
42 *Stone v. Graham*, 449 U.S. 39, Supreme Court of the United States, November 17, 1980. http://caselaw.lp.findlaw.com/scripts/getcase.pl?court=US&vol =449&invol=39
43 "ACLU Sues Judge Over Ten Commandments, Prayer," Center for Reclaiming America for Christ, July 1, 1995.

http://www.reclaimamerica.org/PAGES/NEWS/news. aspx?story=142

44   "Alabama's Conspiracy of Ignorance," *Freethought Today*, March 1997.
http://ffrf.org/fttoday/1997/march97/alabama.html

45   Randy Hall, "Lawsuit Seeks to Restore Moore as Alabama Chief Justice," *CNS News*,
November 20, 2003. http://www.cnsnews.com/ViewNation.asp?Page=%5CNation
%5Carchive%5C200311%5CNAT20031120a.html

46   "Moore Puts God's Law in Alabama Supreme Court," Coral Ridge Ministries *Impact*
newsletter, September 2001. http://www.coralridge.org/impact/2001_Sept_Pg1.htm

47   *Glassroth v. Moore*, No. 01-T-1268-N, U.S. District Court for Middle Alabama, November 18, 2002.
http://www.almd.uscourts.gov/Opinions/Glassroth%20v %20Moore%20Opinion.pdf

48   The Declaration of Independence, The Avalon Project, July 4, 1776.
http://www.yale.edu/lawweb/avalon/declare.htm

49   Ibid.

50   "Court Rejects Commandments," *Impact* newsletter, Coral Ridge Ministries, August
2003, p. 5. http://www.coralridge.org/impact/2003_Aug_Pg5.htm

51   Ibid.

52   "Ten Commandments Judge Removed From Office," CNN Law Center, November 14,
2003. http://www.cnn.com/2003/LAW/11/13/moore.tencommandments/

53   "Duluth Monument in Latest Ten Commandments Debate," *CBS News*, February 12,
2004. http://www.reclaimamerica.org/Pages/NEWS/news.aspx?story=1558

54   "ACLU of Montana Challenges County Creche Display," ACLU Press Release, December 21, 1999. http://www.aclu.org/religion/gen/16139prs19991221.html

55   "Ten Commandments Litigation Runs Rampant," Center for Reclaiming America for
Christ, April 13, 2004. http://www.reclaimamerica.org/PAGES/NEWS/news.aspx?
story=1663

56   "Missionaries, Monuments, and Courts," *Voice of Reason: The Newsletter of Americans
for Religious Liberty*, No. 1 [78], 2002, p. 7. http://www.arlinc.org/newsletters/arl-spring02.pdf

57   "Ten Commandments Litigation Runs Rampant," Center for Reclaiming America for
Christ, April 13, 2004.
http://www.reclaimamerica.org/PAGES/NEWS/news.aspx? story=1663

58   *McCreary County v. ACLU*, No. 03-1693, Supreme Court of the United States, March
2005. http://www.aclu.org/FilesPDFs/mcreary.pdf

59   *McCreary County v. ACLU*, No. 03-1693-P.
http://www.law.cornell.edu/supct/pdf/03-1693P.ZO

60   *McCreary County v. ACLU*, No. 03-1693, http://www.law.cornell.edu/supct/pdf/03-1693P.ZD

61   "D. James Kennedy Responds to Ten Commandments Rulings," Coral Ridge Ministries
Press Release, June 27, 2005.
http://www.coralridge.org/specialdocs/PR_10Commandments Res.htm

62   *Elk Grove v. Newdow*, ACLU Amicus Brief, February 13, 2004.
http://www.aclu.org/FilesPDFs/elkgrove.pdf

63   "ACLU Challenges Colorado's Pledge of Allegiance Law," First Amendment Center,
August 13, 2003. http://www.firstamendmentcenter.org/news.aspx?id=11816

64   *Newdow v. U.S. Congress*, No. 00-16423, Ninth U.S. Circuit Court of Appeals, June 26,
2002. http://www.ca9.uscourts.gov/ca9/newopinions.nsf/FE05EEE7
9C2A97B688256BE3007FEE32/$file/0016423.pdf

65   Greg Hoadley, "A Godly Mother Takes a Stand," Center for Reclaiming America for
Christ, May 9, 2003.
http://www.reclaimamerica.org/Pages/NEWS/news.aspx?story=1204

66   *Elk Grove v. Newdow*, ACLU Amicus Brief, February 13, 2004.
http://www.aclu.org/FilesPDFs/elkgrove.pdf

67   Suzanne Herel, "Judge Rules Pledge of Allegiance Unconstitutional," *San Francisco Chronicle*, September 14, 2005.
     http://www.sfgate.com/cgi-bin/article.cgi?file=/chronicle/archive/2005/09/14/MNpledge14.DTL

68   Kimberly Edds, "Cross in Mojave Desert Barred," *The Washington Post*, June 8, 2004.
     http://www.washingtonpost.com/wp-dyn/articles/A26255-2004Jun8.html

69   "Omnibus Consolidated and Emergency Supplemental Appropriations for Fiscal Year 2001: Conference Report," U.S. House of Representatives, December 15, 2000.
     http://thomas.loc.gov/cgi-bin/cpquery/T?&report=hr1033&dbname=106&

70   *Buono v. Norton*, NO. EDCV 01-216 RT, U.S. District Court for Southern California, July 2002.
     http://www.cacd.uscourts.gov/CACD/RecentPubOp.nsf/bb61c530eab0911c882567cf005ac6f9/9e471f4e9f52a5d488256c0200517e79/$FILE/EDCV01-216RT.pdf

71   *Buono v. Norton*, No. 03-55032, Ninth U.S. Circuit Court of Appeals, June 7, 2004.
     http://www.ca9.uscourts.gov/ca9/newopinions.nsf/F2DC42822BDB96A688256EAC0059531F/$file/0355032.pdf?openelement

72   Dana Wilkie, "Hint to Mt. Soledad Cross's Fate Lies in Desert," *San Diego Union-Tribune*, July 27, 2006.
     http://www.signonsandiego.com/news/metro/20060727-9999-1n27crosses.html

73   "Court: Cross in Mojave Park Is Unconstitutional," *CNN News*, June 8, 2004.
     http://www.cnn.com/2004/LAW/06/08/mojave.cross.ap/index.html

74   "ACLU Sues Federal Government Over Christian Cross in Mojave National Preserve," ACLU of Southern California News Release, March 22, 2001.
     http://www.aclu.org/religion/discrim/16319prs20010322.html

75   "State Considering Memorial for Gay Veterans," *The Desert Sun*, January 13, 2004.
     http://www.thedesertsun.com/news/stories2004/local/20040113003421.shtml

76   Matthew T. Hall, "Soledad Cross Protected by Voters; Court Fights Looming," *San Diego Union-Tribune*, July 26, 2005.
     http://www.signonsandiego.com/news/politics/20050726-2342-1n27cross.html

77   "Judge Rules That Overwhelmingly Approved Mount Soledad Cross Ballot Measure Unconstitutional," *North County Times*, October 7, 2005.
     http://www.nctimes.com/articles/2005/10/08/news/sandiego/15_55_0410_7_05.txt

78   Onell R. Soto, "City Has 90 Days to Remove Mt. Soledad Cross," *San Diego Union-Tribune*, May 4, 2006.
     http://www.signonsandiego.com/uniontrib/20060504/news_1n4soledad.html

79   *San Diegan for the Mt. Soledad National War Memorial v. Phillip Paulson*, No. 05A1233, U.S. Supreme Court Justice Anthony Kennedy, July 7, 2006.   http://www.scotusblog.com/movabletype/archives/Kennedy%20on%20A-1234.pdf

80   Sarah Larkins, "Efforts to Save Mount Soledad Memorial Face Deadline," *CNS News*, July 02, 2006
     http://www.cnsnews.com/ViewCulture.asp?Page=/Culture/archive/200607/CUL20060702a.html

81   Dana Wilkie, "Senate Votes to Put Mount Soledad Cross in Federal Hands," *San Diego Union-Tribune*, August 1, 2006.
     http://www.signonsandiego.com/news/metro/20060801-1730-cnssoledad.html

82   "Policy Statement on H.R. 5683 – Acquisition of Mt. Soledad Veterans Memorial," Executive Office of the President, July 19, 2006.
     http://www.whitehouse.gov/omb/legislative/sap/109-2/hr5683sap-h.pdf

83   Dana Wilkie, "House OKs Plan to Keep Cross on Mount Soledad," *San Diego Union-Tribune*, July 20, 2006.
     http://www.signonsandiego.com/uniontrib/20060720/news_1n20cross.html

84   Allan Turner, "Houston Faces Own Biblical Battle," *Houston Chronicle*, August 8, 2003.

http://www.chron.com/CDA/archives/archive.mpl?id=2003_3683143

85   *Kay Staley v. Harris County*, No. H-03-3411, U.S. Southern District of Texas, August 10, 2004. http://www.alliancealert.org/aa2004/2004_08_11.pdf

86   "5th Circuit Upholds Bible Removal From Courthouse," The First Amendment Center, August 16, 2006.
      http://www.firstamendmentcenter.org/news.aspx?id=17280

87   "Harris County Appeals Monument Bible Ruling," *Dallas Morning News*, August 31, 2006
      http://www.dallasnews.com/sharedcontent/dws/news/texassouthwest/stories/DN-bible_31tex.ART.State.Edition1.3dfdcda.html

88   *Allegheny v. ACLU*, 492 U.S. 573, Supreme Court of the United States, July 3, 1989.

89   Dana Blanton, "Majority OK With Public Nativity Scenes," *Fox News*, June 18, 2004.
      http://www.foxnews.com/story/0,2933,105272,00.html

90   Don Feder, "Public Schools and the ACLU Play Scrooge This Christmas," *Front Page Magazine*, November 24, 2004.
      http://frontpagemag.com/Articles/ReadArticle.asp?ID=16091

91   "Away From the Manger: Creche, Candy, Cookies With Religious Symbolism Barred From Colo. Classroom," Alliance Defense Fund Press Release, December 19, 2005.
      http://www.alliancedefensefund.org/news/pressrelease.aspx?cid=3633

92   Lowell Ponte, "The Christmas Tree Ban," *Front Page Magazine*, December 20, 2000.
      http://www.frontpagemag.com/Articles/ReadArticle.asp?ID=3837

93   Jan LaRue, "ACLU: Guardians of Liberty or 'Card-Carrying' Hypocrites?" Concerned Women for America, September 2, 2004.
      http://cultureandfamily.org/articledisplay.asp?id=6270&department=LEGAL&categoryid=misc

94   "ACLJ Offers to Defend Any School That Displays 'God Bless America,'" American Center for Law & Justice, October 2001.
      http://www.aclj.org/News/Read.aspx?ID=317

95   Dennis Prager, "A Grand Victory at the Grand Canyon," *WorldNetDaily*, August 5, 2003.
      http://www.worldnetdaily.com/news/article.asp?ARTICLE_ID=33917

96   "ACLU Forces City to Remove Cross From Logo," Center for Reclaiming America for Christ, May 3, 2004.
      http://www.reclaimamerica.org/Pages/News/newspage.asp?story=1700

97   "Judge dismisses L.A. County seal lawsuit," The First Amendment Center, October 22, 2004. http://www.fac.org/news.aspx?id=14241

98   "ACLU Battles City Over Christian Calendar," Center for Reclaiming America for Christ, January 31, 2005.
      http://www.reclaimamerica.org/Pages/NEWS/newspage.asp?story=2427

99   "ACLU threat nixes 23rd Psalm display," *WorldNetDaily*, September 14, 2005.
      http://www.worldnetdaily.com/news/printer-friendly.asp?ARTICLE_ID=46307

100   Karen Turni Bazile, "ACLU Wants Parish to Forget Cross," *The Times-Picayune*, August 6, 2006. http://www.nola.com/news/t-p/metro/index.ssf?/base/news-16/1154844074102520.xml&coll=1

101   "Civil Liberties Union Urges Mayor to Withdraw Threats to Brooklyn Museum Over Art Controversy," ACLU News Release, September 24, 1999.
      http://www.aclu.org/freespeech/govtfunding/11030prs19990924.html

102   Phil Hirschkorn, "New York, Brooklyn Museum Settle Funding Dispute," *CNN News*, March 27, 2000.
      http://archives.cnn.com/2000/STYLE/arts/03/27/museum.flap/index.html

103   *National Endowment for the Arts v. Finley*, ACLU Amicus Brief, No. 97-371, Fall Term 1997. http://www.aclu.org/scotus/1997/22767lgl19980206.html

104   *ACLU of Kentucky v. Mercer County*, No. 03-5142, Sixth U.S. Circuit Court of Appeals,

December 20, 2005.
http://www.ca6.uscourts.gov/opinions.pdf/05a0477p-06.pdf

105   Ibid.

106   Peter Smith, "Commandments Display Upheld," *The Courier-Journal*, April 26, 2006.
http://www.courierjournal.com/apps/pbcs.dll/article?AID=/20060425/NEWS01/60
4250370

107   "Pro-Family Attorney Sees Tide Turning Against ACLU's Anti-Religion Efforts," Agape
Press, January 26, 2006. http://headlines.agapepress.org/archive/1/afa/252006a.asp

108   Mat Staver, Letter to Supporters, Liberty Counsel, January 23, 2006.

Chapter Two

1   Jamie Glazov, "The ACLU vs. America: An Interview With Alan Sears," *Front Page Magazine*, September 26, 2005. http://frontpagemag.com/Articles/ReadArticle.asp?ID=19607

2   "Introduction to the *Engel v. Vitale* Court Case," U.S. Department of State, 2006.
http://usinfo.state.gov/usa/infousa/facts/democrac/47.htm

3   *Engel v. Vitale*, 370 U.S. 421, Supreme Court of the United States, June 25, 1962.
http://supct.law.cornell.edu/supct/html/historics/USSC_CR_0370_0421_ZO.html

4   "New York Civil Liberties Union: Championing Civil Rights and Civil Liberties for 50
Years," New York Civil Liberties Union, September 2003.
http://www.nyclu.org/nyclu_50th_anniversary_book.pdf

5   *Engel v. Vitale*, 370 U.S. 421.

6   Ibid.

7   "New York Civil Liberties Union Endorses Supreme Court Ruling," *Newsday*, June 26,
1962.
http://www.people.hofstra.edu/faculty/alan_j_singer/Docket/4%202%20%20Brown.pdf

8   "Gallup Poll Says 81% Endorse School Prayer," *The New York Times*, September 11, 1983.
http://query.nytimes.com/gst/fullpage.html?res=9802E7D91338F932A2575AC0A9659
48260

9   "Poll: Americans Believe Religion Is 'Under Attack' — Majority Says Religion is 'Losing Influence' In American Life," Anti-Defamation League Press Release, November 21, 2005.
http://www.adl.org/PresRele/RelChStSep_90/4830_90.htm

10   *Allegheny County v. ACLU*, 492 U.S. 573, Supreme Court of the United States, July 3,
1989.
http://caselaw.lp.findlaw.com/scripts/getcase.pl?court=US&vol=492&invol=573

11   Jason DeParle, "In Battle to Pick Next Justice, Right Says, Avoid a Kennedy," *The New York
Times*, June 27, 2005.
http://www.nytimes.com/2005/06/27/politics/27kennedy.html?ei=5088&en=f62730bb
f055c497&ex=1277524800&partner=rssnyt&emc=rss&pagewanted=all

12   *Lee v. Weisman*, 505 U.S. 577, Supreme Court of the United States, June 24, 1992.
http://caselaw.lp.findlaw.com/scripts/getcase.pl?court=US&vol=505&invol=577

13   Ibid.

14   *McComb v. Crehan*, Case 2:06-cv-00852, U.S. District Court of Nevada, July 13, 2006.
http://www.rutherford.org/pdf/mccomb.pdf

15   "One Girl's Testimonial or School-Sponsored Religion?" *Las Vegas Review-Journal*, June
20, 2006. http://www.reviewjournal.com/lvrj_home/2006/Jun-20-Tue-2006/opin-
ion/8027170.html

16   *Tinker v. Des Moines*, 393 U.S. 503, Supreme Court of the United States, February 24,
1969. http://caselaw.lp.findlaw.com/scripts/getcase.pl?court=US&vol=393&invol=503

17   Antonio Planas, "District Pulls Plug on Speech," *Las Vegas Review-Journal*, June 17, 2006.
http://www.reviewjournal.com/lvrj_home/2006/Jun-17-Sat-2006/news/8014416.html

18   Antonio Planas, "Group Files Lawsuit, Alleges School Officials Violated Teen's Rights," *Las
Vegas Review Journal*, July 14, 2006.

http://www.reviewjournal.com/lvrj_home/2006/Jul-14-Fri-2006/news/8491786.html

19   Ibid.
20   "Federal Judge Rules Against School-Mandated Prayer at Kentucky High School Gradua-
      tion Ceremony," ACLU News Release, May 19, 2006.
      http://www.aclu.org/religion/schools/25616prs20060519.html
21   Peter Smith, "Graduates Stage Protest Prayer," *The Louisville Courier-Journal*, May 20,
      2006. http://www.courier-journal.com/apps/pbcs.dll/article?AID=/20060520/
      NEWS01/605200365
22   "Tangipahoa School Board Prayers Ruled Illegal," ACLU of Louisiana Press Release, Feb-
      ruary 25, 2005. http://www.laaclu.org/News/2005/Feb25DoeDecision.htm
23   "ACLU Sues Board for School Prayers," *Daily Star*, October 15, 2003.
      http://www.zwire.com/site/news.cfm?newsid=10323195&BRD=1423&PAG=461&dept
      _id=169546&rfi=6
24   *Doe v. Tangipahoa Parish School District*, No. 03-2870, February 23, 2005.
      http://www.laaclu.org/DoevTangiDec.pdf
25   "ACLU: Punish Officials for 'Un-American' Prayer," *WorldNetDaily*, April 7, 2005.
      http://www.worldnetdaily.com/news/article.asp?ARTICLE_ID=43677
26   *Doe v. Tangipahoa Parish School Board*, No. 03-2870-C-1, Motion for Contempt, May 18,
      2005. http://www.laaclu.org/DoeFourthContempt051805.pdf
27   Ibid.
28   "Praying School Board Likened to Terrorists," *WorldNetDaily*, August 17, 2005.
      http://www.worldnetdaily.com/news/article.asp?ARTICLE_ID=45807
29   "ACLU Announces Opposition to Alito Nomination," ACLU Press Release, January 9,
      2006. http://www.aclu.org/scotus/2005/23387res20060109.html
30   *Pelphrey v. Cobb County*, ACLU of Georgia, August 2005.
      http://www.acluga.org/briefs/cobb.county.pelphrey/complaint.pdf
31   Bill Rankin, "Cobb Allowed to Keep Prayers," *The Atlanta Journal-Constitution*, January
      15, 2006.
      http://www.ajc.com/search/content/auto/epaper/editions/sunday/metro_34ac60f4e00
      ed0220052.html
32   Susanna Capelouto, "Georgia County Panel's Prayers Contested," NPR: Weekend Edition
      Sunday, August 28, 2005.
      http://www.npr.org/templates/story/story.php?storyId=4820857
33   "VMI, Virginia Attorney General, ACLU Exchange Words Over Evening Prayers," Virginia
      Military Institute, *The Institute Report*, Volume XXVIII, Number 7, April 13, 2001.
      http://www.vmi.edu/media/cm_publications/Institute%20Report/2000/IR%20Apr01.p
      df
34   "Virginia Military Institute Must Discontinue Dinner Prayers," The First Amendment enter,
      January 25, 2002. http://www.firstamendmentcenter.org//%5Cnews.aspx?id=4260
35   *Mellen v. Bunting*, 02-1215(L), April 30, 2003.
      http://pacer.ca4.uscourts.gov/opinion.pdf/021215.P.pdf
36   David Barton, *Original Intent*, WallBuilder Press, Aledo, Texas, 2000, p. 115.
37   Thomas Jefferson, *Memoirs, Correspondence, and Miscellanies from the Papers of Thomas Jef-
      ferson*, editor: Thomas Jefferson Randolph, 1830.
38   "ACLU Targets Navy," *The Washington Times*, December 29, 2003.
      http://www.washtimes.com/commentary/20031228-104220-9622r.htm
39   H.R. 3430, 109th Congress, Legislation Introduced by Walter Jones, July 26, 2005.
      http://frwebgate.access.gpo.gov/cgi-
      bin/getdoc.cgi?dbname=109_cong_bills&docid=f:h3430ih.txt.pdf
40   "Jones Introduces Bill To Protect Prayer In Our Military Academies," Senator Walter Jones
      Press Release, September 4, 2003. http://jones.house.gov/html/release.cfm?id=176
41   Representative Walter Jones, H.R. 2999, 108th Congress, September 4, 2003.
      http://frwebgate.access.gpo.gov/cgi-

bin/getdoc.cgi?dbname=108_cong_bills&docid=f:h2999ih.txt.pdf

42 "Lawmaker Sued Over Use of 'Jesus,'" *WorldNetDaily*, June 7, 2005.
http://www.worldnetdaily.com/news/article.asp?ARTICLE_ID=44628

43 *Marsh v. Chambers*, 463 U.S. 783, Supreme Court of the United States, July 5, 1983.
http://caselaw.lp.findlaw.com/cgi-bin/getcase.pl?court=us&vol=463&invol=783

44 Vic Ryckaert and Tom Spalding, "Speaker of House Defends Prayers," *The Indianapolis Star*, June 2, 2005.
http://www.indystar.com/apps/pbcs.dll/article?AID=/20050602/NEWS02/506020465

45 *Hinrichs v. Bosma*, No. 1:05-cv-0813-DFH-TAB, U.S. District Court for Southern Indiana, November 30, 2005. http://www.insd.uscourts.gov/News/1-05-cv-0813%20Opinion.pdf

46 House Resolution 1, Indiana House of Representatives, February 13, 2006.
http://www.in.gov/legislative/bills/2006/HRESP/HR0001.html

47 "House Passes Resolution Supporting Uncensored Prayer," Indiana House of Representatives News Release, February 13, 2006.
http://www.state.in.us/legislative/house_republicans/newsroom/060213bosmaprayerresolution.html

48 "Speaker Bosma Files Appeal With Seventh Circuit Court on Prayer Lawsuit," Indiana House of Representatives New Release, May 12, 2006.
http://www.state.in.us/legislative/house_republicans/newsroom/060512bosma7ca.html

49 "Daily Observance of One Minute of Silence," Virginia Code Annotated § 22.1-203.
http://leg1.state.va.us/cgi-bin/legp504.exe?000+cod+22.1-203

50 "ACLU Challenges Virginia's Minute of Silence Law," ACLU Press Release, June 22, 2000.
http://www.aclu.org/religion/schools/16287prs20000622.html

51 Reverend Jerry Falwell, "You Can't Think That Way," *WorldNetDaily*, September 8, 2001.
http://www.worldnetdaily.com/news/article.asp?ARTICLE_ID=24389

52 Brooke A. Masters, "Va. Moment of Silence in Schools Is Upheld," *The Washington Post*, July 25, 2001.
http://www.washingtonpost.com/ac2/wp-dyn?pagename=article&node=&contentId=A45861-2001Jul24

53 Ibid.

54 "High Court Rejects 'Moment of Silence' Case," *CNN Law Center*, October 29, 2001.
http://archives.cnn.com/2001/LAW/10/29/moment.silence/

55 "ACLU, Children Services Deadlock Over Concert," *Ohio News*, August 2004.
www.onnnews.com/global/story.asp?s=2186170&ClientType=Printable

56 "ACLU of Ohio Demands Cancellation of Franklin County Sponsored 'Faith Based' Concert," ACLU News Release, August 21, 2004.
http://www.aclu.org/religion/govtfunding/16348prs20040816.html

57 Felix Hoover, "Judge OKs Government Agency's Gospel Concert," *The Columbus Dispatch*, August 21, 2004. http://www.religionandsocialpolicy.org/news/article.cfm?id=1864

58 Ibid.

59 Josh McDowell, *The New Evidence That Demands A Verdict*, Thomas Nelson Publishers, Nashville, Tennessee, 1999, p. 4.

60 "Florida Citizens Challenge Unconstitutional 'Bible History' Classes," ACLU News Release, February 21, 2002. http://www.aclu.org/religion/gen/16147res20020221.html

61 *Gibson v. Lee County School Board*, No. 97-529-CIV-FTM-17D, U.S. District Court for the Middle District of Florida, January 20, 1998.
http://www.aclufl.org/legislature_courts/legal_department/briefs_complaints/leedecision.cfm?print=true

62 Sam Kastensmidt, "ACLU Threats Cause Dismissal of Adult Christian Course," Center for Reclaiming America for Christ, September 23, 2003.
http://www.reclaimamerica.org/Pages/NEWS/news.aspx?story=1379

63 *The Good News Club v. Milford*, No. 98-9494, Second U.S. Circuit Court of Appeals, February 3, 2000.

http://supreme.lp.findlaw.com/supreme_court/briefs/99-2036/opinion.html
64   "Supreme Court Hears Arguments Today in After-School Evangelism Case," ACLU Press Release, February 28, 2001.
      http://www.aclu.org/religion/schools/16314prs20010228.html
65   *Good News Club v. Milford*, No. 99-2036, ACLU Amicus Brief, January 12, 2001.
      http://www.aclu.org/images/asset_upload_file553_22253.pdf
66   *Good News Club v. Milford*, 533 U.S. 98, Supreme Court of the United States, July 11, 2001. http://supct.law.cornell.edu/supct/pdf/99-2036P.ZO
67   Ibid.

Chapter Three

1   "ACLU's Defense of Religious Liberty," ACLU, March 2, 2005.
     http://www.aclu.org/religion/tencomm/16254res20050302.html
2   Ronald Reagan, "California and the Problem of Government Growth," The Heritage Foundation, January 5, 1967. http://www.reaganheritage.org/html/reagan01_05_67.shtml
3   Erwin W. Lutzer, *Hitler's Cross*, Chicago: Moody Press, 1995, p. 131.
4   Lutzer, p. 143.
5   Lutzer, p. 144-145.
6   Lt. (jg) Carl E. Schorake to Major William Coogan, "Nazi Master Plan: The Persecution of the Christian Churches," Office of Strategic Services, Research and Analysis No. 3114.4, Draft for the War Crimes Staff, July 6, 1945.
     http://www.camlaw.rutgers.edu/publications/law-religion/nuremberg/nazimaster-plan01.pdf
7   "World War II Casualties," *Wikipedia*, July 30, 2006.
     http://en.wikipedia.org/wiki/World_War_II_casualties
8   Patrick L. O'Daniel, "More Honored in the Breach: A Historical Perspective of the Permeable IRS Prohibition on Campaigning of Churches," *Boston College Law Review*, April 2001. http://www.bc.edu/bc_org/avp/law/lwsch/journals/bclawr/42_4/01_TXT.htm
9   Houses of Worship Free Speech Restoration Act, H.R. 235, Introduced by Representative Walter Jones, 108th Session of Congress, January 8, 2003.
     http://frwebgate.access.gpo.gov/cgi-bin/getdoc.cgi?dbname=108_cong_bills&docid=f:h235ih.txt.pdf
10   "Letter to the House Urging Opposition to H.R. 235, the Houses of Worship Free Speech Restoration Act," ACLU Press Release, May 25, 2003.
     http://www.aclu.org/religion/gen/16219leg20030525.html
11   "Statement of D. James Kennedy, President, Coral Ridge Ministries, Fort Lauderdale, Florida, and Senior Minister, Coral Ridge Presbyterian Church," Testimony Before the Subcommittee on Oversight of the House Committee on Ways and Means, May 14, 2002.
     http://www.coralridge.org/DrKennedyTestimonyBeforeCongress.htm
12   Bill O'Reilly, "Another Victory for the ACLU and Its War on Christianity," *The O'Reilly Factor*: Talking Points, June 28, 2004.
     http://www.foxnews.com/story/0,2933,124012,00.html
13   "What's Wrong With the World?" Belief Net, 2004.
     http://www.beliefnet.com/story/6/story_642_1.html
14   D. James Kennedy and Jerry Newcombe, *What If Jesus Had Never Been Born?*, Thomas Nelson Publishers, Nashville, Tennessee, 1994, p. 52.
15   Executive Order # 13199, "Establishment of White House Office of Faith-Based and Community Initiatives," The White House Press Secretary, January 29, 2001.
     http://www.whitehouse.gov/news/releases/2001/01/20010129-2.html
16   "White House Faith-Based & Community Initiative," White House Office for Faith-Based and Community Initiative, 2006.
     http://www.whitehouse.gov/government/fbci/president-initiative.html

17   President George W. Bush, "President Highlights Faith-Based Results at National Confer-
      ence," Office of the White House Press Secretary, March 9, 2006. http://www.white-
      house.gov/news/releases/2006/03/20060309-5.html
18   *Bowen v. Kendrick*, 487 U.S. 589, Supreme Court of the United States, June 29, 1988.
      http://caselaw.lp.findlaw.com/cgi-
      bin/getcase.pl?friend=nytimes&navby=case&court=us&vol=487&invol=589
19   "ACLU of Florida for Local Comment on President Bush's Executive Order on Faith-Based
      Initiatives," ACLU of Florida Press Release, December 12, 2002.
      http://www.aclufl.org/news_events/archive/2002/faith-basedprograms121202.cfm
20   "ACLU Says Latest Faith-Based Bill Supports White House Push for Taxpayer-Funded
      Discrimination," ACLU News Release, January 30, 2003.
      http://www.aclu.org/religion/govtfunding/16184prs20030130.html
21   *Lown v. The Salvation Army*, New York Civil Liberties Union Amended Complaint,
      September 23, 2004.
      http://www.nyclu.org/pdfs/salvation_army_amnd_complaint_092304.pdf
22   Ibid.
23   Barbara Bradley Hagerty, "Judge: Use of Religion in Hiring Decisions OK," National
      Public Radio: *All Things Considered*, October 4, 2005.
      http://www.npr.org/templates/story/story.php?storyId=4945299
24   *Lown v. The Salvation Army*, 04 Civ. 1562 (SHS), U.S. District Judge Sidney H. Stein,
      September 30, 2005.
      http://indianalawblog.com/documents/salvationarmy.pdf
25   Teresa Mendez, "Can Competition Really Improve Schools," *Christian Science Monitor*,
      September 7, 2004. http://www.csmonitor.com/2004/0907/p12s01-legn.html
26   Terry Frieden, "Supreme Court Affirms School Voucher Program, CNN, June 27, 2002.
      http://archives.cnn.com/2002/LAW/06/27/scotus.school.vouchers/index.html
27   "High Court Hears Arguments on Ohio Vouchers; ACLU Says Decision Will Have Nation-
      wide Impact," ACLU News Release, February 19, 2002.
      http://www.aclu.org/religion/vouchers/16124prs20020219.html
28   Thomas L. Krannawitter, "The ACLU's Assault on Religion and Morality," The Claremont
      Institute, June 24, 2002.
      http://www.claremont.org/writings/precepts/20020624krannawitter.html
29   The Northwest Ordinance, Article III, U.S. Congress, 1787.
      http://usinfo.state.gov/usa/infousa/facts/democrac/5.htm
30   *Zelman v. Simmons-Harris*, No. 00-1751, Supreme Court of the United States, June 27,
      2002. http://supct.law.cornell.edu/supct/pdf/00-1751P.ZO
31   "ACLU Calls Supreme Court Ruling on Vouchers 'Bad for Education, Bad for Religious
      Freedom,'" ACLU Press Release, June 27, 2002.
      http://www.aclu.org/scotus/2001/16052prs20020627.html
32   "Boy Scout Oath, Law, Motto, and Slogan," *Boy Scouts of America Fact Sheet*, 2005.
      http://www.scouting.org/factsheets/02-503a.html
33   "Action Alert: Urge the City Council to Seek the Termination of the Boy Scouts' Lease in
      Balboa Park," The ACLU of San Diego, August 2003.
      http://www.aclusandiego.org/pdf/ScoutLeasesActionAlert.pdf
34   "Judge Rules Scouts 'Religious' Group," *WorldNetDaily*, August 6, 2003.
      http://www.wnd.com/news/article.asp?ARTICLE_ID=33941
35   "Boy Scouts' Use of Balboa Park Land Ruled Unconstitutional," *San Diego Union-Tribune*,
      July 31, 2003.
      http://www.signonsandiego.com/news/metro/20030731-1629-aclu-scouts.html
36   "Action Alert: Urge the City Council to Seek the Termination of the Boy Scouts' Lease in
      Balboa Park," The ACLU of San Diego, August 2003.
      http://www.aclusandiego.org/pdf/ScoutLeasesActionAlert.pdf
37   "S.D. Agrees to Pay ACLU $950,000, Will Cancel Pact Over Balboa Park Site," *The San*

Diego Union-Tribune, January 9, 2004.
http://www.signonsandiego.com/news/metro/20040109-9999-7m9scouts.html
38   Donna Miles, "DoD Support for Boy Scouts to Continue, Rumsfeld Says," American
      Forces Press Service, December 6, 2004.
      http://www.defenselink.mil/news/Dec2004/n12062004_2004120609.html
39   "Pentagon Agrees to End Direct Sponsorship of Boy Scout Troops in Response to Religious
      Discrimination Charge," ACLU News Release, November 15, 2004.
      http://www.aclu.org/religion/discrim/16382prs20041115.html
40   "Transcript of Interview Between Bill O'Reilly and Secretary of
      Defense Donald Rumsfeld From the *O'Reilly Factor,*" Boy Scouts
      of America National Council, December 3, 2004.
      http://www.bsalegal.org/rumsfeld-195.htm
41   Hans Zeiger, "The ACLU vs. The Boy Scouts," *Renew America,* January 14, 2004.
      http://www.renewamerica.us/columns/zeiger/040114
42   "Judge: Evolution Stickers Unconstitutional," *CNN News,* January 13, 2005.
      http://www.cnn.com/2005/LAW/01/13/evolution.textbooks.ruling/index.html
43   *Selman v. Cobb County,* Case No. 1 02-CV-2325-CC, January 13, 2005.
      http://www.aclu.org/FilesPDFs/cobb%20county%20decision.pdf
44   Max Jammer, *Einstein and Religion: Physics and Theology.* Princeton: Princeton University
      Press, 1999. http://www.quotationspage.com/quotes/Albert_Einstein/
45   "The Genome Doctor," *Christianity Today,* October 1, 2001.
      http://www.christianitytoday.com/ct/2001/012/2.42.html
46   *Selman v. Cobb County,* No. 05-10341, Eleventh U.S. Circuit Court of Appeals, May 25,
      2006. http://www.ca11.uscourts.gov/opinions/ops/200510341.pdf
47   *Davey v. Locke,* No. 00-35962, Ninth U.S. Circuit Court of Appeals, July 18, 2002.
      http://caselaw.lp.findlaw.com/data2/circs/9th/0035962p.pdf
48   *Locke v. Davey,* No. 02-1315, Supreme Court of the United States, February 25, 2004.
      http://www.supremecourtus.gov/opinions/03pdf/02-1315.pdf
49   *Locke v. Davey,* No. 02-1315, Supreme Court of the United States, February 25, 2004.
      http://www.law.cornell.edu/supct/pdf/02-1315P.ZD
50   "The Liberty Letter," Piedmont Chapter of the American Civil Liberties Union, April 2005.
      http://www.aclusc.org/Chapters/Piedmont/LibLetterApr2005.pdf
51   Mike Cubelo, "A Bullet Memo to the Right," *The Common Voice,* November 26, 2004.
      http://www.commonvoice.com/article.asp?colid=1776
52   "Bible Verses Regarded as Hate Literature," *WorldNetDaily,* February 18, 2003.
      http://www.worldnetdaily.com/news/article.asp?ARTICLE_ID=31080
53   "Swedish Pastor Sentenced to Month in Prison for Preaching Against Homosexuality," *Life-
      Site Daily News,* July 5, 2004. http://www.lifesite.net/ldn/2004/jul/04070505.html
54   "Trial Over Italian Islam Insult," *BBC News,* May 24, 2005.
      http://news.bbc.co.uk/2/hi/europe/4576663.stm
55   Richard Alleyne, "Bishop's Anti-Gay Comments Spark Legal Investigation," *The London
      Telegraph,* October 11, 2003.
      http://www.telegraph.co.uk/news/main.jhtml?xml=/news/2003/11/10/nbish10.xml&s
      Sheet=/portal/2003/11/10/ixportal.html
56   "Leading Catholic Bishop in Spain Speaks Out Despite Threat of Losing Public Funding,"
      LifeSite Daily News, July 6, 2004.
      http://www.zenit.org/english/visualizza.phtml?sid=56388
57   "What Happens in Countries with Hate Crimes Laws?" Center for Reclaiming America for
      Christ, September 15, 2005.
      http://www.reclaimamerica.org/Pages/News/news.aspx?story=2918
58   "Profile in Persecution: An Interview With Pastor Daniel Scot," Center for Reclaiming
      America for Christ, August 21, 2003.
      http://www.reclaimamerica.org/Pages/NEWS/news.aspx?story=1338

59   David Miller, "Distributing Bible Tracts Is Not a Hate Crime: Brazilian Court," *Compass Direct*, July 16, 2004.
      http://www.biblenetworknews.com/southamerica/071604_brazil.html

60   "In Focus: Hate Crimes," *Media Reference Guide, Gay & Lesbian Alliance Against Defamation*, 2005. http://www.glaad.org/media/guide/infocus/crimes.php

61   Bill Toland, "In-Your-Face Evangelist Challenges Hate-Crime Law's Limits," *Pittsburgh Post-Gazette*, January 23, 2005. http://www.post-gazette.com/pg/05023/446796.stm

62   Kelli Samantha Hewett, "Two Men Preparing to Carry Crosses Charged With Disorderly Conduct," *The Tennessean*, May 9, 2004.
      http://www.tennessean.com/local/archives/04/05/51062556.shtml?Element_ID=5106 2556

63   Ed Vitagliano, "Using Caesar's Sword," *American Family Association Journal*, March 2004. http://www.afajournal.org/2004/march/304religious_freedom.asp

64   Senator Edward Kennedy, "Local Law Enforcement Enhancement Act of 2005," S. 1145, 109th Congress, May 26, 2005. http://frwebgate.access.gpo.gov/cgi-bin/getdoc.cgi?db-name=109_cong_bills&docid=f:s1145is.txt.pdf

65   Gregory T. Nojeim and Christopher E. Anders, "RE: Local Law Enforcement Hate Crimes Prevention Act," ACLU Letter to U.S. House of Representatives, May 25, 2005.
      http://www.aclu.org/FilesPDFs/hate%20crimes.pdf

66   Bill Fancher and Jenni Parker, "CFI: Hate Crime Bill Could Criminalize Biblical Truth," *Agape Press*, May 28, 2004. http://www.crosswalk.com/news/1265152.html

67   Ted Olsen, "Judge Calls Denial of Communion 'Tremendous Violence,'" *Christianity Today* Weblog, January 31, 2003.
      http://www.christianitytoday.com/ct/2003/104/51.0.html

68   "Fast Facts: Hate Crimes," Center for Reclaiming America for Christ, 2005.
      http://www.reclaimamerica.org//pages/fastfacts/HateCrimes.pdf

69   Thomas Jefferson, "Jefferson's Letter to the Danbury Baptists," Library of Congress, January 1, 1802. http://www.loc.gov/loc/lcib/9806/danpre.html

70   Dan Albertson, "Publicly Funded Chaplains," *Civil Liberties Newspaper*, July 1, 1997.
      http://www.aclu-wa.org/detail.cfm?id=148

71   *Harland Malyon v. Pierce County*, No. 63664-8, Washington Supreme Court, April 24, 1997. http://mail.tvw.org/modules/opinions/636648_o.htm

72   *Harland Malyon v. Pierce County*, No. 63664-8, Washington Supreme Court, April 24, 1997. http://mail.tvw.org/modules/opinions/636648_o.htm

73   Stephanie Strom, "A.C.L.U. Board Members Debate Limits on Their Own Speech," *The New York Times*, June 18, 2006.
      http://select.nytimes.com/gst/abstract.html?res=F70912F63A550C7B8DDDAF0894DE 404482

74   Stephanie Strom, "ACLU Withdraws Proposals to Limit Public Criticism by Board Members," *The New York Times*, July 12, 2006.
      http://select.nytimes.com/gst/abstract.html?res=F30A12F63A540C718DDDAE0894DE 404482

75   "ACLU Demands Recall of State Health Department Religious AIDS Brochure," ACLU of Florida News Release, April 3, 2003.
      http://www.aclufl.org/news_events/archive/2003/aidshealthdeptletter.cfm

76   Jim Brown and Jenni Parker, "School Officials Censor Biblical Views on Homosexuality," *Agape Press*, July 1, 2004.
      http://headlines.agapepress.org/archive/7/12004c.asp

77   ACLU Troubled by Court's Refusal to Hold Louisiana Governor's Program on Abstinence in Contempt for Continuing to Preach With Taxpayer Dollars," ACLU Press Release, June 24, 2005.
      http://www.aclu.org/reproductiverights/gen/12641prs20050624.html

78   Ray Henry, "Rhode Island Bans Private Group's Abstinence Program," *The Boston Globe*,

March 22, 2006.
http://www.boston.com/news/local/rhode_island/articles/2006/03/22/rhode_island_bans_private_groups_abstinence_program/
79   "Court Throws Out Challenge to Ohio's 'Choose Life' Tags," *CNS News*, October 6, 2005.
        http://www.cnsnews.com/news/viewstory.asp?Try=No&Page=\Culture\archive\200510\C
        UL20051006c.html
80   "ACLU of Alaska Says Tax Exemption Favors Religious Groups Over Other Charitable Organizations," ACLU News Release, June 12, 2006.
        http://www.aclu.org/religion/govtfunding/26028prs20060612.html
81   Alan Sears, "The ACLU's War on Religion," *WorldNetDaily*, September 22, 2005.
        http://www.worldnetdaily.com/news/article.asp?ARTICLE_ID=46454
82   "Judge Rules Islamic Education OK in California Classrooms," *WorldNetDaily*, December 13, 2003. http://www.worldnetdaily.com/news/article.asp?ARTICLE_ID=36118

Chapter Four

1   "Sexually Transmitted Diseases: Questions and Answers for Federal Bureau of Prisons Facility Staff Members," The U.S. Department of Justice, 2000.
        http://www.cdc.gov/nchstp/od/cccwg/includes/FacilityStaff.pdf
2   "Genital HPV Infection," CDC Fact Sheet, 2005. http://www.cdc.gov/std/HPV/hpv.pdf
3   "Tracking the Hidden Epidemics: Trends in STDs," Centers for Disease Control, September 2002. http://www.cdc.gov/nchstp/dstd/Stats_Trends/Trends2000.pdf
4   "More Than a Million Americans Living With HIV," *MSNBC News*, June 13, 2005.
        http://msnbc.msn.com/id/8203052/
5   Terry Wynn, "USA's Youth at High Risk for Venereal Diseases," *USA Today*, February 24, 2004.
        http://www.usatoday.com/news/health/2004-02-24-american-stds_x.htm?csp=22_tnt
6   "Social Issues Linked to Rise in STDs," *MSNBC*, April 19, 2005.
        http://www.msnbc.msn.com/id/7268133/
7   "Births: Final Data for 2003," *National Vital Statistics Report*, Centers for Disease Control, September 8, 2005. http://www.cdc.gov/nchs/data/nvsr/nvsr54/nvsr54_02.pdf
8   George A. Akerlof and Janet L. Yellen, "An Analysis of Out-Of-Wedlock Births in the United States," The Brookings Institution, August 1996.
        http://www.brookings.edu/comm/policybriefs/pb05.htm
9   "White House Briefing," CNN Transcripts, January 27, 2003.
        http://edition.cnn.com/TRANSCRIPTS/0301/27/se.08.html
10   "ACLU Letter to the House of Representatives Urging Opposition to Extending the Federal Refusal Clause and Appropriation of Money for Abstinence-Only-Until Marriage Programs," ACLU Press Release, June 15, 2005.
        http://www.aclu.org/reproductiverights/sexed/12636leg20050615.html
11   "ACLU Announces Nationwide Action Aimed at Combating Dangerous Abstinence-Only-Until-Marriage Curricula in the States," ACLU Press Release, September 21, 2005.
        http://www.aclu.org/reproductiverights/gen/20117prs20050921.html
12   "About Us: ACLU Lesbian & Gay Rights Project," ACLU Website, 2006.
        http://www.aclu.org/getequal/aboutpage.htm
13   J. Vincelette, "Predicators of Chlamydial Infection and Gonorrhea Among Patients Seen by Private Practitioners," *Canadian Medical Association Journal* 144 (1995): 713-721.
        http://www.frc.org/get.cfm?i=IS01B1#edn26
14   "Characteristics of Patients with Syphilis Attending Baltimore STD Clinics," *Archives of Internal Medicine*, 1991. http://www.ncbi.nlm.nih.gov/entrez/query.fcgi?cmd=Retrieve&db=PubMed&list_uids=2001134&dopt=Abstract
15   Todd Henneman, "Scared of Sex," *The Advocate*, August 17, 2004.

http://findarticles.com/p/articles/mi_m1589/is_2004_August_17/ai_n6148237

16   "Young People at Risk: HIV/AIDS Among America's Youth," Division of HIV/AIDS
      Prevention (Centers for Disease Control), November 14, 2000.
      http://www.cdc.gov/hiv/pubs/facts/youth.htm

17   "Viral Hepatitis B: Frequently Asked Questions," National Center for Infectious Diseases,
      Centers for Disease Control and Prevention, September 29, 2000.
      http://www.cdc.gov/ncidod/diseases/hepatitis/b/faqb.htm#gen

18   J.M. Palefsky, "Prevalence and Risk Factors for Human Papillomavirus Infection of the Anal
      Canal in HIV-Positive and HIV-Negative Homosexual Men," *Journal of Infectious Diseases*,
      February 1998.
      http://www.ncbi.nlm.nih.gov/entrez/query.fcgi?cmd=Retrieve&db=PubMed&list_uids=9
      466522&dopt=Abstract

19   Michael King, M.D. and Eamonn McKeown, Ph.D., "Mental Health and Quality of Life of
      Gay Men and Lesbians in England and Wales," *The British Journal of Psychiatry* 183: 552-
      558, December 2003.
      http://bjp.rcpsych.org/cgi/content/abstract/183/6/552?ijkey=41e175a2972ac95a6c2ab
      961ea84dd1439eca426&keytype2=tf_ipsecsha

20   *Bowers v. Hardwick*, 478 U.S. 186, Supreme Court of the United States, June 30, 1986.
      http://caselaw.lp.findlaw.com/scripts/getcase.pl?court=US&vol=478&invol=186

21   *Bowers v. Hardwick*, No. 85-140, U.S. Supreme Court, June 30, 1986.
      http://www.law.ukmc.edu/faculty/projects/ftrials/conlaw/bowers.html

22   "Getting Rid of Sodomy Laws: History and Strategy that Led to the Lawrence Decision,"
      ACLU News Release, June 26, 2003.
      http://www.aclu.org/lgbt/crimjustice/11886res20030626.html

23   "Brief Amici Curiae of the ACLU and the ACLU of Texas in Support of Petitioner,"
      Delivered to U.S. Supreme Court, January 16, 2003.
      http://www.aclu.org/FilesPDFs/garner.pdf

24   *Lawrence v. Texas*, No. 02-102, U.S. Supreme Court, June 26, 2003.
      http://supct.law.cornell.edu/supct/html/02-102.ZO.html

25   *Planned Parenthood of Southern Pennsylvania v. Casey*, No. 91-744. U.S. Supreme Court,
      June 29, 1992. http://www.law.cornell.edu/supct/html/91-744.ZS.html

26   "Age of Consent," *Wikipedia*, March 13, 2006.
      http://en.wikipedia.org/wiki/Age_of_consent

27   "Sweden highlights bestiality problem," *The Local News*, April 29, 2005.
      http://www.thelocal.se/article.php?ID=1357&date=20050429

28   "Prostitution," *Wikipedia*, March 14, 2006. http://en.wikipedia.org/wiki/Prostitution

29   "Same-Sex Marriage," *Wikipedia*, March 14, 2006.
      http://en.wikipedia.org/wiki/Same-sex_marriage

30   "ACLU Letter to the House of Representatives Regarding H.Res. 97 and the Interpretation
      of the Constitution in International Law," ACLU Press Release, September 27, 2005.
      http://www.aclu.org/crimjustice/gen/20038leg20050927.html

31   Ibid.

32   *Lawrence v. Texas*, No. 02-102, U.S. Supreme Court, June 26, 2003.
      http://supct.law.cornell.edu/supct/html/02-102.ZO.html

33   Justice Antonin Scalia, Dissenting Opinion in *Lawrence v. Texas*, June 26, 2003.
      http://supct.law.cornell.edu/supct/pdf/02-102P.ZD

34   Ibid.

35   Phyllis Schlafly, "Isn't Turnabout Fair Play," Eagle Forum, August 24, 2005.
      http://www.eagleforum.org/column/2005/aug05/05-08-24.html

36   "Managers of Spa Prostitution Fronts Arrested for Unlicensed Massages," *The Brown Daily
      Herald*, November 28, 2005.
      http://www.browndailyherald.com/media/paper472/news/2005/11/28/Metro/Man-
      agers.Of.Spa.Prostitution.Fronts.Arrested.For.Unlicensed.Massages-

1114084.shtml?norewrite&sourcedomain=www.browndailyherald.com

37   "Police in U.S. state R.I. seek stricter anti-prostitution laws," *Police One*, September 11, 2005. http://www.policeone.com/news/118773/

38   "ACLU Questions Call for New Prostitution Laws Based on Providence Police 'Spa' Raids," ACLU of Rhode Island News Release, May 26, 2005. http://www.riaclu.org/20050526.html

39   ACLU of Rhode Island Executive Director Steven Brown, Letter Sent to Rhode Island Senator Rhoda Perry, May 24, 2005. http://www.riaclu.org/friendly/documents/prostitu-tion_laws.pdf

40   "*The Advocate* Sex Poll," *The Advocate*, August 20, 2002. http://www.findarticles.com/p/articles/mi_m1589/is_2002_August_20/ai_90164066

41   *Little Black Book: This One Will Keep You Out of Trouble*, Lambda Legal. http://www.lambdalegal.org/binary-data/LAMBDA_PDF/pdf/262.pdf

42   "Detroit Settles ACLU Lawsuit Challenging Police Sting Operation Against Gay Men," ACLU Press Release, July 23, 2002. http://www.aclu.org/lgbt/crimjustice/12010prs20020723.html

43   "Lawsuit Prompts New DOC Policy on Medical Treatment for Transgendered Prisoners," ACLU of Virginia News Release, September 24, 2004. http://www.acluva.org/newsreleases2004/Sep24.html

44   Ann Babe, "ACLU Sues Over Sex-Change Ban," *The Badger-Herald*, February 6, 2006. http://badgerherald.com/news/2006/02/06/aclu_sues_over_sexc.php

45   Gina Barton, "Inmate Can Still Take Hormones for Now," *Milwaukee Journal Sentinel Online*, January 24, 2006. http://www.jsonline.com/story/index.aspx?id=387447

46   Ann Babe, "ACLU Sues Over Sex-Change Ban," *The Badger-Herald*, February 6, 2006. http://badgerherald.com/news/2006/02/06/aclu_sues_over_sexc.php

47   "Yale Professors' Brief on Solomon Amendment," Yale Law School, September 22, 2005. http://www.law.yale.edu/outside/html/Public_Affairs/650/yls_article.htm

48   Solomon Amendment, January 2002. http://frwebgate6.access.gpo.gov/cgi-bin/wais-gate.cgi?WAISdocID=523352218204+0+0+0&WAISaction=retrieve

49   Amicus Brief filed in *Rumsfeld v. Forum for Academic and Institutional Rights*, ACLU, September 21, 2005. http://www.aclu.org/images/asset_upload_file710_21337.pdf

50   *Rumsfeld v. F.A.I.R.*, No. 04–1152, Supreme Court of the United States, March 6, 2006. http://a257.g.akamaitech.net/7/257/2422/06Mar20061300/www.supremecourtus.gov/opinions/05pdf/04-1152.pdf

51   "View Homosexual Film or School Faces Lawsuit," *WorldNetDaily*, November 28, 2004. http://www.worldnetdaily.com/news/article.asp?ARTICLE_ID=41667

52   "ACLU Hails Federal Court Ruling on School Trainings Aimed at Reducing Anti-Gay Harassment," ACLU Press Release, February 18, 2006. http://www.aclu.org/lgbt/youth/24215prs20060218.html

53   "Don't Say They're Wrong," ADF Press Release, February 15, 2005. http://www.alliancedefensefund.org/news/story.aspx?cid=3338

54   "Don't Say They're Wrong," ADF Press Release, February 15, 2005. http://www.alliancedefensefund.org/news/story.aspx?cid=3338

55   "Ky. Students Can't Skip Anti-Gay Harassment Training," First Amendment Center, February 20, 2006. http://www.firstamendmentcenter.org/news.aspx?id=16508

Chapter Five

1   "U.S. Department of Education, Office of the Under Secretary, *Educator Sexual Misconduct: A Synthesis of Existing Literature*, Washington, D.C., 2004. http://www.ed.gov/rschstat/research/pubs/misconductreview/index.html

2   *Educator Sexual Misconduct*, p. 17.

3   *Educator Sexual Misconduct*, p. 18.

4   *Educator Sexual Misconduct*, p. 44.
5   Sam Kastensmidt, "America's Universities Promoting Pedophilia," Center for Reclaiming
     America for Christ, January 17, 2005.
     http://www.reclaimamerica.org/Pages/News/news.aspx?story=2364
6   Michael Capel, "Pedophilia 101 at Cornell," *Accuracy in Academia*, February 1998.
     http://www.academia.org/campus_reports/1998/october_1998_1.html
7   Scott Hogenson, "APA Under Fire for Child Sex Abuse Report," *CNS News*, March 31,
     1999.
     http://www.cnsnews.com/InDepth/archive/199903/IND19990331c.html
8   "Sex Bias in the U.S. Code," A Report of the U.S. Commission on Civil Rights, April 1977,
     p. 102.
9   Appellant's Opening Brief on Rehearing, *Kansas v. Limon*, No. 00-85898-A.
     http://www.aclu.org/FilesPDFs/ACF4B93.pdf
10   "Sex Assault Convictions May Be Thrown Out," *Family News in Focus*, September 25,
     2003. http://www.family.org/cforum/fnif/news/a0028075.cfm
11   "Kline Appears on National Talk Show," *Topeka-Capital Journal*, October 1, 2003.
     http://www.cjonline.com/stories/100103/leg_kline.shtml
12   *Commonwealth v. Charles Jaynes*, Docket 00-P-578, June 21, 2002.
     http://caselaw.lp.findlaw.com/scripts/getcase.pl?court=ma&vol=appslip/appJune02y&inv
     ol=1
13   Deroy Murdock, "No Boy Scouts: The ACLU Defends NAMBLA," *National Review On-
     line*, February 27, 2004.
     http://www.nationalreview.com/murdock/murdock200402270920.asp
14   Ibid.
15   "ACLU Defends Child Molester Group," *WorldNetDaily*, December 13, 2000.
     http://www.worldnetdaily.com/news/article.asp?ARTICLE_ID=18029
16   "ACLU Asks Federal Judge to Dismiss Case Against Man-Boy Sex Group," Associated
     Press, July 18, 2001.
     http://www.freedomforum.org/templates/document.asp?documentID=14432
17   "Parents of Murdered Child Sue Child-Sex Advocates," *CNN*, January 8, 2001.
     http://archives.cnn.com/2001/LAW/01/08/nambla.suit.crim/
18   *Curley v. NAMBLA*, *Wikipedia*, March 21, 2006.
     http://en.wikipedia.org/wiki/Curley_v._NAMBLA
19   Brief for the Petitioners, *Ashcroft v. Free Speech Coalition*, submitted by Former Acting Solic-
     itor General Barbara D. Underwood, April 2001.
     http://www.usdoj.gov/osg/briefs/2000/3mer/2mer/2000-0795.mer.aa.pdf
20   W. L. Marshall, "The Use of Sexually Explicit Stimuli by Rapists, Child Molesters, and
     Nonoffenders," *The Journal of Sex Research 25*, no.2 (May 1988): 267-88.
21   "Let's Fight This Terrible Crime Against Our Children," *Parade Magazine*, February 16,
     2006.
     http://www.parade.com/articles/editions/2006/edition_02-19-2006/Andrew_Vachss
22   ACLU Brief, *Ashcroft v. Free Speech Coalition*, No. 00-795.
     http://www.aclu.org/FilesPDFs/ACF8690.pdf
23   "Supreme Court Strikes Down Ban on 'Virtual Child Porn,'" *CNN Law Center*, April 18,
     2002.
     http://archives.cnn.com/2002/LAW/04/16/scotus.virtual.child.porn/
24   *Ashcroft v. Free Speech Coalition*, No. 00-795, U.S. Supreme Court, April 16, 2002.
     http://supct.law.cornell.edu/supct/pdf/00-795P.ZO
25   Matthew Sostrin, "Private Writings and the First Amendment: The Case of Brian Dalton,"
     University of Illinois Law Review, September 9, 2003, pp. 887-912.
     http://home.law.uiuc.edu/lrev/publications/2000s/2003/2003_3/sostrin.pdf
26   "Court Reverses Ohio Man's 11-Year Prison Term for Sexually Explicit Diary," ACLU Press
     Release, March 5, 2004.

http://www.aclu.org/freespeech/gen/11213prs20040305.html
27   Ibid.
      http://www.aclu.org/freespeech/gen/11213prs20040305.html
28   Virginia Code § 35.1-18, Virginia General Assembly Statutes, 2004.
      http://leg1.state.va.us/cgi-bin/legp504.exe?000+cod+35.1-18
29   "ACLU Challenges Virginia Ban on Teen Nudist Camps," ACLU of Virginia Press Release,
      June 29, 2004. http://www.acluva.org/newsreleases2004/Jun29.html
30   "Appeals Court to Hear Arguments Tomorrow in Challenge to Law Banning Teen Nudist
      Camps," ACLU of Virginia Press Release, March 15, 2005.
      http://www.acluva.org/newsreleases2005/Mar15.html
31   *White Tail Park v. Stroube*, ACLU Opening Brief, November 15, 2004.
      http://www.acluva.org/docket/pleadings/whitetail_openingbrief.pdf
32   "ACLU Seeks to Reinstate Suit Over Teen Nudist Camp," *The Washington Times*, March
      17, 2005.
      http://www.washingtontimes.com/metro/20050316-102512-6855r.htm
33   *White Tail Park v. Stroube*, Fourth U.S. Circuit Court of Appeals, July 5, 2005.
      http://pacer.ca4.uscourts.gov/opinion.pdf/042002.P.pdf
34   Frank J. Murray, "Lifting of Ban on Sex Predator in Parks to Be Appealed," *The Washington
      Times*, July 2, 2003.
      http://www.washtimes.com/national/20030702-113116-8223r.htm
35   "Lafayette Can't Ban Sex Offender From Parks," *The Indianapolis Star*, June 28, 2003.
      http://www.indystar.com/print/articles/4/054015-1794-009.html
36   Frank J. Murray, "Lifting of Ban on Sex Predator in Parks to Be Appealed," *The Washington
      Times*, July 2, 2003.
      http://www.washtimes.com/national/20030702-113116-8223r.htm
37   *John Doe v. City of Lafayette*, No. 01-3624, 7th U.S. Circuit Court of Appeals, June 27,
      2003. http://caselaw.lp.findlaw.com/data2/circs/7th/013624p.pdf
38   Ibid.
39   "Child Molester Can Be Banned From City Parks," First Amendment Center, August 2,
      2004. http://www.fac.org/news.aspx?id=13811
40   Nicole Service, "Proposed City Ban Concerns ACLU," *The Daytona Beach News-Journal*,
      August 2, 2005.
      http://www.news-
      journalonline.com/special/sexualoffenders/03FlaglerFLAG01080205.htm
41   "ACLU Asks U.S. Supreme Court to Review Iowa's Sex Offender Residency Restriction,"
      ACLU Press Release, September 29, 2005.
      http://www.aclu.org/crimjustice/gen/20127prs20050929.html
42   "New Bills Target Released Sex Offenders," *The Times*, January 26, 2006.
      http://www.peopleforeddy.com/articles/1_31_06_target_offenders.pdf
43   "Coalition Letter to the House Urging Opposition to H.R. 2146, the 'Two Strikes You're
      Out Child Protection Act,'" ACLU Press Release, March 12, 2002.
      http://www.aclu.org/crimjustice/sentencing/10093leg20020312.html
44   "Uncompassionate Sex Offender Registration Impedes Individual's Efforts to Gain Educa-
      tion, Earn Honest Pay," ACLU of Louisiana, April 8, 2003.
      http://www.laaclu.org/News/2003/April%208%20Sex%20Offender%20Reg.html
45   Ibid.
46   "The Honorable Mark Foley Testimony Before the House Judiciary Subcommittee on
      Crime, Terrorism, and Homeland Security Hearing on The Sex Offender Registration and
      Notification Act (H.R. 2423)," U.S. House Committee on the Judiciary, June 9, 2005.
      http://judiciary.house.gov/HearingTestimony.aspx?ID=285
47   "Online Victimization: A Report on the Nation's Youth," National Center for Missing &
      Exploited Children, June 2000.
      http://www.missingkids.com/en_US/publications/NC62.pdf

48 "Sexual Violence: Fact Sheet," Centers for Disease Control, 2004. http://www.cdc.gov/ncipc/factsheets/svfacts.htm

49 U.S. Department of Education, Office of the Under Secretary, *Educator Sexual Misconduct: A Synthesis of Existing Literature*, Washington, D.C., 2004, p. 24. http://www.ed.gov/rschstat/research/pubs/misconductreview/index.html

50 "Understanding Child Sexual Abuse," The American Psychological Association, 2001. http://www.apa.org/releases/sexabuse/effects.html

51 "Bureau of Justice Statistics Bulletin: Women in Prison," U.S. Department of Justice, March 1994. http://www.ojp.usdoj.gov/bjs/pub/ascii/wopris.txt

52 Matthew 18:5-6 (NKJV)

Chapter Six

1   Tamar Lewin, "Untying the Knot: For Better or Worse: Marriage's Stormy Future," *The New York Times*, November 23, 2003.   http://www.nytimes.com/2003/11/23/weekinreview/23LEWI.html?ei=5035&en=1e400aeec892c652&ex=1155963600&adxnnl=1&partner=MARKETWATCH&adxnnlx=1143648321-MNPE2PBA5hzOXNYnilYRNA

2   Alan Sears and Craig Osten, *ACLU v. America: Exposing the Agenda to Redefine Moral Values*, Broadman and Holman Publishers, Nashville, Tennessee, 2005 p. 12-13.

3   Stanley Kurtz, "The End of Marriage in Scandinavia," *The Weekly Standard*, February 2, 2004.   http://www.weeklystandard.com/Content/Public/Articles/000/000/003/660zypwj.asp?pg=2

4   Ibid.

5   Ibid.

6   "Parliamentary Report on the Family and the Rights of Children," French National Assembly, January 26, 2006.   http://www.marriageinstitute.ca/images/PARLIAMENTARY%20REPORT%20ON%20THE%20FAMILY%20AND%20THE%20RIGHTS%20OF%20CHILDREN.pdf

7   Wade F. Horn, Ph.D. and Tom Sylvester, National Fatherhood Initiative, *Father Facts*, Fourth Edition, 2002. http://www.fatherhood.org/fatherfacts_t10.asp

8   "Same-Sex Marriage in the United States," *Wikipedia*, 2006. http://en.wikipedia.org/wiki/Same-sex_marriage_in_the_United_States

9   "Study Finds Gay Unions Brief," *The Washington Times*, July 11, 2003. http://www.washtimes.com/national/20030711-121254-3711r.htm

10 Ibid.

11 Ibid.

12 *Murphy v. Ramsey*, 114 U.S. 15, U.S. Supreme Court, March 23, 1885. http://caselaw.lp.findlaw.com/scripts/getcase.pl?navby=search&court=US&case=/us/114/15.html

13 "ACLU Cheers Massachusetts High Court Decision Not to Deny Same-Sex Couples Right to Marry," ACLU Press Release, November 18, 2003. http://www.aclu.org/lgbt/relationships/11935prs20031118.html

14 *Hillary Goodridge v. Department of Public Health*, SJC-08860, Massachusetts Supreme Judicial Court, November 18, 2003. http://www.lc.org/ProFamily/goodridge.pdf

15 Constitution of the Commonwealth of Massachusetts, Chapter III, Article 5. http://www.mass.gov/legis/const.htm

16 "Mass. Court Will Hear Arguments on Its Homosexual Marriage Decision," *CNS News*, February 11, 2005. http://www.cnsnews.com//ViewCulture.asp?Page=\Culture\archive\200502\CUL200502 11a.html

17 "Federal Court Strikes Down Nebraska's Anti-Gay-Union Law Banning Protections for Same-Sex Couples," ACLU Press Release, May 12, 2005. http://www.aclu.org/lgbt/relationships/12201prs20050512.html

18   "Lawsuits in 8 States Seek Same-Sex 'Marriage' Legalization," *Baptist Press,* July 21, 2004.
      http://www.bpnews.net/bpnews.asp?ID=18727
19   "ACLU Files Challenge to Misleading Arkansas 'Marriage' Ballot Initiative," ACLU Press
      Release, August 26, 2004.
      http://www.aclu.org/lgbt/relationships/12395prs20040826.html
20   "Six Same-Sex Couples Urge Florida Supreme Court to Strike Initiative Threatening Fami-
      lies of Same-Sex Couples," ACLU Press Release, February 28, 2006.
      http://www.aclu.org/lgbt/relationships/24103prs20060208.html
21   "ACLU of Tennessee Files Lawsuit Challenging State Amendment Banning Marriages for
      Same-Sex Couples," ACLU Press Release, April 21, 2005.
      http://www.aclu.org/lgbt/relationships/12233prs20050421.html
22   "ACLU and the History of LGBT Rights & HIV/AIDS," ACLU Press Release, March 16,
      2006. http://www.aclu.org/lgbt/gen/24578res20060316.html
23   "Marriage in the 50 States," The Heritage Foundation, 2006.
      http://www.heritage.org/Research/Family/Marriage50/Marriage50States.cfm
24   Ibid.
25   S.J. 30, The Marriage Protection Amendment, Introduced by Senator Allard.
      http://thomas.loc.gov/cgi-bin/query/z?c108:S.J.RES.30
26   "ACLU: Federal Marriage Amendment 'Harmful to Children,'" *CNS News,* July 13, 2004.
      http://www.cnsnews.com//ViewCulture.asp?Page=\Culture\archive\200407\CUL200407
      13a.html
27   "Federal Court Rules Against Nebraska's Marriage Amendment, *CNS News,* May 12, 2005.
      http://www.cnsnews.com/ViewCulture.asp?Page=%5CCulture%5Carchive%5C200505%5
      CCUL20050512b.html
28   "ACLU and Lambda Legal Urge Federal Court to Strike Down Nebraska Law Banning
      Recognition of Gay Couples," ACLU Press Release, October 15, 2004.
      http://www.aclu.org/lgbt/relationships/12417prs20041015.html
29   Ibid., "Federal Court Rules Against Nebraska's Marriage Amendment.
30   "Federal Court Strikes Down Nebraska's Anti-Gay-Union Law Banning Protections for
      Same-Sex Couples," ACLU Press Release, May 12, 2005.
      http://www.aclu.org/lgbt/relationships/12201prs20050512.html
31   Ibid., "Federal Court Rules Against Nebraska's Marriage Amendment.
32   *Citizens for Equal Protection v. Bruning,* No. 05-2604, the Eighth U.S. Circuit Court of
      Appeals, July 14, 2006. http://www.ca8.uscourts.gov/opndir/06/07/052604P.pdf
33   *Singer v. Hara,* Court of Appeals of Washington: Division One, May 20, 1974.
      http://qrd.org/qrd/usa/legal/singer-v-hara-05.20.74
34   Revised Code of Washington §26.04.010
      http://apps.leg.wa.gov/RCW/default.aspx?cite=26.04.010
35   Revised Code of Washington §26.04.020
      http://apps.leg.wa.gov/RCW/default.aspx?cite=26.04.020
36   "King County judge rules in favor of same-sex marriage," *Seattle Post-Intelligencer,* August
      4, 2004. http://seattletimes.nwsource.com/html/localnews/2001996456_webgaymar-
      riage04m.html
37   "Supreme Court to Rule on Marriage Equality," ACLU of Washington State, March 9,
      2005. http://www.aclu-wa.org/detail.cfm?id=88
38   *Castle v. State,* No. 04-2-00614-4, Washington State Superior Court Judge Richard D.
      Hicks, September 7, 2004.
      http://www.marriageequalityca.com/politics/court-cases/us/castle-vs-wa-state/castle-vs-
      state-opinion.pdf
39   Opening Brief in *Castle v. State,* No. 75934-1, ACLU of Washington, February 15, 2005.
      http://www.aclu-wa.org/library_files/Castle%20Corrected%20Brief%20of%20Respon-
      dents.pdf
40   *Andersen v. King County,* No. 75934-1, Supreme Court of Washington, July 26, 2006.

http://seattlepi.nwsource.com/dayart/pdf/andersenvking.pdf

41 Defense of Marriage Act, Public Law 104-199, Enacted September 21, 1996. http://frwebgate.access.gpo.gov/cgi-bin/getdoc.cgi?dbname=104_cong_public_laws&docid=f:publ199.104.pdf

42 Supplemental Brief in Support of Petitioner's Appeal, No. A95-076-067, U.S. Department of Justice Executive Office for Immigration Review, ACLU Foundation, December 16, 2004. http://www.aclu.org/FilesPDFs/lovolara_supbrief.pdf

43 "In re Jose Mauricio LOVO-Lara, Beneficiary of a Visa Petition Filed by Gia Teresa LOVO-Ciccone, Petitioner," Decision 746 (Board of Immigration Appeals), May 18, 2005. http://www.usdoj.gov/eoir/vll/intdec/vol23/3512%20.pdf

44 "Jury Trial Sought in Transsexual Case," *The Leavenworth Times*, April 1, 2004. http://www.leavenworthtimes.com/articles/2004/04/01/news/news06.txt

45 "Transsexual Arrested For Trying To Marry Partner," KMBC-TV, March 22, 2004. http://www.thekansascitychannel.com/news/2936700/detail.html

46 "ACLU Victor in Transgender Case," ACLU Press Release, November 30, 2004. http://www.acluozarks.org/news/gast_11_04.html

47 Edward Wheelan, "The Ginsburg Record and Standard," *The National Review*, July 26, 2005. http://www.nationalreview.com/whelan/whelan200507260753.asp

48 "ACLU of Utah to Join Polygamists in Bigamy Fight," ACLU Press Release, July 16, 1999. http://www.aclu.org/religion/frb/16163prs19990716.html

49 "Survey: 90 Percent of Utahans Want Crackdown on Crimes Within Polygamy," *Provo Daily Herald*, 2000. http://www.polygamyinfo.com/media%20plyg%20218herald.htm

50 "History of the Church of Jesus Christ of Latter-day Saints," Wikipedia, 2006. http://en.wikipedia.org/wiki/History_of_the_Church_of_Jesus_Christ_of_Latter-day_Saints

51 "Past Convention Highlights," *CNN*, 2000. http://www.cnn.com/ELECTION/2000/conventions/republican/features/convention.history/index.html

52 *United States v. Reynolds*, 98 U.S. 145, U.S. Supreme Court, October 1878. http://caselaw.lp.findlaw.com/scripts/getcase.pl?navby=search&court=US&case=/us/98/145.html

53 *Davis v. Beason*, 133 U.S. 333, U.S. Supreme Court, February 3, 1890. http://caselaw.lp.findlaw.com/scripts/getcase.pl?navby=search&court=US&case=/us/133/333.html

54 W. Jean Yeung, "Fathers: An Overlooked Resource for Children's Educational Success," New York University. http://www.nyu.edu/fas/cassr/yeung/yeung_after_the_bell.pdf

55 Wade F. Horn, Ph.D. and Tom Sylvester, National Fatherhood Initiative, *Father Facts*, Fourth Edition, 2002. http://www.fatherhood.org/fatherfacts_t10.asp

56 "A Blueprint for New Beginnings: A Responsible Budget for America's Priorities," U.S. Department of Health and Human Services: Fatherhood Initiative, February 28, 2001. http://fatherhood.hhs.gov/index.shtml

57 "Fatherhood Initiative," The U.S. Department of Health and Human Services, February 28, 2001. http://www.nationalreview.com/comment/comment-fumento050902.asp

58 "Gay Parenting Does Affect Children Differently, Study Finds," National Association for Research and Therapy of Homosexuality, September 21, 2004. http://www.narth.com/docs/does.html

59 *Lawrence v. Texas*, Human Rights Campaign Amicus Brief, No. 02-102, March 26, 2003, P. 16 (footnote 42). http://www.hrc.org/Content/NavigationMenu/HRC/Get_Informed/Issues/Privacy_Issues/Friend_of_Court_Brief_Summary.htm

60 Ibid., "Gay Parenting Does Affect Children Differently, Study Finds."

61 "Rosie O'Donnell—In Her Own Words," Concerned Women for America, April 3, 2002. http://www.cwfa.org/articles/579/CFI/cfreport/index.htm

62 "ACLU Challenges Florida Ban on Lesbian and Gay Adoption," ACLU Press Release, May 26, 1999. http://www.aclu.org/lgbt/parenting/11857prs19990526.html
63 Appellant's Brief, *Lofton v. Kearney*, No. 01-16723-DD, February 13, 2002. http://www.aclufl.org/pdfs/Lofton%20Appeals%20Brief.pdf
64 "ACLU Argues Case Challenging Florida's Gay Adoption Ban," ACLU Press Release, March 4, 2003. http://www.aclu.org/lgbt/parenting/12039prs20030304.html
65 *Lofton v. Secretary of the Department of Children and Family Services*, No. 01-16723, Eleventh U.S. Circuit Court of Appeals, January 28, 2004. http://www.ca11.uscourts.gov/opinions/ops/200116723.pdf
66 Charles Lane, "Gay-Adoption Ban in Florida to Stand," *Washington Post*, January 11, 2005. http://www.washingtonpost.com/wp-dyn/articles/A62672-2005Jan10.html
67 "Drives to Ban Gay Adoption Heat Up in 16 States," *USA Today*, February 20, 2006. http://www.usatoday.com/news/nation/2006-02-20-gay-adoption_x.htm
68 "Supreme Court to Hear Lesbian Custody Petition," *The Gay & Lesbian Times*, September 9, 2004. http://www.gaylesbiantimes.com/?id=3377&issue=872
69 *Tina Birch v. Paul Smarr*, No. 31855, Justice Benjamin Dissenting, August 8, 2005. http://www.state.wv.us/wvsca/docs/spring05/31855c2.pdf
70 "ACLU Applauds Child Custody Award for Surviving Lesbian Mom in West Virginia," ACLU Press Release, June 17, 2005. http://www.aclu.org/lgbt/parenting/12242prs20050617.html
71 "Washington Appeals Court Allows Non-Biological Mother in Same-Sex Relationship to Seek Parental Rights After Breakup, ACLU Press Release, May 4, 2004. http://www.aclu.org/lgbt/parenting/12083prs20040504.html
72 State of the Union Address, President Theodore Roosevelt, December 3, 1906. http://www.reclaimamerica.org/download/ProtectingMarriage.pdf

Chapter Seven

1   "Supreme Court to Revisit Child Porn Law," Interview with Ann Beeson, *The Washington Post*, October 14, 2003. http://www.washingtonpost.com/ac2/wp-dyn/A24167-2003Oct14?language=printer
2   "Generation M: Media in the Lives of 8-18 Year-Olds," Kaiser Family Foundation, Executive Summary, March 2005, p. 6. http://www.kff.org/entmedia/upload/Executive-Summary-Generation-M-Media-in-the-Lives-of-8-18-Year-olds.pdf
3   "Sexuality, Contraception, and the Media," *Pediatrics*, American Academy of Pediatrics, Volume 107, January 2001, p. 191-194. http://pediatrics.aappublications.org/cgi/content/full/107/1/191
4   "Generation M: Media in the Lives of 8-18 Year-Olds," Kaiser Family Foundation, Executive Summary, March 2005, p. 19. http://www.kff.org/entmedia/upload/Executive-Summary-Generation-M-Media-in-the-Lives-of-8-18-Year-olds.pdf
5   Ibid.
6   George Raine, "Annual Ad Spending Exceeds $141 Billion," *San Francisco Chronicle*, March 10, 2005. http://www.sfgate.com/cgi-bin/article.cgi?f=/c/a/2005/03/10/BUG7TBN0JP1.DTL
7   Ibid.,"Sexuality, Conception, and the Media" http://pediatrics.aappublications.org/cgi/content/full/107/1/191
8   "Teen Sex Linked to Racy TV Programs," *MSNBC*, September 7, 2004. http://www.msnbc.msn.com/id/5930891/
9   Ibid., "Sexuality, Contraception, and the Media."
10 "Number of Sexual Scenes on TV Nearly Double Since 1998," The Kaiser Family Foundation, November 9, 2005. http://www.kff.org/entmedia/entmedia110905nr.cfm

11   "Notice of Apparent Liability for Forfeiture," Federal Communications Commission, March 15, 2006. http://hraunfoss.fcc.gov/edocs_public/attachmatch/FCC-06-18A1.pdf

12   "Janet Jackson's Super Bowl Show Promises 'Shocking Moments'" *MTV News*, January 28, 2004. http://www.mtv.com/news/articles/1484644/20040128/jackson_janet.jhtml?headlines=true

13   "Jackson Overexposure: TV Feels Heat," *CNN*, February 5, 2004. http://www.cnn.com/2004/SHOWBIZ/TV/02/05/superbowl.jackson/

14   "FCC Chair 'Outraged' by Breast Stunt," *World Net Daily*, February 2, 2004. http://www.worldnetdaily.com/news/article.asp?ARTICLE_ID=36894

15   "FCC Chief Blasts Jackson Halftime Show," *Fox News*, February 2, 2004. http://www.foxnews.com/story/0,2933,110114,00.html

16   Mark Rahner, "FCC Indecency Fight Chilling Free Speech?" *The Seattle Times*, April 24, 2004. http://seattletimes.nwsource.com/html/localnews/2001911494_fcc24.html

17   "FCC Acknowledges Hundreds of Thousands Who Have Complained About Super Bowl Halftime Show," Federal Communications Commission, February 6, 2004. http://hraunfoss.fcc.gov/edocs_public/attachmatch/DOC-243648A1.pdf

18   Geraldine Fabrikant, "CBS Is Fined $550,000 for Super Bowl Incident," *The New York Times*, September 23, 2004 http://www.nytimes.com/2004/09/23/business/media/23fine.html?ex=1144382400&en=3bdc51bf8ae8e17d&ei=5070

19   "Poll: Parents Want Feds to Tame TV," *CBS News*, September 23, 2004. http://www.cbsnews.com/stories/2004/09/23/entertainment/main645195.shtml

20   "ACLU Letter to the House Subcommittee on Telecommunications and the Internet Expressing Concerns About H.R. 3717, the Broadcast Decency Enforcement Act of 2004," ACLU Press Release, February 10, 2004. http://www.aclu.org/freespeech/commercial/10964leg20040210.html

21   "House Passes Indecency Bill," *The Christian Post*, June 8, 2006. http://www.christianpost.com/article/culture/1765/section/house.passes.indecency.bill.christians.celebrate/1.htm

22   "Protecting Freedom in Perilous Times: The ACLU's Legislative Advocacy in the 108th Congress," ACLU Washington Legislative Office, January 2005. http://www.aclu.org/FilesPDFs/protecting%20freedom%20in%20perilous%20times.pdf

23   "ACLU Joins Media Giants and Performers in Asking FCC to Reconsider Indecency Ruling on Bono Remark," ACLU Press Release, April 19, 2004. http://www.aclu.org/freespeech/gen/11196prs20040419.html

24   "FCC OK's Bono's F-Word Slip," *CBS News*, October 7, 2003. http://www.cbsnews.com/stories/2003/09/17/entertainment/main573729.shtml

25   "FCC Flip-Flops On Bono F-Word," *CBS News*, March 12, 2004. http://www.cbsnews.com/stories/2004/02/25/tech/main602251.shtml

26   "FCC Indecency Enforcement Called Confusing, Burdensome," *CNS News*, January 12, 2005. http://www.cnsnews.com/ViewSpecialReports.asp?Page=%5CSpecialReports%5Carchive%5C200501%5CSPE20050112a.html

27   "4 TV Networks Challenge FCC on Indecency," *Los Angeles Times*, April 6, 2006. http://www.latimes.com/news/printedition/front/la-fi-indecency15apr15,1,4085491,full.story?coll=la-headlines-frontpage

28   David Hudson, "Distributor Asks State High Court to End Prohibition of 'Vulgar' Beer Label," *The Freedom Forum*, November 9, 2000. http://www.freedomforum.org/templates/document.asp?documentID=3554

29   "Brewery Gets Go-Ahead to Use Once-Banned Label," *Freedom Forum*, April 11, 2001. http://www.freedomforum.org/templates/document.asp?documentID=13656

30   Gordon Y.K. Pang, "ACLU Sues City Over Nude Art," *The Honolulu Star*, August 15,

2001. http://starbulletin.com/2001/08/15/news/story7.html

31 Rosemarie Bernardo, "City Allows Display of Banned Nude Art," *The Honolulu Star*, March 7, 2002. http://starbulletin.com/2002/03/07/news/story3.html

32 "Federal Court Prohibits State From Blocking Protest Involving 'Living Nude Peace Symbol,'" ACLU of Florida News Release, February 13, 2003. http://www.aclufl.org/news_events/archive/2003/natureprotest021303.cfm

33 *Wyner v. Struhs*, U.S. District Court for the Southern District of Florida, February 13, 2003. http://www.aclufl.org/pdfs/Peace_Symbol_preliminary_injunction.pdf

34 "Children's Internet Protection Act: FCC Consumer Facts," Federal Communications Commission, January 12, 2006. http://www.fcc.gov/cgb/consumerfacts/cipa.html

35 U.S. Senate Roll Call, 106th Congress/2nd Session, Vote 149, June 27, 2000. http://www.senate.gov/legislative/LIS/roll_call_lists/roll_call_vote_cfm.cfm?congress=106&session=2&vote=00149

36 Plaintiffs' Joint Pretrial Brief, ACLU, *Multnomah County Public Library v. United States*, Civil Action No. 01-CV-1322, March 20, 2002. http://www.aclu.org/FilesPDFs/multnomah_pretrial_brief.pdf

37 *United States v. American Library Association*, No. 02-361. U.S. Supreme Court, June 23, 2003. http://www.supremecourtus.gov/opinions/02pdf/02-361.pdf

38 "Losing It—All About Virginity," Teenwire.com, April 13, 2004. http://www.teenwire.com/infocus/2004/if-20040413p282-virginity.php

39 "Are You Experienced," Teenwire Website, June 8, 2004. http://www.teenwire.com/infocus/2004/if-20040608p296-experience.php

40 "Ask the Experts: Does Swallowing Sperm Make You Fat," Teenwire.com, October 9, 2003. http://www.teenwire.com/ask/2003/as-20031009p660-semen.php

41 Ibid.

42 "Ask the Experts: How to Give Oral Sex, Teenwire.com, July 10, 2001. http://www.teenwire.com/ask/2001/as-20010710p244.php

43 "Ask The Experts: How to Enjoy Anal Sex, Teenwire.com, April 25, 2003. http://www.teenwire.com/ask/2003/as-20030425p552-anal.php

44 "Ask the Experts: What Happens to Semen After Sodomy, Teenwire.com, October 6, 2005. http://www.teenwire.com/ask/2005/as-20051006p1129-anus.php

45 Maggie Gallagher, "South Dakota Library Removing Abortion Link Causes Controversy," *Life News*, July 22, 2004. http://www.lifenews.com/state650.html

46 *Ashcroft v. ACLU*, No. 00-1293, ACLU Brief for the Respondents, U.S. Supreme Court. http://www.aclu.org/FilesPDFs/aclu_v_ashcroft_1_brief.pdf

47 "Supreme Court to Revisit Child Porn Law," Interview with Ann Beeson, *The Washington Post*, October 14, 2003. http://www.washingtonpost.com/ac2/wp-dyn/A24167-2003Oct14?language=printer

48 *Ashcroft v. ACLU*, No. 03–218. U.S. Supreme Court, June 29, 2004. http://www.cdt.org/speech/copa/20040629copadecision.pdf

49 "Oregon's Unique Constitutional Protection of Free Expression Is Challenged," ACLU of Oregon, October 31, 2004. http://www.aclu-or.org/litigation/Oregon's%20Unique%20Constitutional.html

50 Oregon Revised Statute 167.062, Oregon State Legislature, 2003 Edition. http://www.leg.state.or.us/ors/167.html

51 *Oregon v. Ciancanelli*, Supreme Court of Oregon, September 29, 2005. http://www.publications.ojd.state.or.us/S49707.htm

52 "Preemptive State Smoke-Free Indoor Air Laws – United States, 1999—2004," Centers for Disease Control, March 18, 2005. http://www.cdc.gov/mmwr/preview/mmwrhtml/mm5410a4.htm

53 "Bill O'Reilly Comments on ACLU," *Jewish World Review*, October 17, 2005. http://www.jewishworldreview.com/cols/oreilly101705.asp

54 Ken Kusmer, "DOC Sued Over New Policy Barring Nude, Sexual Material," *Fort Wayne News Sentinel*, July 11, 2006.
http://www.fortwayne.com/mld/newssentinel/15015455.htm
55 "Indiana Inmates Sue for Porn Magazines," *Citizen Link*, July 13, 2006.
http://www.family.org/cforum/news/a0041225.cfm
56 *Barnes v. Glen Theatre, Inc.*, 501 U.S. 560, Supreme Court of the United States, June 21, 1991. http://caselaw.lp.findlaw.com/scripts/getcase.pl?court=US&vol=501&invol=560
57 *Paris Adult Theatre I v. Slaton*, 413 U.S. 49, Supreme Court of the United States, June 21, 1973. http://caselaw.lp.findlaw.com/scripts/getcase.pl?court=US&vol=413&invol=49
58 Penny Nance, "Predators & Pornography," *The National Review*, May 19, 2005.
https://www.nationalreview.com/comment/nance200505190815.asp

Chapter Eight

1 D. James Kennedy and Jerry Newcombe, *What If Jesus Had Never Been Born?*, Thomas Nelson Publishers, Nashville, Tennessee, 1994, p. 11.
2 Ibid.
3 "Standards for Life: Abortion," Christian Medical Association, 2006.
4 "The Death Toll of *Roe v. Wade*," The Family Research Council, 2003.
http://www.stthomasmore.org/pdf/RespectLife/DeathTollRoevWade.pdf
5 "Abortion in the United States: Statistics and Trends," National Right to Life, 2004.
http://www.nrlc.org/abortion/facts/abortionstats.html
6 "The ACLU And Women's Rights: Proud History, Continuing Struggle," ACLU Reproductive Rights Project, March 12, 2002.
http://www.aclu.org/womensrights/gen/13150res20020312.html
7 Ibid.
8 *Roe v. Wade*, 410 U.S. 113, U.S. Supreme Court, January 22, 1973.
http://caselaw.lp.findlaw.com/scripts/getcase.pl?court=US&vol=410&invol=113
9 Ibid.
10 Ibid.
11 Jan LaRue, "It's Time to Reject *Roe v. Wade* as Invincible Precedent," Concerned Women for America, November 22, 2005.
http://www.cwfa.org/articles/9491/LEGAL/scourt/index.htm
12 "Senators Launch 2nd Round of Questioning in Alito Confirmation Hearings," *CNN*, January 11, 2006. http://transcripts.cnn.com/TRANSCRIPTS/0601/11/se.01.html
13 Edward Lazarus, "Was Justice Blackmun Correct, or Is the Decision Still Troubling," Find Law, January 23, 2003. http://writ.news.findlaw.com/lazarus/20030123.html
14 "*Roe v. Wade* Abortion Case Was Poorly Reasoned," Traditional Values Coalition, December 8, 2005. http://www.traditionalvalues.org/modules.php?sid=2525
15 "Standards for Life: Abortion," Christian Medical Association, 2006.
16 Ibid.
17 Mother Teresa, "Notable and Quotable," *Wall Street Journal*, p. A14, February 25, 1994.
18 Kathryn Hooks, "Results of a Thirty Year Experiment on Women," The Beverly LaHaye Institute, July 23, 2003.
http://www.beverlylahayeinstitute.org/articledisplay.asp?id=4321&department=BLI&categoryid=dotcommentary
19 "Biased Counseling Against Abortion," The ACLU Reproductive Freedom Project, April 11, 2001.
http://www.aclu.org/reproductiverights/abortion/16402res20010411.html
20 Ibid.
21 "Report of the South Dakota Task Force to Study Abortion," South Dakota Task Force to Study Abortion, December 2005.
http://www.dakotavoice.com/Docs/South%20Dakota%20Abortion%20Task%20Force%20

Report.pdf
22   "Laws Restricting Teenagers' Access to Abortion," ACLU Reproductive Freedom Project, April 1, 2001.
      http://www.aclu.org/reproductiverights/youth/16388res20010401.html
23   "Poll: Americans Back Abortion Limits, Oppose Ban," CNN, November 27, 2005.
      http://www.cnn.com/2005/US/11/27/abortion.poll/index.html
24   "Laws Requiring Parental Consent or Notification for Minors' Abortions," Planned Parenthood, June 2006.
      http://www.plannedparenthood.org/pp2/portal/files/portal/medicalinfo/abortion/fact-parental-consent.xml
25   "Florida Supreme Court Denies Motion Overturning Abortion Notification Vote," *Life News*, January 13, 2005.
      http://www.lifenews.com/state839.html
26   "In A Victory for Privacy Rights, Florida Supreme Court Strikes Down Parental Notification Law," ACLU News Release, July 10, 2003.
      http://www.aclu.org/reproductiverights/youth/16434prs20030710.html
27   Florida Statute 877.04 (3)
28   Florida Statute 381.0075 (7)
29   Florida Statute 985.03 (25a)
30   Florida Statute 743.0645 (4)
31   *North Florida Women's Health and Counseling Services, v. State of Florida*, No. SC01-843, Florida Supreme Court, July 10, 2003.
      http://www.floridasupremecourt.org/decisions/pre2004/ops/sc01-843.pdf
32   Ibid.
33   "Florida Voters Approve Parental Notice Amendment," *The Florida Baptist Witness*, November 4, 2004. http://www.floridabaptistwitness.com/3442.article
34   PATH Project: Providing Access to Teen Health, Homepage, 2006.
      http://www.pathproject.net/
35   "The American Civil Liberties Union of Florida Launches Teen Health Website, Toll-free Legal Helpline," ACLU of Florida News Release, March 16, 2006.
      http://www.aclufl.org/news_events/index.cfm?action=viewRelease&emailAlertID=1728
36   "Using Illegal Street Drugs During Pregnancy," The American Pregnancy Association, 2006.
      http://www.americanpregnancy.org/pregnancyhealth/illegaldrugs.html
37   "Leading MD Physicians, Drug Treatment Providers, and Public Health Advocates Condemn Prosecution of Pregnant Woman," ACLU Media Advisory, July 19, 2005.
      http://www.aclu-md.org/aPress/Press%202005/71905_Cruz.html
38   *Kelly Lynn Cruz v. Maryland*, No. 1478, ACLU of Maryland Amicus Brief, November 29, 2005. http://www.aclu-md.org/aPress/PJC_Amicus_Brief_FINAL.pdf
39   "ACLU of Maryland Declares Victory as High Court Unanimously Rules Pregnancy Prosecutions Are Illegal," ACLU News Release, August 3, 2006.
      http://www.aclu.org/privacy/medical/26389prs20060803.html
40   *Ward v. Texas, Smith v. Texas*, ACLU Brief of Amicus Curiae, Seventh Circuit Court of Appeals of Texas, April 18, 2005. http://www.aclu.org/pdfs/rfp_ward_amicus_brief.pdf
41   Texas Health and Safety Code, Texas Controlled Substance Act, 481.122.
42   *Ward v. Texas, Smith v. Texas*, ACLU Brief of Amicus Curiae, Seventh Circuit Court of Appeals of Texas, April 18, 2005. http://www.aclu.org/pdfs/rfp_ward_amicus_brief.pdf
43   "ACLU Applauds Court Decision Reversing Conviction Denying Pregnant Women in Texas Their Rights" ACLU News Release, March 30, 2006.
      http://www.aclu.org/reproductiverights/fetalrights/24836prs20060330.html
44   "Clinton Claims on Partial-Birth Abortion *Still* Not True – Not Even 'Legally Accurate,'" U.S. Senate Republican Policy Committee, September 15, 1998.
      http://www.senate.gov/~rpc/releases/1998/partial-birth.htm

45 Dr. D. James Kennedy, *Today's Conflict, Tomorrow's Crisis*, Coral Ridge Ministries, Fort Lauderdale, Florida, 2000, p. 181.

46 "Clinton Claims on Partial-Birth Abortion *Still* Not True – Not Even 'Legally Accurate,'" U.S. Senate Republican Policy Committee, September 15, 1998. http://www.senate.gov/~rpc/releases/1998/partial-birth.htm

47 "Abortion Bans: An Affront to Women's Health and Rights," ACLU Website, 2006. http://www.aclu.org/reproductiverights/abortionbans/index.html

48 ACLU Amicus Brief filed with the Supreme Court of the United States, *Stenberg v. Carhart*, No. 99-830, March 29, 2000, p. 184. http://www.aclu.org/scotus/1999/22416lgl19990329.html

49 Ibid.

50 *Stenberg v. Carhart*, No. 99-830, Supreme Court of the United States, June 28, 2000. http://www.law.cornell.edu/supct/pdf/99-830P.ZO

51 *Stenberg v. Carhart*, Justice Antonin Scalia's Dissenting Opinion, No. 99-830, Supreme Court of the United States, June 28, 2000. http://www.law.cornell.edu/supct/pdf/99-830P.ZD1

52 Amy Fagan, "Senate Targets Abortion Method," *The Washington Times*, October 22, 2003. http://www.washtimes.com/national/20031021-112742-9765r.htm

53 "President Bush Signs Partial Birth Abortion Ban Act of 2003," The White House Press Release, November 5, 2003. http://www.whitehouse.gov/news/releases/2003/11/20031105-1.html

54 "Groups Sue to Block Abortion Procedure Ban," *CNN Law Center*, December 17, 2003. http://www.cnn.com/2003/LAW/11/01/abortion.lawsuit/index.html

55 "U.S. Judges Block Ban on Late-Term Abortions, Rulings in S.F., N.Y. Come One Day After Bush Signed Law," *The San Francisco Chronicle*, November 7, 2003. http://www.sfgate.com/cgi-bin/article.cgi?file=/c/a/2003/11/07/MNG4Q2SGC81.DTL

56 Transcripts from *National Abortion Federation v. Ashcroft*, Southern District Court of New York, March 30, 2004. http://www.aclj.org/media/pdf/NYhighlightsPBADoc.pdf

57 Transcripts from *National Abortion Federation v. Ashcroft*, Southern District Court of New York, March 30, 2004. http://www.aclj.org/media/pdf/NYhighlightsPBADoc.pdf

58 "CWA Says Nebraska Judge Is Partial to Abortionists," Concerned Women for America, September 8, 2004. http://www.cwfa.org/articledisplay.asp?id=6326&department=MEDIA&categoryid=life

59 "President Bush Signs Partial Birth Abortion Ban Act of 2003," The White House Press Release, November 5, 2003. http://www.whitehouse.gov/news/releases/2003/11/20031105-1.html

60 "D. James Kennedy Responds to Ruling on Partial-Birth Abortion," Coral Ridge Ministries Press Release, August 26, 2004. http://www.coralridge.org/specialdocs/PR_CaseyPartialBirthAbortionUnconstitutional.htm

61 Bill Mears, "Justices Tackle Late-Term Abortion Issue," *CNN*, February 28, 2006. http://www.cnn.com/2006/LAW/02/21/scotus.latetermabortion/index.html

62 Ibid.

63 "Joint Consideration: Abortion Funding," U.S. Department of Health and Human Services, February 26, 1982. http://www.hhs.gov/dab/decisions/dab260.html

64 "Public Funding for Abortion," ACLU Position Statement, July 21, 2004. http://www.aclu.org/reproductiverights/lowincome/16393res20040721.html

65 *Feminist Women's Health Center v. Burgess*, ACLU's Memorandum of Law in Support of Plaintiff's Motion for a Temporary Restraining Order and Preliminary Injunction, December 2003. http://www.acluga.org/briefs/abortions.pdf

66 Ibid.

67 "ACLU Seeks Order to Fund Medically Necessary Abortions Under Medicaid," Associated

Press, December 2003.

http://www.accessnorthga.com/news/ap_newfullstory.asp?ID=27295

68   "Public Funding for Abortion: Medicaid and the Hyde Amendment," National Abortion Federation, 2006.

http://www.prochoice.org/pubs_research/publications/downloads/about_abortion/public_funding.pdf

69   Francis Schaeffer, *The Great Evangelical Disaster*, Crossway, 1984.

70   "High Court Rejects Constitutional Right to Doctor-Assisted Suicide," ACLU Press Release, June 26, 1997.

http://www.aclu.org/scotus/1996/23013prs19970626.html

71   American Medical Association Code of Ethics, # E-2.211, June 1994.

http://www.ama-assn.org/ama/pub/category/8459.html

72   C. Everett Koop, Testimony Before the Vermont House Human Services Committee Concerning the Rights of Mentally Competent Patients Suffering a Terminal Condition, April 14, 2005.

http://www.vaeh.org/resources/VT-HHS-Testimony-2005-04.doc

73   *Washington v. Glucksberg*, No. 96-110, U.S. Supreme Court, June 26, 1997.

http://www.law.cornell.edu/supct/html/96-110.ZS.html

74   Ibid.

75   *Gonzales v. Oregon*, No. 04-623, Supreme Court of the United States, January 17, 2006.

http://www.supremecourtus.gov/opinions/05pdf/04-623.pdf

76   "Brief of the ACLU and the ACLU of Oregon as Amici Curiae in Support of Respondents," American Civil Liberties Union, July 2005.

http://www.aclu.org/images/asset_upload_file516_21277.pdf

77   "Privacy Issue Is Central to Oregon's Assisted-Suicide Law But Is Not Defined in U.S. Constitution," Death With Dignity National Center, October 3, 2005.

http://www.deathwithdignity.org/news/news/statesmanjournal.10.03.05.asp

78   *Gonzales v. Oregon*, Supreme Court of the United States, January 17, 2006.

http://www.law.cornell.edu/supct/pdf/04-623P.ZD

79   "'Euthanasia' and T-4," *The Holocaust Chronicle*, 2002.

http://www.holocaustchronicle.org/staticpages/169.html

80   "National Sanctity of Human Life Day, 2002," The White House, January 18, 2002.

http://www.whitehouse.gov/news/releases/2002/01/20020118-10.html

Chapter Nine

1   John Perazzo, "*The New York Times*-ACLU War on National Security," *FrontPage Magazine*, December 21, 2005.

http://www.frontpagemag.com/Articles/ReadArticle.asp?ID=20630

2   "Man of the Year: The Mystic Who Lit the Fires of Hatred," *Time*, January 7, 1980.

http://www.library.cornell.edu/colldev/mideast/1979.htm

3   "All Jihad All the Time," *The Weekly Standard*, January 30, 2006.

http://www.weeklystandard.com/Content/Public/Articles/000/000/006/576bjtmp.asp

4   "Address to a Joint Session of Congress and the American People," The White House, September 20, 2001.

http://www.whitehouse.gov/news/releases/2001/09/20010920-8.html

5   "Significant Terrorist Incidents, 1961-2003: A Brief Chronology," U.S. Department of State, March 2004.

http://www.state.gov/r/pa/ho/pubs/fs/5902.htm

6   *Hamdi v. Rumsfeld*, No. 03-6696, Supreme Court of the United States, June 28, 2004.

http://www.supremecourtus.gov/opinions/03pdf/03-6696.pdf

7   "Financial Anti-Terrorism Act of 2001," Library of Congress, October 17, 2001.

http://thomas.loc.gov/cgi-bin/query/C?c107:./temp/~c107qfJOZd

8   "Letter to the House Urging Opposition to the 'Financial Anti-Terrorism Act of 2001'; the
     Oxley Bill," ACLU Press Release, October 16, 2001.
     http://www.aclu.org/natsec/emergpowers/14411leg20011016.html
9   Representative Michael Oxley, "Financial Anti-Terrorism Act of 2001, October 26, 2001.
     http://thomas.loc.gov/cgi-bin/bdquery/z?d107:HR03004:@@@X
10   *Rumsfeld v. Padilla*, No. 03-1027, Supreme Court of the United States, June 28, 2004.
     http://www.supremecourtus.gov/opinions/03pdf/03-1027.pdf
11   *Rasul v. Bush*, No. 03-334, Supreme Court of the United States, June 28, 2004.
     http://www.supremecourtus.gov/opinions/03pdf/03-334.pdf
12   "A Mixed Verdict on the Terror War," *CNN News*, July 6, 2004.
     http://www.cnn.com/2004/LAW/06/28/scotus.terror.cases
13   "Wife of Solicitor General Alerted Him of Hijacking From Plane," *CNN News*, September
     12, 2001. http://archives.cnn.com/2001/US/09/11/pentagon.olson/
14   "Excerpts From Supreme Court Arguments on Detainees at Guantánamo," *The New York
     Times*, April 21, 2004.
     http://www.nytimes.com/2004/04/21/national/21STEX.html?ex=1139979600&en=c9
     bbcbd7907f0f8f&ei=5070
15   "Supreme Court Says Courts Can Review Bush Administration Actions in Terrorism Fight,"
     ACLU Press Release, June 28, 2004.
     http://www.aclu.org/safefree/detention/18470prs20040628.html
16   "Petition to the United Nations Working Group on Arbitrary Detention," ACLU Press Re-
     lease, January 27, 2004.
     http://www.aclu.org/FilesPDFs/complaint.final.012704.pdf
17   "Organizers of the September 11, 2001, Attacks," *Wikipedia Encyclopedia*, February 7,
     2006.
     http://en.wikipedia.org/wiki/Organizers_of_the_September_11,_2001_attacks
18   "ACLU Files Complaint with United Nations in Geneva Seeking Justice for Immigrants
     Detained and Deported after 9/11," ACLU Press Release, January 27, 2004.
     http://www.aclu.org/safefree/general/16908prs20040127.html
19   "Rights Body Harshly Criticizes U.S. Human Rights Record," ACLU News Release, July
     18, 2006.
     http://www.aclu.org/intlhumanrights/gen/26167prs20060718.html
20   "Treason," *American Heritage Dictionary of the English Language*, 2000.
     http://dictionary.reference.com/search?q=treason
21   "United Nations Security Council Meeting #4971," United Nations Press Release, May 19,
     2004. http://www.un.org/News/Press/docs/2004/sc8097.doc.htm
22   "Abu Ghraib Torture and Prisoner Abuse, *Wikipedia Encyclopedia*, February 14, 2006.
     http://en.wikipedia.org/wiki/Abu_Ghraib_prisoner_abuse
23   "Defense Department Files Secret Arguments in Further Attempt to Suppress Abu Ghraib
     Photos," ACLU Press Release, July 29, 2005.
     http://www.aclu.org/safefree/detention/20250prs20050729.html
24   "Judge: Release Abu Ghraib Photos," *Fox News*, September 29, 2005.
     http://www.foxnews.com/story/0,2933,170796,00.html
25   *ACLU v. Department of Defense*, U.S. District Court of Southern New York, September 29,
     2005. http://www.nysd.uscourts.gov/courtweb/pdf/D02NYSC/05-05912.PDF
26   "Federal Court Orders Government to Turn Over Videos and Photos Showing Detainees
     Abuse," ACLU Press Release, June 2, 2005.
     http://www.aclu.org/safefree/general/17637prs20050602.html
27   "Utopia's Victims," The Claremont Institute, November 24, 2003.
     http://www.claremont.org/writings/crb/winter2003/alexander.html
28   "Freedom in the U.S.A. and the U.S.S.R.," *The Soviet Russia Today*, September 1934.
     http://www.law.ucla.edu/volokh/blog/baldwin.pdf
29   "Roger Nash Baldwin," Wikipedia Encyclopedia, February 6, 2006.

http://en.wikipedia.org/wiki/Roger_Nash_Baldwin

30   "Bombers Target London," *CNN News*, July 2005.
      `http://www.cnn.com/SPECIALS/2005/london.bombing/

31   "In New Security Move, New York Police to Search Commuters' Bags," *The New York Times*, July 21, 2005. http://www.nytimes.com/2005/07/21/nyregion/21cnd-security.html?ex=1279598400&en=63c8013bebf1fce7&ei=5088&partner=rssnyt&emc=rss

32   "NYCLU Sues New York City Over Subway Bag Search Policy," ACLU Press Release, August 4, 2005. http://www.nyclu.org/mta_searches_suit_pr_080405.html

33   "The Right Way to Profile in NYC," *Front Page Magazine*, August 17, 2005. http://www.frontpagemag.com/Articles/ReadArticle.asp?ID=19163

34   "CAIR-NY Rep Discusses Profiling on MSNBC's *Hardball*," Council on American Islamic Relations, August 5, 2005.
      http://www.cair-net.org/default.asp?Page=articleView&id=37375&theType=NB

35   "Judge OKs Random Police Bag Searches on NYC Subway," *The Boston Globe*, December 2, 2005.
      http://www.boston.com/news/nation/articles/2005/12/02/judge_oks_random_police_bag_searches_on_nyc_subway/

36   "Feds Agree to Pay ACLU Over No Fly List," *ABC News*, January 24, 2006.
      http://abcnews.go.com/US/wireStory?id=1538342&CMP=OTC-RSSFeeds0312

37   "Statement of Timothy D. Sparapani," ACLU Press Release, February 9, 2006.
      http://www.aclu.org/safefree/general/24113leg20060209.html

38   "ACLU and Diverse Coalition of National Non-Profits Win Major Victory in Challenge to Misguided CFC Government Watch List and Contribution Policies," ACLU Press Release, November 9, 2005. http://www.aclu.org/natsec/emergpowers/21264prs20051109.html

39   *ACLU v. National Security Agency*, Complaint for Declaratory and Injunctive Relief, January 17, 2006. http://www.aclu.org/images/nsaspying/asset_upload_file137_23491.pdf

40   "Gonzales Defends NSA Wiretaps," *Fox News*, February 7, 2006.
      http://www.foxnews.com/story/0,2933,183902,00.html

41   "National Security Agency," *Rasmussen Reports*, December 28, 2005.
      http://www.rasmussenreports.com/2005/NSA.htm

42   Gadhafi: Islam Taking Over Europe," *WorldNetDaily*, May 3, 2006.
      http://www.worldnetdaily.com/news/article.asp?ARTICLE_ID=50020

43   "Madrid Train Station Blasts Kill 190," *Fox News*, March 11, 2004.
      http://www.foxnews.com/printer_friendly_story/0,3566,113887,00.html

44   "Gunman Kills Dutch Film Director," *BBC News*, November 2, 2004.
      http://www.bbc.co.uk/go/pr/fr/-/1/hi/world/europe/3974179.stm

45   "London Death Toll Rises to 52," *The Guardian Unlimited*, July 11, 2005.
      http://www.guardian.co.uk/attackonlondon/story/0,16132,1525961,00.html

46   "Iranian President Calls for Israel's Destruction: Responses From World Leaders," Anti-Defamation League, October 27, 2005.
      http://www.adl.org/main_Anti_Semitism_International/iran_responses.htm

47   "France Lifts State of Emergency," *BBC News*, January 4, 2006.
      http://www.bbc.co.uk/go/pr/fr/-/2/hi/europe/4576430.stm

48   "The Cartoon That Shook the World," *WorldNetDaily*, February 5, 2006.
      http://www.worldnetdaily.com/news/article.asp?ARTICLE_ID=48674

49   "Joint Statement by the Secretary General of the United Nations, the Secretary General of the Organization of the Islamic Conference and the High Representative for Common Foreign and Security Policy of the European Union," United Nations Press Release, February 7, 2006.
      http://ue.eu.int/ueDocs/cms_Data/docs/pressdata/EN/declarations/88344.pdf#search=%22%22damage%20the%20image%20of%20a%20peaceful%20Islam%22%22

Chapter Ten

1   "Guardians Of Freedom," The ACLU Website, July 2006.
      http://www.aclu.org/about/faqs/21419res20051115.html
2   "American Civil Liberties Union Foundation, Inc.," The Capital Research Center, 2006.
      http://www.capitalresearch.org/search/orgdisplay.asp?Org=ACL100#grant
3   "About Us," ACLU Website, July 2006. http://www.aclu.org/about/
4   *Florida Bar Foundation: Annual Report 2003-2004*, The Florida Bar Foundation, June 30,
      2004. http://www.flabarfndn.org/communication/fbf2004a.pdf
5   The Florida Bar Foundation Articles of Incorporation, The Florida Bar Foundation, June 8,
      2004. http://flabarfndn.org/governance/incorp.asp
6   Letter Regarding the Foundation Grants to the American Civil Liberties Union Foundation
      of Florida, Florida Bar Foundation, September 25, 2003.
      http://www.reclaimamerica.org/download/FLBarFndn.pdf
7   "Planned Parenthood and ACLU Hail Florida Appeals Court Decision Striking Down Law
      that Would Have Forced Physicians to Give Patients Irrelevant Information, ACLU News
      Release, October 13, 2004.
      http://www.aclu.org/reproductiverights/medical/12731prs20041013.html
8   "In a Victory for Privacy Rights, Florida Supreme Court Strikes Down Parental Notification
      Law," ACLU of Florida Press Release, July 10, 2003.
      http://www.aclufl.org/news_events/archive/2003/parentalrights071003.cfm
9   "Hearing Set for Court Challenge to Florida's Ban on Medicaid-Funded Abortions,"
      ACLU of Florida News Release, June 16, 2003.
      http://www.aclufl.org/news_events/archive/2003/medicaiddcahearing.cfm
10   "ACLU Says Florida's Proposed Marriage Ban Threatens Health Benefits for Thousands of
      Families in Florida," ACLU of Florida, April 6, 2005.
      http://www.aclufl.org/news_events/?action=viewRelease&emailAlertID=961
11   "ACLU Asks U.S. Supreme Court to Hear Appeal in Challenge to Florida Gay Adoption
      Ban," ACLU of Florida Press Release, October 1, 2004.
      http://www.aclufl.org/news_events/index.cfm?action=viewRelease&emailAlertID=490
12   "ACLU Hails Court Decision Striking Down Florida School Voucher Program," ACLU of
      Florida News Release, August 5, 2002.
      http://www.aclufl.org/news_events/archive/2002/voucherruling080502.cfm
13   "ACLU Statement on Approval by Polk County Commission to Post Ten
      Commandments," ACLU of Florida Statement, October 18, 2001.
      http://www.aclufl.org/news_events/archive/2001/tencommandments.cfm
14   "ACLU to Appeal Court Ruling on Jacksonville School Prayer," ACLU of Florida News
      Release, March 16, 2000. http://www.aclufl.org/news_events/archive/2000/adlerrul-
      ing0300.cfm
15   "ACLU Letter to Miami-Dade School Board Urging Reconsideration of Proposed Bible
      Curriculum," ACLU of Florida News Release, June 20, 2002.
      http://www.aclufl.org/news_events/archive/2002/dadebiblecurriculum062002.cfm
16   42 U.S.C. 1983
      http://www.law.cornell.edu/uscode/html/uscode42/usc_sec_42_00001983——
      000-.html
17   42 U.S.C. 1988 (b).
      http://www.law.cornell.edu/uscode/html/uscode42/usc_sec_42_00001988——
      000-.html
18   "Bill Would Drop Lawyer Fee Damages in Religious Battles," *CNS News*, June 26, 2006.
      http://www.cnsnews.com/ViewCulture.asp?Page=/Culture/archive/
      200606/CUL20060626a.html
19   "Ex-ACLU Attorney: Group 'Terrorizing' U.S.," *WorldNetDaily*, December 28, 2005.
      http://www.worldnetdaily.com/news/article.asp?ARTICLE_ID=48098
20   "Bill Would Drop Lawyer Fee Damages in Religious Battles," *CNS News*, June 26, 2006.

http://www.cnsnews.com/ViewCulture.asp?Page=/Culture/archive/200606/CUL20060
626a.html

21   "Mat Staver to Testify Before Congress in Support of Bill That Prohibits Damages and
Attorney's Fees in Establishment Clause Cases," Liberty Counsel News Release, June 21,
2006.

22   "Bill Would Drop Lawyer Fee Damages in Religious Battles," *CNS News*, June 26, 2006.
http://www.cnsnews.com/ViewCulture.asp?Page=/Culture/archive/200606/CUL20060
626a.html

23   "Judge Orders Library Board to Pay Attorneys Fees," Press Release from Mainstream
Loudoun, April 1, 1999.
http://lists.webjunction.org/wjlists/publib/1999-April/088488.html

24   "ACLU of Ohio Declares Victory in School Prayer Case," ACLU of Ohio Press Release,
October 19, 1999.
http://www.acluohio.org/press_releases/1999_press_releases/1999.10.19.htm

25   "Kentucky Cannot Erect Ten Commandments, Judge Rules," ACLU News Release,
July 25, 2000.
http://www.aclu.org/religion/tencomm/16282prs20000725.html

26   "State Pays ACLU $121,500 in Ten Commandments Fight," *The Cincinnati Enquirer*,
July 9, 2003.
http://www.enquirer.com/editions/2003/07/09/loc_kytencommandments09.html

27   "ACLU Wins $10,000 in Damages for High School Student in Web Parody Case," ACLU
News Release, February 20, 2001.
http://www.aclu.org/freespeech/youth/11103prs20010220.html

28   "State Pays ACLU $121,500 in Ten Commandments Fight," *The Cincinnati Enquirer*,
July 9, 2003.
http://www.enquirer.com/editions/2003/07/09/loc_kytencommandments09.html

29   Rees Lloyd, "Judicial Voodoo vs. The Cross," *WorldNetDaily*, April 15, 2005.
http://www.worldnetdaily.com/news/article.asp?ARTICLE_ID=43799%20

30   *Buono v. Norton*, NO. EDCV 01-216 RT, U.S. District Court for Southern California,
July 2002.
http://www.cacd.uscourts.gov/CACD/RecentPubOp.nsf/bb61c530eab0911c882567cf0
05ac6f9/9e471f4e9f52a5d488256c0200517e79/$FILE/EDCV01-216RT.pdf

31   Ray Huard, "Mt. Soledad Cross Case Seems Settled," *San Diego Union-Tribune*, March 31,
2004. http://www.signonsandiego.com/uniontrib/20040331/news_7m31soledad.html

32   "ACLU Fights Pennsylvania Police on Profanity Arrests," Freedom Forum, July 10, 2002.
http://www.freedomforum.org/templates/document.asp?documentID=16529

33   *Powell v. Portland Public Schools*, The ACLU of Oregon, March 2006. http://www.aclu-
or.org/site/PageServer?pagename=Lit_tp_powell&JServSessionIdr004=hvpdemeu93.
app1b

34   "Detroit Settles ACLU Lawsuit Challenging Police Sting Operation Against Gay Men,"
ACLU News Release, July 23, 2002.
http://www.aclu.org/lgbt/crimjustice/12010prs20020723.html

35   Jannell McGrew, "State to Pay Legal Fees of $549,000," *The Montgomery Advertiser*,
April 15, 2004.
http://www.montgomeryadvertiser.com/specialreports/TENcommandments/StoryAlaba-
mamoore415w.htm

36   "Pasco Apologizes to Artists for Censoring Their Works," ACLU of Washington News
Release, March 3, 2003.
http://www.aclu-wa.org/detail.cfm?id=70

37   "ACLU Secures Sweeping Changes in Arkansas School District," ACLU News Release,
July 17, 2003.
http://www.aclu.org/lgbt/youth/11881prs20030717.html

38   "Boy Scouts' Use of Balboa Park Land Ruled Unconstitutional," *San Diego Union- Tribune*,

July 31, 2003.
http://www.signonsandiego.com/news/metro/20030731-1629-aclu-scouts.html

39   "Pots of Gold Behind Crosses," *The Phyllis Schlafly Report*, Volume 38; No. 2, September 2004.
      http://www.eagleforum.org/psr/2004/sept04/psrsept04.html

40   *Kay Staley v. Harris County*, No. H-03-3411, U.S. Southern District of Texas, August 10, 2004. http://www.alliancealert.org/aa2004/2004_08_11.pdf

41   *Selman v. Cobb County*, No. 02-02325-CV-CC-1, Eleventh U.S. Circuit Court of Appeals, May 25, 2006. http://www.ca11.uscourts.gov/opinions/ops/200510341.pdf

42   Butch Mabin, "Judge Awards 416 Opponents Legal Fees," *Lincoln Journal Star*, August 2, 2005.
      http://www.journalstar.com/articles/2005/08/02/local/doc42efae0b8e7f7297850171.txt

43   "Court Reinstates Nebraska Gay Marriage Ban; Tennessee to Vote on Issue," *Fox News*, July 14, 2006. http://www.foxnews.com/story/0,2933,203600,00.html

44   *John Doe v. Barrow County*, U.S. District Court for the Northern District of Georgia, July 18, 2005. http://www.acluga.org/briefs/10.commandments.barrow/order.pdf

45   "2003-2005 Litigation/Advocacy Docket," ACLU of Georgia, 2005.
      http://www.acluga.org/docket.html

46   Paula Reed Ward, "District in Evolution Debate to Pay $1 Million in Legal Fees," *Pittsburgh Post-Gazette*, February 23, 2006. http://www.postgazette.com/pg/06054/659758.stm

47   "School Board Approves Payment to Intelligent Design Legal Team," PR Newswire, February 21, 2006.
      http://www.prnewswire.com/cgi-bin/stories.pl?ACCT=104&STORY=/www/story/02-21-2006/0004286486&EDATE

48   Clarke D. Forsythe, "A Pro-Life Mistake," *National Review Online*, December 16, 2004.
      http://www.nationalreview.com/comment/forsythe200412160851.asp

49   "Federal Court Tosses Challenge to Utah City's Commandments Display," The First Amendment Center, June 3, 2004.
      http://www.firstamendmentcenter.org/news.aspx?id=13463

50   "Utah City to Remove Ten Commandments Monument," First Amendment Center, November 30, 2002. http://www.firstamendmentcenter.org/news.aspx?id=3178

51   *Stone v. Graham*, 449 U.S. 39, Supreme Court of the United States, November 17, 1980.
      http://caselaw.lp.findlaw.com/scripts/getcase.pl?court=us&vol=449&invol=39

52   "Commandments Display Is Upheld," *Louisville Courier-Journal*, December 21, 2005.
      http://www.courier-journal.com/apps/pbcs.dll/article?AID=/20051221/NEWS01/512210407

53   "Atheist Director Loses Suit as Judge Rules Indiana Ten Commandments Display Must Remain," American Atheists, December 29, 1999.
      http://www.atheists.org/flash.line/tenco10.htm

54   "Atheist Director Wins as Federal Court Strikes Ten Commandments Monument in Indiana," American Atheists, December 14, 2000.
      http://www.atheists.org/flash.line/tenco21.htm

55   "Ten Commandments Plaque Ordered out of Pennsylvania Courthouse," The First Amendment Center, March 7, 2002.
      http://www.freedomforum.org/templates/document.asp?documentID=15834

56   "3rd Circuit: Ten Commandments Plaque Can Remain on Courthouse," The First Amendment Center, June 27, 2003.
      http://www.firstamendmentcenter.org/news.aspx?id=11651

57   Bill Rankin, "Court Allows County Seal's Commandments," *The Atlanta-Journal Constitution*, June 3, 2003. http://pewforum.org/news/display.php?NewsID=2276

58   *Glassroth v. Moore*, No. 01-01268-CV-T-N, Eleventh U.S. Circuit Court of Appeals, July 1,

2003. http://news.lp.findlaw.com/hdocs/docs/religion/glsrthmre70103opn.pdf
59   "High Court Split on Ten Commandments," *CNN Law Center*, June 27, 2005.
      http://www.cnn.com/2005/LAW/06/27/scotus.ten.commandments/index.html
60   "Testimony of Mathew D. Staver Before House Judiciary Subcommittee on the Constitu-
      tion," Liberty Counsel, June 22, 2006. http://www.lc.org/attachments/congress_testi-
      mony_PERA.pdf
61   The Public Expression of Religion Act of 2005, H.R. 2679, Introduced by Representative
      John Hostettler, May 26, 2005. http://frwebgate.access.gpo.gov/cgi-bin/getdoc.cgi?db-
      name=109_cong_bills&docid=f:h2679ih.txt.pdf
62   Jody Brown, "Sen. Brownback: ACLU – Not Taxpayers – Should Foot the Bill for Church-
      State Lawsuits," American Family Association, August 3, 2006.
      http://headlines.agapepress.org/archive/8/afa/32006a.asp
63   "Text of Congressman John Hostettler's Remarks to the American Legion National Wash-
      ington Conference in Washington, D.C., on February 28, 2006," Rep. John Hostettler,
      March 2, 2006.
      http://www.house.gov/apps/list/press/in08_hostettler/pr_060302_alnwc.html
64   Ibid.
65   "Legislative Goal of the American Legion Family," The American Legion, February 17,
      2006. http://www.legion-aux.org/files/pera_final.pdf
66   "Center Petitions Congress to Stop Tax Dollars to ACLU," Coral Ridge Ministries Press
      Release, December 13, 2005.
      http://www.reclaimamerica.org/pages/NEWS/news.aspx?story=2958
67   Ibid.

Chapter Eleven

1   Matthew 5:13
2   Ibid.
3   "National Day of Prayer 2006: A Proclamation by the President of the United States of
      America," The White House Press Secretary, May 3, 2006.
      http://www.whitehouse.gov/news/releases/2006/05/20060503-14.html
4   Matthew 5:43-44
5   1 Corinthians 1:18
6   John 3:36
7   Matthew 28:19-20
8   Matthew 5:16
9   Ephesians 6:4
10   Kyle Smith, "C.S. Lewis Scholar Hopes 'Narnia' Helps PostModerns Find God," Baptist
      Press, 2006.
      http://www.christianity.com/faith/1371705.aspx
11   "The Importance of Voting and Christian Involvement in the Political Arena," WallBuilders,
      2003. http://www.wallbuilders.com/resources/search/detail.php?ResourceID=22
12   Exodus 18:21
13   Proverbs 29:2
14   C.S. Lewis, *Mere Christianity*, HarperCollins Publishers, New York, 1952.

Index

O'Reilly, Bill 78, 85, 122, 178

P

parental consent 17, 190, 191
parental notification 190, 191, 192, 230
partial-birth abortion 16, 195, 196, 197, 198, 199
Patriot Act 213
pedophile 120, 123
Pentagon 85, 209, 213
Pfeffer, Leo 32
Planned Parenthood 106, 174, 198
Plato 21
Pledge of Allegiance 17, 48, 52, 240
polygamy 20, 29, 110, 138, 152, 153, 154, 161
pornography 14, 16, 20, 86, 125, 126, 127, 163, 164, 173, 174, 175, 176, 177, 179, 180, 231, 232
Powell, Michael 166, 167
Princeton University 24, 26
Public Expression of Religion Act 240, 241, 242

R

racial profiling 218
Reagan, Ronald 73
Rehnquist, William 34, 83, 173, 174, 203
Rind Report 120
Roberts, John 48, 116, 199
Roe v. Wade 106, 185, 188, 199
Roosevelt, Franklin 30
Roosevelt, Theodore 161
Rundquist, George 53

S

Salvation Army 80, 81
Scalia, Antonin 38, 55, 88, 109, 110, 197, 205
Schaeffer, Francis 23, 201, 202
school vouchers 82
Sears, Alan 51, 96
sex offender registries 133
sexually transmitted diseases 99, 100, 165
Shapiro, Steven R. 54, 70, 82, 202
Simon, Howard 69, 157, 191
Solomon Amendment 115, 116
stare decisis 106, 107
Staver, Mat 49, 50, 232, 239

Stenberg v. Carhart 196
Story, Joseph 28

T

Tangipahoa Parish 58
Ten Commandments 9, 16, 27, 34, 35, 36, 37, 38, 48, 49, 97, 171, 230, 233, 235, 236, 237, 238, 239, 240
Thomas, Clarence 71
Thompson, Gordon 42
Thompson, Myron 36, 235

U

United Nations 214, 215, 221, 225

V

Veterans of Foreign Wars 40
Virginia Military Institute 61, 62

W

wall of separation 27, 34, 48, 49, 53, 186
Walpole, Horace 25
Washington, George 9, 14, 27, 244
White, Byron 104
Whitehead, John 57
Willis, Kent 66, 113, 128, 129
Wilson, James 27
wiretapping 222, 223
Witherspoon, John 24, 25, 26
World Trade Center 208, 211